"A breathless and fun-to-read, yet sobering, tour through the worlds we built. The depth of culture, subculture, and fascinating history that comes alive in this book captures a world before the internet, before corporate whitewashing obscured the complexity of our connections and experiences. *A Place of Our Own* illustrates a time when each woman had to venture out into the world of the unknown to create her lesbian life and all the unforeseen adventures she encountered and created. Bravo!"

—Sarah Schulman, author of
Let the Record Show

"*A Place of Our Own* is a wonderfully rangy, conversational, and thoughtful exploration of lesbian geographies. It's particularly enriched by the quantity and quality of personal interviews, which range from the delightful, to the curious, to the heartbreaking. It is optimistic without collapsing into coziness or cliché, animated by affection but not lacking in rigor, comprehensive yet brisk, and I only wish there was more of it."

—Daniel Lavery, author of *Something That
May Shock and Discredit You*

"In the words of Joan Baez, action is the antidote to despair. Immensely readable, *A Place of Our Own* charts the inventive actions of queer women in the latter half of the twentieth century. Far more than an elegy for past times, this book is a warts-and-all how-to guide to forging community in the face of what seem like insurmountable obstacles. It's a celebration of what was—and can be—built, with all its hurdles and ecstasies. Ultimately encouraging and empowering, *A Place of Our Own* is a reminder that you can't change the world, but you can change your neighborhood."

—Rosie Garland, novelist,
poet, and singer

"Thomas's meticulously researched book pulses with delicious dykes and the spaces we have made for ourselves over the years. It is a timely reminder that many lesbian spaces have always welcomed trans women, and also that few lesbian spaces ever included all of us—women of color, women without disposable income, women who didn't look 'lesbian enough' or who looked 'too lesbian' have been excluded accidentally or intentionally. While not every space was as hopefully inclusive as we might now desire, it is important to recognize how we got to where we are now and those who paved the way. I welcome this story, and I very much look forward to one set on this side of the Atlantic."

—Stella Duffy, author of *Theodora*

"Thomas's lively, hugely engaging book is a fascinating chronicle of the courage, tenacity and vision with which queer women have carved out spaces for themselves in an often less than friendly world. An inspiring celebration of lesbian camaraderie, activism and fun."

—Sarah Waters, author of
The Little Stranger

A PLACE OF OUR OWN

SIX SPACES THAT SHAPED
QUEER WOMEN'S CULTURE

JUNE THOMAS

SEAL PRESS

New York

Seal Press

Hachette Book Group

1290 Avenue of the Americas, New York, NY 10104

www.sealpress.com

@sealpress

Printed in the United States of America

First Edition: May 2024

Published by Seal Press, an imprint of Hachette Book Group, Inc. The Seal Press name and logo is a registered trademark of the Hachette Book Group.

The Hachette Speakers Bureau provides a wide range of authors for speaking events. To find out more, go to hachettespeakersbureau.com or email HachetteSpeakers@hbgusa.com.

Seal books may be purchased in bulk for business, educational, or promotional use. For information, please contact your local bookseller or Hachette Book Group Special Markets Department at special.markets@hbgusa.com.

The publisher is not responsible for websites (or their content) that are not owned by the publisher.

Print book interior design by Amy Quinn.

Library of Congress Control Number: 2024934187

ISBNs: 9781541601741 (hardcover), 9781541601765 (ebook)

LSC-C

Printing 1, 2024

For Rosemary

CONTENTS

INTRODUCTION

LESBIANS GET OUR NAME FROM AN ISLAND: LESBOS, THE Mediterranean homeland of the poet Sappho, who lived and loved there more than twenty-six hundred years ago. It's a place few of us will ever visit. I've never been, and I've never seen a photo of Mytilene, its capital, in any of our bars. Lesbians are a people without a home. Perhaps that's why the ones we make for ourselves are so important.

My own life has been defined by a search for lesbian spaces. In the early 1980s, shortly after I headed off to college, I bought a gay travel guide to the United States. Some of the activities catalogued in that little brick of a book were either downright terrifying or completely inapplicable to an awkward young feminist like me—so many "cruisy areas" and adult bookstores! Still, I studied that tome like a holy text. I spent more time thinking about the abbreviations used in its listings than I did about my major, though I never fully unlocked their secrets. "L/W: Leather/Western." Like John

1

Wayne? "N: Nudity permitted in some areas." Those were areas I definitely needed to avoid. "AYOR: At your own risk." Wasn't it all? But occasionally I would light upon a "W," which meant "Mostly women (lesbians)." That letter kept me reading.

Since I grew up in England, my interest in the bars of Athens, Georgia, or the erotica emporia of Modesto, California, was largely academic. I wasn't going to cruise Tujunga Canyon or attend a denim/uniform night in Dallas, but the existence of this decidedly unslim volume, dense with agate type, gave me hope. Even if I couldn't go there, the fact that there was a bar for W's on Capitol Hill in Washington, DC, meant there must be dykes who drank there. If Provincetown, Massachusetts, had a lesbian craft store, there had to be women who shopped there. Here at last was the proof I needed that there was more to lesbian life than the two other dykes in the college gay group and that one bar in town that hosted a women's night on the last Tuesday of every month.

In the decades since, many of the dreams that were hatched while I was poring over that ancient guidebook have come true. I made awkward conversation with dozens of women in lesbian bars, and despite some near misses, I avoided being injured by an errant pool cue. I spent untold hours browsing the shelves of women's bookstores; attended feminist bookfairs in Montreal, Barcelona, and Amsterdam; and eventually worked at a feminist publisher in Seattle. I became an American. I communed with thousands of naked women at music festivals, learning that I was happier if I kept my socks on. I attended heart-stoppingly thrilling sporting events and went home realizing that the best part was bonding with all the other dykes in the stands. I spent ecstatic nights on dance floors, long evenings in collective meetings, and rejuvenating weeks in gay resorts. It was all exactly like I hoped it would be, and it was all completely different.

Since the proverbial dawn of civilization, some of those drawn to the "opposite" sex for love, passion, and partnership have felt a need to restrict the options of the rest of humanity, to instill feelings of shame, fear, and self-loathing in the people we now call lesbian, gay, bisexual, or transgender. Institutions that were supposed to provide support—religious groups, the criminal justice system, and the nuclear family, to name but a few—instead targeted their queer brethren, telling them they must transform or at least deny their true selves if they wanted to avoid banishment. To retain their place in the family, the church, and the community, they would need to conform.

Many did. But the queer people who didn't—those who refused to see themselves as sick, who failed in their attempts to pass themselves off as straight, or who decided that the pain caused by suppression and deception was worse than the punishment they would receive if the truth came out—were forced to find new homes: Neighborhoods where they could live and socialize relatively safely. Venues where they could meet and mate. Spots where they could generate and share new ideas to challenge the old ideologies. Parks where they could play together. Places where they wouldn't be alone. In the twentieth and early twenty-first centuries, these spaces planted their rainbow flags on the map, at first tentatively and clandestinely, then with growing out-and-proud visibility. Making solitude a choice rather than an unavoidable fate has been the greatest achievement of the gay civil rights movement.

The journey from isolation to community—from the well of loneliness to the gayborhood—required the construction of numerous way stations. Some blossomed and faded; some have endured, albeit in forms that look very different from their original manifestations; and others have become so integrated into society that their queer origins have been forgotten.

For queer people, these spaces hold an outsized significance. We aren't born into the LGBTQ community. Unlike other minority groups (which many of us also belong to), where parents teach their children about family history, religious traditions, and systemic prejudice, our birth families are generally ignorant of queer codes and culture. We have to work out their rules, rituals, and rich history for ourselves. For that to happen, we need places where we can find our new, queer families. Covid-related lockdowns reminded everyone of the importance of "third places"—the informal settings beyond home and work that foster community life and satisfy people's need for human interaction. Yet, even under normal circumstances, the third place is especially precious for LGBTQ people, who may be rejected by their families or shunned by their coworkers.

Lesbian and bisexual women have experienced extra challenges in finding an alternative home base. Although we make up as much as 5 percent of the population, we're diverse in our interests and enthusiasms, and we tend to have less disposable income than gay men, making it challenging for commercial enterprises targeting queer women to succeed.[1] It sometimes feels as if at least four-fifths of the media coverage of lesbian institutions consists of eulogies for newly shuttered bars, bookstores, and businesses.

This book isn't a lament for those lost locations. Rather, it is a joyful celebration of the dream palaces queer women have built: places to meet, share ideas, form teams, create utopias, find G-spots, and get away from it all. Although we *are* everywhere, I focus on six key locations where contemporary lesbian culture was created and shaped, primarily in America, starting in the 1950s and 1960s: the lesbian bar (and its less celebrated cousins, the women's coffeehouse and restaurant), the feminist bookstore, the softball diamond, the rural commune, the feminist sex-toy store, and the vacation destination.

Starting in the 1970s, lesbians transformed bars from spaces where they were barely tolerated to locations where they were welcomed and respected. Energized by feminist activism and the potential of lesbian organizing, women established bookstores where lesbians could access the latest publications and where they could meet and exchange ideas. Even softball, a sociable summer pastime played in parks and popular with working-class women—in part because it didn't require expensive equipment—took a political turn in that same decade. Activists realized that the softball field provided a venue where they could promote their organizations, model lesbian camaraderie, build physical strength, and even yell "queer cheers" in very public settings. Some women were so determined to sever their ties with men that they turned to each other for love and support, forming separatist communes on "lesbian land" in rural areas across America, where men, and often straight and bisexual women, were not welcome. Women in New York and San Francisco founded the first feminist, sex-positive vibrator stores focused on helping women have better sex, launching a movement that was especially valuable to people whose experiences had been overlooked in sex-ed classes. All the while, resorts such as Provincetown and Cherry Grove and the dozens of women's music festivals that sprang up around the country provided a temporary refuge from the heterosexual, male gaze.

Even as queer women made space for themselves, the larger world continued to be full of perils. Gathering under the same roof was risky, but so were the most basic forms of communication. In the 1950s, it was dangerous to broach queer topics in newsletters, magazines, or even personal correspondence sent through the US mail. Early civil rights organizations couldn't avoid the post office—indeed, setting up a PO box as a point of contact was still safer than using a home address or renting an office—but every interaction carried considerable risk.[2] Post office officials were authorized to seize mail they considered obscene, a label some bureaucrats automatically applied to anything related to homosexuality, and individuals caught sending or receiving "obscene" mail were subject to fines and public shaming.[3] Institutions from national civil rights organizations to groups arranging social gatherings in private homes effectively imperiled their members' welfare every time they wrote their address on an envelope.

Fear of post office interference even shaped literary history. In the early 1950s, when Marijane Meaker sat down to write a novel about her lesbian experiences at boarding school, her straight, male editor gave her two editorial notes: she should move the action to a college setting, and she must present homosexuality in a negative light.[4] The latter requirement wasn't just a matter of maintaining mid-century mores; it was designed to avoid distribution problems. If postal authorities inspected a shipment and discovered even one title with gay content, they were liable to confiscate the entire delivery. Consequently, Meaker explained to me in 2016, "You had to censor yourself, because you didn't want other authors to be punished for something you wrote."[5] The best way to keep the authorities at bay was to deprive queer characters of anything resembling a happy ending. Meaker's novel, *Spring Fire*, published under the pseudonym Vin Packer in 1952, ends with Leda, a bisexual college student, committed to a psychiatric hospital. The book was a massive hit, selling nearly 1.5 million copies in its first year of publication and unleashing a flood of pulp lesbian fiction, almost all of which ended in tragedy.[6] Queer readers, skilled in the art of translating straight narratives to fit the contours of their own lives, learned to enjoy the love story that preceded the mandatory misery.

In the mid-1950s, gay rights group ONE, Inc., exasperated when Los Angeles postal officials seized every copy of two separate issues of its monthly magazine, fought the confiscation all the way to the Supreme Court. In 1958, in *One, Inc. v. Olesen*, the court ruled that homosexuality was not inherently obscene.[7] This provided some relief to groups wanting to communicate with potential members, but it certainly didn't mean that queer activists could let down their guard. Long after the 1950s, obscenity was used as a pretext to restrict the distribution of sex-toy catalogs (and sex toys) through the mail, for customs authorities to seize LGBTQ books crossing international borders, and in the 2020s to prohibit librarians from providing queer books to children.[8]

Deep into the 1960s, a sense of uncertainty pervaded businesses that catered to the queer community. In the world of nightlife, this took the form of vague rules, inconsistently applied. Even in a relatively liberal state like New York, the selective prosecution of ambiguous offenses like disorderly or indecent conduct meant that no one was absolutely certain whether it was legal to serve liquor to openly gay patrons or exactly how many items of women's clothing people assigned female at birth must be wearing to avoid arrest for "masquerading" as men.[9] No legitimate operator would want anything to do with such an unpredictable business. In the mid-twentieth century, the twilight world of queer bars provided a welcoming home for the Mafia, which took advantage of this semilegal environment to charge exorbitant prices for watered-down liquor, sell untaxed cigarettes, and run prostitution, blackmail, and other illegal rackets. To keep their bars open, the Mob paid off the police. That would bring a temporary respite, but the cops always returned. Raids happened when police wanted a bigger payoff, when a bar was operating too brazenly, or when mayoral elections loomed and the administration craved newspaper headlines about cleanups and clampdowns. They were an inconvenience for bar operators and an absolute catastrophe for patrons. Newspapers routinely listed the names of those rounded up by the cops, which meant that a night in a bar could cost a lonely lesbian her job, home, or family.

Even if lesbians could avoid losing everything, the economic circumstances they lived under made it almost impossible to establish a women's space—much less a lesbian one. Before the Equal Credit Opportunity Act (ECOA) passed in 1974, only women of independent means or with connections to deep-pocketed men could dream of setting up a bar, bookstore, or any other kind of meeting place. Until then, it was perfectly legal for lenders to deny loans to women.[10] When they married, women's credit histories were routinely subsumed by those of their husbands: if a woman had a credit card in her own name before she got hitched, it would be canceled and the woman directed to reapply under her husband's name (pending his permission, of course). When a couple divorced, many lenders had a blanket policy of refusing to extend credit to the woman for up to a year after the separation. Even after the ECOA became law, women still had problems accessing capital. The founders of Sisterhood Bookstore in Los Angeles, who were all married to men when they started the store, couldn't get a bank loan until they found a female bank manager who was willing to help.[11] (There were exceptions, though, as the 1970s also saw the creation of explicitly feminist funding institutions. San Francisco's Old Wives' Tales bookshop was able to open in 1976 thanks to a loan from the San Francisco Feminist Federal Credit Union.)[12]

Still, generations of queer people persevered and carved out spaces through unimaginable difficulty, ultimately creating not just individual institutions but complex lesbian scenes that were hotbeds of political action. When we think of such scenes, the first association is probably Paris in the 1920s, New York's Greenwich Village in the 1950s, or the Los Angeles of *The L Word* in the 2000s, but a robust lesbian infrastructure also drew women to places like Eugene, Oregon; Park Slope, Brooklyn; and Gainesville, Florida.

In Gainesville, starting in the late 1960s, women created consciousness-raising groups, formed early lesbian-land projects, and founded women's arts festivals. One group bought an old house, which became the home of an organization called Women Unlimited, housing a bookstore, a radical newsletter, and a counseling center.[13] Another, the Feminist Action Network, begat Lesbians Empowered for Action and Politics, which organized annual retreats attracting hundreds of women from around the South to spend a weekend camping on women's land.[14] There, they expanded their social circles as well as their understanding of what lesbian-feminist community might encompass.

These new institutions, often small and informally operated, were nevertheless powerful enough to draw women clear across the country. Barb Ryan was in her mid-twenties, living in Reading, Pennsylvania, when she decided to go to college.[15] Word of Mother Kali's Books and the presence of radical hippies in Eugene, as well as the string of lesbian-land groups just a few miles down the highway, made her decision easy: She applied to just one school, the University of Oregon, despite its being thousands of miles away. Once in Eugene, she also discovered the Riviera Room bar, local cafés like Mama's Home Fried Truck Stop, and, of course, a softball team. She was active in a lesbian mothers' support group and later became a counselor. Four decades after moving to Eugene because of its radical reputation, Ryan was still part of the community.

Although these institutions operated independently, they were deeply embedded within their communities. Soon after archivist Linda Long and her late partner moved to Eugene, she learned that artist Tee Corinne was part of the vibrant lesbian-separatist communities in southern Oregon.[16] Long was familiar with Corinne's photography and realized her personal papers would be a valuable research collection for the University of Oregon Special Collections and University Archives. Lacking a way to contact the artist, Long knew who would have that information. She headed to Mother Kali's Books, and after she had demonstrated her connection to the local community and spelled out her plans to develop a manuscript collection for the lesbian-land movement, store manager Izzie Harbaugh shared Corinne's contact information with her. That interaction set in motion the creation of the Oregon Lesbian Land Manuscript Collections, one of the most significant centers of lesbian scholarship in the United States.

As Long and Corinne demonstrate, the women whose energy fueled hubs like Eugene were often involved in multiple projects. Before she became the first openly gay mayor of a major US city in 2010, Annise Parker was a co-owner of Inklings, Houston's feminist bookstore, and she was active in the local lesbian softball league.[17] Driving to a meeting in the state capital, Parker met Phyllis Frye, who soon became the first trans woman to play in the softball league. Years later, Parker helped Frye break another barrier when she appointed her as the first openly transgender judge in the United States.

There are countless examples of how the existence of spaces like these led women to community activism. Because ACT UP New York held its meetings at New York's Lesbian and Gay Community Services Center, now known simply as The Center, it became a powerful activation point. Garance Franke-Ruta was a seventeen-year-old high school dropout attending a queer youth meeting in the center when an ACT UP member, who was systematically visiting every room in the building looking for people to attend an upcoming action at the Food and Drug Administration headquarters, stopped by.[18] After that first protest, Franke-Ruta spent the next four years of her life as a full-time AIDS activist. Others joined ACT UP because they were at the center for health-care appointments, Alcoholics Anonymous meetings, or other political events when they chanced upon the Monday night gatherings.

All these physical, in-person meetings might feel like a dream from a bygone era—and in some respects, they are. The internet has revolutionized lesbian culture in undeniably positive ways. We can now connect and scheme with others who share our obsessions, concerns, and creative interests, regardless of geography, in ways that were unimaginable before the mid-1990s. Podcasts, videos, and internet publications have a potentially limitless reach. People all over the world can shop at queer-owned websites, discuss their lives in forums with other queer people, and share a Zoom room with trailblazing writers and thinkers.

Still, it would be a shame to lose the physical spaces that shaped late twentieth-century lesbian culture and a tragedy to forget them. Even a tech-obsessed hermit like me would rather browse brick-and-mortar places—for objects, ideas, and compatible individuals—than be forced to rely on algorithmic search results. Feminist bookstores, to choose one of my favorite hangouts, didn't only change lives because shoppers could find the latest books and magazines within their welcoming walls (though they could, and that alone was transformational). Women could also consult the binders crammed with information about bird-watching clubs, twelve-step programs, and political affinity groups. And most importantly, they could meet and hang out with other members of the community and talk with a staffer who could offer advice about books and relationships. That bookstore worker might even play a role that is essential in every lesbian's life: the first dyke—a role model, a crush, a potential friend. Like the truck driver with her ring of keys in Alison Bechdel's *Fun Home*, but a woman you can talk to any time you walk into the building rather than a figure you can only gaze upon from a distance.[19]

None of these locations—no, not even militantly separatist lesbian land—were exclusively lesbian. Bisexual, asexual, and heterosexual women (including those who applied different labels to themselves over the years) also created and sustained these projects, as did nonbinary people and transgender women and men. When I speak of "queer women," I am using the phrase as an umbrella term for nonstraight people who are not cisgender men. I suspect this imprecision will irritate some readers, but it is the reality of lesbian-feminist organizing and community building, where we have always understood that identity is a fugitive thing.

Big questions emerged in these spaces. Who owns "our" institutions? Can queer feminist ideals thrive in the capitalist marketplace? Do we really all play for the same team? Can we, and should we, separate ourselves from anyone who isn't a lesbian, however that is defined? How important is sex to sexual orientation? Can being in the majority for one week a year fuel us for the other fifty-one? Can an inherently diverse group create a truly equitable community, or is it doomed to replicate the exclusionary dynamics of the larger society?

Lesbian stories are important for anyone who hopes to understand American culture. After all, the forces that are causing lesbian bars to close are also making it harder for *anyone* to find a cozy local spot where they can socialize with friends. The rise and fall of the feminist bookstore and sex-toy boutique runs parallel to the roller-coaster ride all independent bookstores and small businesses have taken over the last thirty years. Lesbians aren't the only adults seeking fellowship in a lonely world; nor are we the only minority group that has tried to form separatist enclaves or establish locations where their community, temporarily at least, makes up the majority.

Some of the sites this book explores are commercial; some are civic spaces; some are collectively owned and operated. Some are for couples and small groups, some for individuals, and some for teams; some are intentional communities, and some are open to anyone who can afford them. But they all shaped what we now think of as lesbian culture, and they all have lessons to teach readers—queer and straight alike—about the history of the late twentieth and early twenty-first centuries, the triumphs and failures of activism, and the ongoing struggle for a more just and loving world.

Dee Meadows and Stormé DeLarverie inside the Cubby Hole, New York City, 1986. © 1986 JEB (Joan E. Biren)

ONE
LESBIAN BARS

WHERE DO YOU GO TO FIND LESBIANS? IF THAT WERE A question on *Family Feud*, the most popular answer would surely be "BAR." For decades, women risked their livelihoods and family ties to spend evenings in lesbian bars. They were—and still are—a place to meet lovers and friends; dance, flirt, and blow off steam; and build community.

For most lesbians and gay men, the bar is the first place we go to find our queer selves. I still remember the terrifying, giddy excitement of my first forays into gay pubs and clubs, the thrill of discovering other lesbians and gay men in all their beautiful, dreary, fabulous, sleazy variety. There, I danced to fifteen-minute techno remixes under spinning disco balls, learned that the proper way to show appreciation to drag performers is to hand them neatly folded paper money, and came to understand the importance of giving the heroines of the pool table plenty of room to make their shots. Lesbian bars are my cultural patrimony and my political heritage.

Although there's no evidence that the world contains more queer men than queer women, there have always been many more bars built for that population.[1] The 2023 edition of the *Gayellow Pages* showed Manhattan as having two lesbian bars but as many as fifty-five catering to gay men.[2] Why the disparity?

Back in 1966, *New York Unexpurgated*, "an amoral guide" to mid-century Manhattan, floated some theories about the scarcity of lesbian bars: "Shyer, more private than fags—[lesbians] don't seek out bars as frequently. Also—their motivations and sex drive are entirely different. The rapacious cruising and turnover necessary for gay men isn't their scene. So fewer clubs are needed. Also—they keep closing because of an overabundance of male spectators, mostly ineffectual sorts who thrive on watching these girls."[3] That's not the language I'd use, but I can't argue with the sentiment.

In the twenty-first century, straight guys spend less time leering at live lesbians, but lesbian couples' homebody tendencies are still terrible for the bar business. According to Maggie Collier, who ran an eponymous New York nightlife promotion company, "Women tend to go out seeking a partner. When they find one, I don't see them for two years. Then all of a sudden, they break up. You see them every single week at every single party until they find the next [girlfriend], and then they disappear, and the pattern continues."[4]

As convincing as these explanations may be, they ignore the historical forces that served to push women away from bars. It's hard for contemporary queers to inhabit the shoes of a lesbian or bisexual woman of the 1950s, 1960s, or 1970s. Those who had what might be described as "middle-class jobs," as civil servants, teachers, librarians, and so forth, lived in fear of losing the positions that allowed them to live outside the family home without the support of a husband. Those fears were well founded. Until quite recently, by choosing to spend an evening in a lesbian bar, women were placing themselves in potentially life-wrecking jeopardy. Being caught up in a raid might cost a woman her job, her apartment, and her reputation. It could cause her nearest and dearest to erase her from their lives. It could result in her losing custody of her kids. And yet women went, drawn like moths to flickering neon flames, because bars offered something no other place could: a guarantee that within those walls, women would— or at least *could*—meet other lesbians.

Starting in the 1950s, millions of copies of a racy new kind of novel were sold across the United States. These "pulps," whose lurid covers shone like spotlights from grocery-store shelves and magazine stands, introduced readers to blissfully happy same-sex couples—even if the rules of the genre required that the relationship end badly. In many of these stories, a lovelorn femme found the butch of her dreams in the bars of Greenwich Village, transforming this downtown neighborhood, whose cheap rents and tolerant bohemian residents had turned it into a cozy haven for homosexuals decades earlier, into the sapphic Shangri-la of the American imagination.[5] In *Beebo Brinker*, Ann Bannon wrote

of the eponymous character's first glimpse of women dancing together in a Village club: "Their cheeks were touching.
Quick light kisses were exchanged. And they were all girls,
every one of them: young and lovely and infatuated with each
other. They touched one another with gentle caresses, they
kissed, they smiled and laughed and whispered while they
turned and moved together."[6] These scenes were so intoxi-
cating that readers wanted to join in the fun. After Marijane
Meaker (as Ann Aldrich) published We Walk Alone, a gay
girl's guide to life in New York, she was deluged with letters
from women wanting to move to the city, asking, "where lesbians could find jobs, where they could find bars, and where
they could live."[7]

Perhaps because the popular image of bar raids is shaped
by representations of the June 1969 unrest at the Stonewall
Inn, where, according to one of its bartenders, the clientele
was 98 percent male, some might assume that the police only
targeted men's bars.[8] This simply isn't true. Women's bars
were raided all the time, and when mixed bars were targeted,
women were arrested along with their male counterparts.
Consider a few examples from the history of Chicago.[9] In the
1930s, the cops raided the Roselle Inn and the Twelve-Thirty
Club, which was said to be popular with "women who dress
as men." In 1949, cops arrested fifteen men and nine women
after raiding several bars along North Clark Street, resulting
in all the detainees being charged with disorderly conduct.
When Mayor Richard J. Daley ordered a cleanup before the
1968 Democratic Convention arrived in town, the cops' first
stop was Maxine's, a lesbian bar.

It also has to be said that the sense of danger, the thrill of the forbidden, was part of the appeal of queer nightlife. By walking through the door of a lesbian bar, even a mild-mannered milquetoast could see herself as an outlaw. Everyone in the place had broken a significant taboo just by being there. They were members of an elite club, a secret sapphic society. Well into the 1970s, intentionally vague laws against gay gatherings, "impersonation" (which is to say wearing garments inappropriate for one's assigned gender), or vagrancy meant there was always a chance that a bar could be raided by the police. The only sure way to avoid that risk was to stay away completely.

Bar-goers faced dangers beyond police crackdowns. The "Red scare" of the 1950s, when politicians stoked and exploited citizens' fear of Communist influence on American life, was accompanied by a "lavender scare," in which politicians pledged to purge "perverts" from government service. Over the course of three decades, this campaign of persecution led to the firing of thousands of government employees and planted a justified seed of paranoia in the mind of every queer civil servant or indeed anyone who dreamed of working for the government or in a job that required a background security check.[10] (Not that gay and bisexual people were the only victims of the purge: since lavender scare dismissals were based on rumor, mischief, and circumstantial "evidence," many heterosexuals became collateral damage.)

The insidiousness of the lavender scare was that it combined the era's most common response to homosexuality—revulsion, fueled by religious and "moral" teaching—with the oft-repeated canard that lesbian, gay, and bisexual people represented a "security risk." (Never mind that the biggest danger, the threat of blackmail, was only present because the dire consequences of discovery obliged queer people to conduct their personal lives in secrecy.) People were deemed security risks based on perceived characteristics rather than their individual beliefs or behaviors. In other words, homosexuals were considered intrinsically untrustworthy because of who they were rather than because of anything they did. Following this line of thinking, it was therefore deemed necessary for all such people to be rooted out of public service.

At the time of the lavender scare, women made up approximately 40 percent of the federal workforce.[11] Still, because lesbian social networks were harder for investigators, almost all of whom were men, to penetrate, and because women tended to hold less powerful positions, gay men were disproportionately targeted for dismissal. That statistical anomaly provided cold comfort to women desperate to retain their reputations and livelihoods. Pervasive fear led to self-censorship and "discretion," the better part of which might involve steering clear of known homosexual haunts like gay and lesbian bars, dressing in a conventional—cis, straight—style, and avoiding friendships with anyone who might be read as stereotypically queer.

Joan Cassidy, who held a civilian post with naval intelligence, considered the bars to be so dangerous that she and her friends socialized exclusively at private parties—and even in those settings, they took extreme pains to restrict the guest list to people in similar professions. "We never invited anyone who didn't have as much to lose as we did," she told author David K. Johnson.[12] (However much sympathy one feels for the women who denied themselves social interaction for the sake of financial security and to maintain the reputational benefits they'd worked hard to build, the constant repetition of "I had too much to lose" rightfully irritated women with less social capital. One working-class woman told academic Marie Cartier, "It's as if they're saying that . . . people like me had nothing to lose. . . . Everyone just has what they have, and everyone has everything to lose.")[13] In 1975, the Civil Service Commission ended its blanket denial of jobs to gay and lesbian people, but the chilling effect of the lavender scare lingered for years in the hearts and minds of anxious federal employees.[14]

Lesbians tended to be more educated than their heterosexual sistren, so they were more likely to have jobs they were desperate to protect. In *Sexual Behavior in the Human Female*, published in 1953, Alfred C. Kinsey noted that the more years a woman spent in formal education, the more likely she was to have same-sex relationships. Kinsey hypothesized that "prolongation of the years of schooling, and the consequent delay in marriage . . . interfere with any heterosexual development of these girls."[15] Let me suggest an alternative explanation: because they knew that in order to live independently or with another woman, they would need to be self-sustaining, lesbians were more motivated to stay in education.

These highly educated women were well-represented among those who joined pioneering lesbian rights groups like the Daughters of Bilitis (DoB) and subscribed to early homophile publications like *The Ladder* and *ONE*. Joining a gay-rights organization might appear to be a high-risk activity, but at the time it was considered safer to take part in activities organized by these mission-driven groups, whose middle-class members met in private homes, than to gather in bars. (In a private home, there was substantially less risk of having your gathering disrupted by police and your name printed in the next day's newspaper.) A survey carried out in 1961 revealed that 20 percent of *ONE*'s readership worked in education, including librarians as well as teachers and professors; 40 percent worked in other white-collar professions; and only 27 percent worked blue-collar or agricultural jobs.[16] Who knows how many of the women in white-collar jobs might have preferred dancing and drinking in seedy bars to wholesome discussion groups in well-lit living rooms, but the scales were weighted in favor of security.

When the Daughters of Bilitis was formed in 1955, the founding members adopted the French phrase *qui vive*, meaning "on the alert" or "on guard," as the organization's motto.[17] From the very beginning, a central tension within DoB was between providing a safe place for queer women to socialize, specifically somewhere safer than the raid-prone bars, and organizing to promote "the integration of the homosexual into society" through education, research, and political organizing. Many potential members who were desperate for the social benefits a group like DoB might provide them—a place to meet other lesbians and to socialize as couples—were nevertheless driven away because they were afraid of the attention such activism might generate. (It's mind-boggling to think that women felt safer inviting complete strangers into their homes than they did gathering in a duly licensed public place. And they were surely aware that summoning a group of women to a private home might attract the attention of nosy neighbors.)

The limitations of bar culture drove many women toward groups like the Daughters of Bilitis. For women who disliked taverns, it was the existence of an alternative—*any* alternative—rather than the specifics of DoB's policies or ideology that drove them to attend (or dream of attending) the Gab 'n' Java discussion sessions that convened in members' homes. In 1958, "Florence Ray" of Minnesota wrote to *The Ladder* to express envy of the San Francisco members who were able to "get together over a cup of coffee rather than a fifth."[18] "Ray" yearned "to discuss the problems that beset us and spend worthwhile time and effort in trying to find a solution rather than the intent of seeing who can drink the most and then so fortified—shake a defiant fist at the world."

Starting in the 1970s, the bars where those drinkers shook defiant fists started to change.

Elaine Romagnoli may well have been the most important lesbian bar operator of the twentieth century, but she didn't go into the hospitality industry to change the world. She just needed a job. Romagnoli's parents were working-class Italian immigrants who saw only one "career" path for women: marriage.[19] To a man. That wasn't in the cards for Elaine, nor was college, and when she graduated high school, she couldn't picture herself in an office. She'd worked as a waitress at Howard Johnson's all through high school, so when she left the family home in Palisades Park, New Jersey, and crossed the George Washington Bridge to New York City, she looked for work as a bartender.

Her first job was at the Horse's Head, a bar at 52nd Street and Eighth Avenue, not far from the cluster of Midtown jazz clubs once known as Swing Street. At that time—around 1960—it was illegal for women to work behind a bar after midnight in New York City, a rule supposedly designed to "protect" female employees but which just happened to ensure that only male bartenders were on duty when patrons left the biggest tips.[20] After spending the first half of her shift slinging drinks, Romagnoli was then obliged to spend the next few hours on the other side of the bar as a "B girl," socializing with male customers. "You had to get them to buy you drinks," she explained to me in 2011. "I would rather have stayed behind the bar, but I tell you something: I made so much money."

A decade into her life behind bars, Romagnoli knew she was very good at running "clubs," as she called them. "I was always being made the manager of something, so I decided, 'Why don't I just do this for myself?'" In 1972, she did just that, transforming a gay bar just below Washington Square Park known as the Tenth of Always into Bonnie & Clyde.[21] Romagnoli chose that name because she hoped to attract both gay men *and* women to the space, but because it was one of the first queer bars known to be managed by a lesbian, it became a de facto women's bar.

Some dispute whether Bonnie & Clyde was the Village's first lesbian-operated bar. At least one had previously been run by a woman: Kooky's on West 14th Street, which was open from 1965 to 1973.[22] The eponymous Kooky was said to be heterosexual, however.[23] According to Martin Duberman's *Stonewall*, she "ran her bar like a tyrannical man, ordering the lesbian patrons around as if they were scum, beneath contempt. She would think nothing of coming up to a woman sitting at the bar, grabbing her glass, and shoving it up to her mouth. 'Drink up, drink up,' she would growl. . . . Then Kooky would turn to the bartender and bark, 'She's buying another drink.'"[24] That was not the atmosphere at Bonnie & Clyde.

Bonnie & Clyde's amenities included a DJ spinning Wednesday through Saturday; a free buffet lunch every Sunday, and a pool table—the first, but definitely not the last, in a New York lesbian bar.[25] They took pool seriously at Bonnie & Clyde. A writeup in the September 1977 issue of *Christopher Street* noted, "People who are so ignorant as to go out of turn at the pool table should carry the best possible medical insurance."[26] The same reviewer described the bar's ambience as ranging "from impressive punky elegance to tinges of Southside Chicago dingeola" and its patrons as women "who feel extremely comfortable being gay in a determined and no-bullshit fashion."

Although the space at 82 West 3rd Street boasted a large window looking onto the street, the glass was covered with an oversized logo, which obscured the bar's interior. The sturdy wooden front door was similarly protective of patrons' privacy—a curious passer-by would have had to peer through a tiny porthole-like window, which was often plastered over with flyers, to catch a glimpse of what was happening inside.

In 1972, *Purple Rage*, a magazine published by the Gay Women's Liberation Front, cited Bonnie & Clyde as a prime example of a positive development in the women's bar scene. "It has a neighborhood bar atmosphere, no syndicate thugs at the door, political women are welcomed instead of banned (as in Kooky's) and drinks ARE NOT PUSHED."[27] This new business model—a supportive space run by an out lesbian rather than open exploitation by hostile straight people—required patrons to adjust their attitudes and change their behavior. *Purple Rage* explained to its readers that they should treat the bar's staff like "sisters, brothers and workers" rather than abusive profiteers: "When you buy drinks at the bar or the tables you should try and tip. This is the way the sisters earn their money."

Unlike the Mafia-run gay bars that traditionally served watered-down booze, Bonnie & Clyde poured the good stuff. This was so unusual that in 1977, eight years after Stonewall, a writeup in the *Women's Gayellow Pages* noted, "They serve genuine drinks, so you really feel like you've had some alcohol."[28] (The reviewer also noted, "The action is fast and the clientele on the younger side. Cruising seems to be a major attraction.")

Like most of the bars Romagnoli would later run in the Village, Bonnie & Clyde was especially popular with women of color. Her explanation for that distinction was straightforward: "It was me not discouraging them." At the time, bar operators—including many who served the lesbian community—weren't particularly subtle in the tactics they used to keep Black and Latina women out of their clubs:

requiring them to present multiple pieces of ID when white women could enter with one, or unevenly applying the dress code so that Black women were turned away while similarly dressed white women were welcomed. Romagnoli's attitude wasn't without business consequences, however. She claimed that once Bonnie & Clyde "started going Black," many of the white lesbian-feminists who had previously patronized the bar stopped drinking there. What's more, she said, when bars have a predominantly Black clientele, they are more likely to draw complaints from neighbors—especially in a gentrifying, mostly white neighborhood like Greenwich Village.

One group of people found Bonnie & Clyde absolutely irresistible and were willing to jump through hoops to gain entry, even though Manhattan already boasted thousands of bars that welcomed them with open arms: straight men. The bar's location across the street from a New York University frat house provided an endless supply of young fellows eager to cross its threshold. The legal situation was clear: anyone who is sober and of age must be admitted to a place of public accommodations. But Romagnoli knew that lesbian and bisexual women saw the bar as a refuge from straight men, whose presence would drive away her primary clientele. Romagnoli implemented a strict dress code as a deterrent, requiring male customers to wear a shirt and tie, but that was a minor hurdle for any guy determined to gain admittance. Nevertheless, men who felt excluded occasionally complained to the city's Division of Human Rights, which meant Romagnoli would have to show up at hearings to defend her bar's policies.

Eventually, knowing that her core demographic would seek out the place regardless of its appearance, Romagnoli tried a bold tactic: She made her establishment visually unappealing, allowing garbage to stack up around the bar's exterior so that anyone outside the magic lesbian circle would ignore it completely. In 1978, the Bonnie & Clyde holiday card acknowledged this unusual business practice.[29] It showed a trim Black woman wearing the classic waiter's uniform of tailored pants, vest, and bowtie, exiting the bar while holding a champagne-laden tray aloft. In contrast to the neat, smiling server, the area around the bar was a disaster scene—trash piled high, and a white woman sprawled on the ground, swigging from a bottle. The card's message read, "Thank you for not judging us by our cover. Happy Holidays, Bonnie & Clyde's."[30]

Bonnie & Clyde's 1978 holiday card acknowledged the bar's unprepossessing exterior. Photo by Joanne Giganti. *Source:* Lesbian Herstory Archives.

The carefully composed trashscape and covered windows weren't exactly an attempt to hide the bar's existence—that would be financial suicide. They were more about making it unattractive to all but the intended clientele. There's a long history of American bars using camouflage to try to outwit the licensing authorities. Saloon keepers put up coverings so that passers-by couldn't see inside their premises from the street, allowing them to flout Sunday and early-closing mandates. These tactics were outlawed by Prohibition-era "screen laws," which prohibited "curtains, screens, blinds, and/or other things in the window . . . which prevented a clear view and full view of the interior." In 1980, the Greenwich Village lesbian bar the Duchess came under fire from the New York State Liquor Authority for violating one of these ordinances.[31] This, along with a series of undercover operations and raids designed to establish that the Duchess refused to serve men, eventually led to the bar losing its license in 1982.[32] For some, obscured windows served a greater purpose than camouflage. In 2022, Sheila Smallman, one of the owners of Herz, a now-shuttered Black-owned lesbian bar in Mobile, Alabama, told writer Krista Burton that the windows were covered to keep politics, religion, and other related annoyances on the other side of the glass. "When you're in here," she said, "you're in your own little world."[33]

Repellent surroundings weren't the only "cover" Bonnie & Clyde was seeking forgiveness for. Patrons were asked to cough up a door charge that ranged between $3 and $4 over the bar's lifetime. Although the cover entitled each customer to two drinks, it wasn't always well received. Romagnoli recalled hearing a customer ask the woman working the door if she had to pay the cover since she didn't drink alcohol. This annoyed Romagnoli, but she realized that customers' economic imperatives didn't always align with hers. She told the nondrinker, "I can fill this place up with people who don't want to spend money. That's not why I'm here. I have a landlord. I have bills to pay."

In January 1981, Romagnoli taped a note to the door of the bar, announcing that Bonnie & Clyde was closing.[34] The lease had expired, and she was no longer "able to continue as a disco, dance operation." Romagnoli told *Womanews* that the closure "was not a result of lesbian harassment from neighbors or the landlord," though she acknowledged that the local community was convinced that discos attracted drug dealers.[35] She added that she intended to open new premises as soon as she found a suitable location.

Romagnoli made good on her promise to return to the lesbian bar scene in 1983, when she opened the Cubby Hole at 438 Hudson Street, a ten-minute walk from Bonnie & Clyde's location. The original Cubby Hole was tiny, just 360 square feet.[36] This meant there really wasn't room for a dance floor. A Canadian publication recommended going there only "if you don't mind not dancing."[37] In Romagnoli's view, this explained why this was her only Manhattan operation that was mostly patronized by white women: "Your Black clientele want a dance bar," she told me in 2011.

In July 1988, the Cubby Hole became the best-known lesbian bar in the world when Madonna made an unconvincing "surprise" appearance on *Late Night with David*

Letterman. Letterman had been jokingly needling regular guest Sandra Bernhard about her rumored relationship with the queen of pop, suggesting that the tabloids were exaggerating their closeness. Bernhard then summoned Madonna, who was dressed in an identical outfit of white T-shirt and denim shorts, and the pair proceeded to act like silly sweethearts. When Letterman asked them to describe a typical night on the town together, Madonna giggled that they caroused "en route to the Cubby," to which Bernhard immediately responded, "Hole."

Long after the messy, mushy *Late Night* segment, people were still buzzing about those two seconds of carefully staged sentence completion.[38] Unfortunately, the bar couldn't take advantage of the spotlight. The minuscule space was already operating at capacity, on weekends at least, and after the *Letterman* incident, Cubby Hole staff had to deal with Madonna fans tying up the phone line with calls from all over the world.

In the summer of 1989, Romagnoli found a much larger space a couple of blocks away at 21 Seventh Avenue South and opened Crazy Nanny's. Not wanting to compete against her own lesbian bar, she tried to rebrand the Cubby Hole as a neighborhood spot for both gay men and women. The experiment was a flop. Bartender Jay Funk, who worked at the Cubby Hole in its all-gender era, told a local gay paper, "I don't think dykes and fags are ready to sit [at a bar] together. A lot of women didn't come here because there were men here, and a lot of men didn't come here because there were women here."[39] To make things even more complicated,

Romagnoli's efforts to reshape the bar's demographics upset lesbian patrons so much that one group of dykes organized a "take back the Cubby night" in November 1990.[40]

Displaying her usual candor—it's clear Romagnoli never underwent media training—she later told *OutWeek*, "The only reason I even tried to keep the Cubby Hole open with boys is because boys spend more money."[41] But there was another motivation for rolling out the welcome mat to male patrons. Although Romagnoli had been dealing with the legal consequences of men complaining about being excluded from her bars since the days of Bonnie & Clyde, the State Liquor Authority had ramped up its persecution of lesbian bars for denying service to men, including the series of undercover stings and raids that led to the Duchess losing its license in 1982.[42] Romagnoli resented the time and expense of having to respond to these claims, but she was equally irritated that women didn't file similar grievances against clubs that excluded women, even if she understood why: "Perhaps because women are themselves discriminated against so often, they are reluctant to bring charges against someone else, especially another gay person."

In December 1990, Romagnoli announced that the Cubby Hole would be closing. The fabled name would live on, however. In 1993, Romagnoli's friend Tanya Saunders, who had been running DT's Fat Cat, a mixed, though mostly lesbian, bar at 281 West 12th Street, had a falling out with her business partner of ten years, Debra Fierro. Fierro left to open a bar and restaurant called Rubyfruit Bar and Grill a few blocks away. According to Romagnoli, Saunders was "distraught about the breakup and was worried that she wasn't going to be able to keep up that place without Debbie." Romagnoli believed Saunders "was hinting that she would like me to come on board," and although she was feeling "over the business" at that point, she agreed to do so. In 1994, she offered to transfer the name—now for some reason styled as the Cubbyhole, one word—to the small space on West 12th Street, leveraging the notoriety that still lingered many years after Madonna had mumbled it on late-night TV. (In yet another beat in this story, longtime Cubby Hole and Crazy Nanny's bartender Lisa Cannistraci expanded the former Cubby Hole space at 438 Hudson and reopened it in 1991 as Henrietta Hudson.[43] "Hens" is still in operation today.)

The cooperation between the "new" Cubbyhole and Crazy Nanny's saw Romagnoli and Saunders running ads in local gay and feminist publications that touted their unity and promoted both bars. In one of these shared display ads, Crazy Nanny's described itself as "A Place for Gay Women, Biological or Otherwise," a strap line that several later commentators have interpreted as an explicit statement of support for transgender customers.[44] There's no reason to think that Crazy Nanny's management or patrons had any animus against trans people, but the "biological or otherwise" phrasing wasn't a reference to trans customers. Instead, it referred to the controversy generated by a 1991 article in *Science* by neurobiologist Simon LeVay, which proclaimed that gay men had different brain anatomy than straight men, and therefore homosexuality was biological.[45] This theory was a big talking point at the time, with many queer people fearing

Inside the ad image:

A Place for
Gay Women

Biological
or Otherwise

Word is out...
THE FAT CAT'S
IN THE CUBBYHOLE!
Come share our New Life,
New Face
Yes! Yes! Yes!
New Exhaust, too!
Same cozy space!

CUBBY HOLE

281 W. 12th Street
Corner of W. 4th St
(212) 243-9041

Crazy Nanny's

2 Bars, Pool Table, Dancing,
Cabaret, Outdoor Cafe

21 7th Avenue South
New York, NY 10014

Events (212) 366-6312
Bar (212) 929-8356
Fax (212) 807-9195

OPEN NOW!

Serving the Gay and Lesbian Community
Tanya Saunders, Elaine Romagnoli

Elaine Romagnoli and Tanya Saunders touted their
bars' unity in shared ads. This ad appeared in the February 1995 issue of *Sappho's Isle.*

that linking homosexuality and biology would have negative
eugenic consequences.

In 1991, Crazy Nanny's advertised itself as "an asylum
from life and its cares, A place to exchange ideas, A neutral
ground where the unrelated can relate."[46] Although the ad
mentioned attractions like two bars and a full line of nonalcoholic beverages, the emphasis was on connection: "You are
invited to join us in a celebration of community, every night
of the week." And if there was any doubt as to which was the

better-known bar, Crazy Nanny's ads explained its location by referencing another club: it was "one block south and one block west of the Cubby Hole."

By 1993, the cover at Crazy Nanny's had risen to $5.[47] The larger space allowed Romagnoli to offer more-varied programming—the bar hosted fund-raisers, presented art shows, and widened its musical offerings to include a country night on Thursdays.

In these years, there was a corridor of dyke bars from Crazy Nanny's past Henrietta Hudson and Rubyfruit to the Cubbyhole—and on weekends, lesbian cruising along that strip was very much a reality. Longtime New York City resident Al Miller remembers women openly "asking for cigarettes and flirting with strangers," almost as if those blocks formed one enormous outdoor lesbian bar.[48] It was a rare time of fully public lesbian socializing—no special reason, no event or festival, just dykes on the street vibing together. The concentration of lesbian and welcoming mixed-gender bars drew more women to the neighborhood. Bars didn't feel that they were competing against each other—the cluster of nightlife options helped everyone's bottom line. Instead, their biggest competition came from one-night "parties" that promoters threw in straight or gay-men's clubs. In a May 1991 letter to *OutWeek*, Romagnoli complained that the lesbian community gave too little thought to why those venues "want you there only one night per week."[49] She also bemoaned the impact the events had on the bottom lines of gay businesses that were committed to opening every night of the year.

In 2011, when we talked in the West Village offices of my then employer *Slate* magazine, just blocks from where her clubs had bustled and thrived, Romagnoli said that in her next life she wanted to come back as a party promoter. "You don't even care about the laws. Your clients want to do coke? You just turn your back. You're not going to lose your license. You'll just move your party to another space." Even four decades after the "party" scene took off, Romagnoli was visibly bitter that so many of her customers had been tempted away by the one-nighters. "They all go to these events and come back at 3 a.m. when you have an hour to go, and they're already trashed."

It's easy to see why bar owners, who are obliged to cover the expense of keeping their establishments open through the doldrums of winter and every wet Wednesday in March, would resent the incursions of party promoters Pied Piper–ing their patrons off to pastures new. It's also clear why bar-goers would welcome the chance to meet and mingle in bigger and better clubs on an irregular basis. These understandings initially led me to dismiss as sour grapes Romagnoli's complaints about party promoters playing fast and loose with the law. That changed when I came across the story of the Shescape 7. When a company is constantly moving around, it's harder to spot patterns of discrimination—unless, of course, lesbians get together to talk about their experiences.

In 1986, a group of women—originally seven, though the list of complainants eventually grew to nine—filed a complaint with New York City's Commission on Human Rights. They claimed that events hosted by Shescape, first at their Midtown

East club, then, after that venue shuttered, at spots around the city, discriminated against Black and Latina patrons. Bouncers and door staff were said to have consistently found fault with the forms of ID shown by women of color; claimed that they didn't meet the dress code, even when white women wearing similar outfits were admitted; and, according to affidavits, repeatedly treated Black and Brown women with contempt. They were by no means the only bar operators alleged to have employed these tactics, but they appear to have been especially unsubtle in their application. One complainant reported hearing a manager tell a bouncer not to let any more Black women into the club because there were already too many inside. Shescape denied the charges, claiming, "Such negative attacks can only work to the detriment of all of us by making our already small community infinitely smaller and less cohesive."[50]

One of the Shescape 7 complainants was four-time Newbery Honor winner, former Young People's Poet Laureate, and MacArthur fellow Jacqueline Woodson. Thirty-five years later, Woodson remembered her days as a club kid. She went to Studio 54 as a teenager and grew up in that scene, eventually becoming part of a posse of young academics and artists who regularly got together for nights of dancing in Manhattan. The original Shescape club on East 58th Street was a great venue, she recalls, with a huge dance floor and excellent DJs. Woodson, who is Black, was admitted on a couple of occasions when she was with a group of predominantly white women. Several other times, though, she says she was left standing outside and had to endure disrespectful behavior from white security guards.

It was only when Woodson and her teammates in Brooklyn's Prospect Park Women's Softball League were talking about their experiences at Shescape events that she says they noticed the pattern. "We realized they were not letting Black women in, especially Black women who were coming in with other Black women."[51] Soon after, the women gathered at Brooklyn Women's Martial Arts in Park Slope, where many of them trained, to strategize about how to proceed. Eventually, they filed a claim.

Frustrated with the sluggish pace of deliberations, especially as Shescape continued to host parties around the city while the process dragged on, Woodson and others founded the Committee of Outraged Lesbians (COOL). COOL picketed and leafleted Shescape-sponsored parties at several clubs throughout 1986 and 1987, asking would-be patrons to stay away from a company that COOL said used racist admission policies. COOL flyers reminded potential attendees that patronizing Shescape events was "synonymous with . . . disrespecting the dignity of fellow human beings . . . and with reaffirming your desire to keep women of color 'out.'"[52] As a result of the protests, at least one venue—gay club the Saint—decided that it would stop renting to Shescape.[53] Woodson says, "I had no intention of being that kind of activist. I just wanted to write my books." But she says that the promoter's behavior was so egregious, she couldn't let it go unchallenged.

In January 1988, a settlement was reached that was widely seen as a victory for the complainants. Over the course of negotiations, Shescape had pledged to clearly state dress code and other admissions policies in the promotional materials for its events and agreed to make a donation to New York's Lesbian and Gay Services Center. In practice, though, the final statement is shockingly tame. Shescape simply "reaffirm[ed]" its commitment to nondiscrimination and said it "regret[ted] the anguish, upset or embarrassment suffered by the complainants as a result of inadvertent misapplication of such policy."[54] Meanwhile, the complainants were obliged to apologize for "any inadvertent inconvenience" their picketing and leafleting may have caused women attending those events.

Woodson says the Shescape 7 were disappointed by the resolution. "We asked, 'What has this changed?' They got to keep on keeping on." Indeed, Shescape stayed in business into the 1990s, organizing regular events at some of New York's swankiest clubs. Decades later, it's clear that the complainants and the women of color they were standing up for did not receive the level of support they deserved. *Gay Community News* reported that at a protest in the middle of February, a small group of picketers "braved the bitter cold" outside a Manhattan bar to distribute leaflets, but they "had difficulty in dissuading women from attending the event."[55] Anyone who entered a lesbian club in this period could see who was allowed in and who was kept out. Still, most white bar-goers prioritized their social lives over social justice and allowed lesbian spaces to operate as de facto white lesbian spaces.

Romagnoli closed Crazy Nanny's in 2004.[56] After 9/11, Romagnoli claimed, "her crowd," which is to say women of color, became more appealing to other bar owners whose businesses suffered after the attacks. That closure didn't officially mark the end of her entrepreneurial career, but it was the end of her run as a manager and owner of lesbian bars.

She held on to the liquor license after Crazy Nanny's closed, when the space became home to predominantly heterosexual clubs Luke and Leroy's (2004–2007) and Le Royale (2007–2009).[57] Romagnoli's "straight-bar years" represented a miserable end to a storied career. Regardless of her level of participation in the business, as far as the state was concerned, she was responsible for conduct in the club. That meant she was on the hook for the $5,000 fine imposed by the state in 2009 after a spot inspection of Le Royale in March of that year revealed a long list of infractions.[58] The bar was too crowded and too noisy, and it was clearly badly run.

Throughout her career, Elaine Romagnoli saw herself as both a businesswoman and an activist, raising the consciousness of her customers and funds for numerous good causes. She considered lesbian bars an almost sacred community resource because they are so often where people go to discover themselves. "You could always tell when someone was coming to a gay bar for the first time because of how frightened and uncomfortable they were as they approached the doorway," she told me. "I made a concerted effort to focus on them and introduce them to my bartender, and my bartender would always introduce them to people." To Romagnoli, owning a lesbian bar was inherently a political act, and her activism relied on her ability to keep the lights on. At the same time, though, Romagnoli didn't express much love for the business she spent fifty years working in. She didn't enjoy being around drunks or feeling trapped behind a bar and "forced" to talk to customers. "Everybody wants to tell you how to run your business, and you have to be polite," she said. "I loved it at first—it's like going to a party every night—but after a while, I just couldn't bear it." Still, she had a good run. "I made my livelihood from it, and I was successful. What I really liked doing was designing spaces. Once they got going, I wanted to move on, but I didn't always have the money to do that."

When I asked Romagnoli, who died in October 2021, about the biggest rewards of running bars, she told me, "I made money, and I had a lot of girlfriends."[59] But the hours were terrible—she would get home from the club at 6 a.m., rise at noon, and be back at work by 4 p.m.—and the obsession was endless. "I may have had a lot of girlfriends, but I never had a long-term relationship. I don't blame people for not wanting to be with me. The restaurant business is brutal if you care about what you're doing."

The lesbian bar business is particularly brutal for a host of economic and psychological reasons, starting with their very location. Romagnoli's clubs were in densely packed Greenwich Village in public-transportation-friendly New York City, but lesbian bars have traditionally been established in out-of-the-way places. Poet Chocolate Waters summarized the situation in most American cities in the opening words of a poem she published in the December 1979 issue of *Big Mama Rag*: "The Trouble with Women's Bars in This

Town / is that they're all across the street from the Pepsi Cola Bottling Company or / Joe's Electrical Heating Service or / right next door to the Climax Lounge."[60]

The month after Waters's poem appeared, Mac McCann, who had run women's bars in Saint Louis for a decade, responded with a long and angry letter to *Big Mama Rag* spelling out the reasons why and how lesbian bars came to be placed on the fringes of city life. "Bars don't grow on quiet cozy corners," she wrote. "To open a bar, isolated from the Pepsi Colas, the Joes Electric Shops of the world, would cost a fortune."[61]

As McCann explained, locations that might seem desirable are often headache inducing. One of her bars was in a progressive gay-friendly neighborhood of Saint Louis, but parking was impossible, and she endured constant conflicts with the men who ran the gay club upstairs. McCann then got a chance to "graduate to a place I felt would be all ours. . . . But it was a predominantly Black neighborhood. Many women would not come in at all because this was true, and many of those women were Black."

Eventually, having built up a decent credit record, McCann opened a new bar, Mor or Les, in a prime spot in South Saint Louis. "Parking was excellent. The place was large and furnished beautifully. The neighborhood was supposedly excellent. We *deserved* this place!" Unfortunately, Mor or Les was subject to intense harassment. In short order, the bar endured having its expensive windows broken, a bomb scare, men exposing themselves to customers, and numerous general disruptions that made business all but impossible. A reporter from the *St. Louis Post-Dispatch* wrote, "The bar does not blend in quietly with the conservative neighborhood. It is obviously different and almost flaunts its difference."[62] Neighbors seemed offended by Mor or Les's lack of discretion. A local businessman told the paper, "They're not at all quiet about it.... They seem to relish all the debate." Eventually, the neighbors took advantage of a city ordinance mandating that if 51 percent of local residents and property owners signed a petition requesting that a bar be closed, it must do so, without need for any further justification. The bar lost its license—and while McCann was fighting the decision, the premises were firebombed, and Mor or Les closed for good.[63]

Running a bar was a lonely job, as Elaine Romagnoli knew all too well. One of the most affecting parts of Mac McCann's letter to *Big Mama Rag* was her acknowledgment of how isolated she felt. It wouldn't be good business practice to tell customers that the guys at the club upstairs were being jerks, that patrons' cars had been broken into, or that neighbors were trying to close down the bar. That information might well cause them to stay away. Even politically conscious lesbian business owners must keep some things to themselves if they want customers to come through the door.

As McCann's experience attests, the trouble with women's bars isn't only that lesbian-owned businesses tend to be undercapitalized and thus find the rents in upscale areas a stretch or that they often face homophobic harassment; it's also that they must cater to multiple audiences under the broad umbrella of queer women. Yes, they have to attract lesbians, a minority of the population, but more challeng-ingly they must satisfy every kind of lesbian. The United States, with a population of more than 333 million, has fewer than thirty lesbian bars, and as of 2023, only six US cities supported more than one.[64] Consequently, bar owners must please rowdy young party dykes and older women who'd pre-fer a quiet conversation with friends; pool sharks and dancing queens; women who want to invite straight friends, fam-ily members, and coworkers to the bar; and customers who would prefer if it were just for queers.

Lesbian bars must be all things to all queer women. Straight establishments can be cocktail bars, fern bars, pickup bars, dive bars, or any other kind of bar their pro-prietors can dream up; dyke joints almost never get to spe-cialize. That means our bars must appeal to women of all ages, even though economic imperatives mean that younger patrons, who go out more frequently and buy more drinks, are more valuable customers. Back in 1958, a reader wrote to *ONE* imploring an entrepreneurial type to open a club for older women, because, she said, "the usual bars for lesbians are frequented by teen-agers, as far as I can determine. An older woman, without a companion, feels something like an old granny, and very much out of place."[65] Straight people aren't obliged to keep patronizing the bar they stumbled into at twenty-one, but because of the lack of alternative options, lesbians are supposed to remain loyal for life.[66]

If all this makes the lesbian bar seem like an all-inclusive resort that provides for its customers' every need, well, that's a fantasy, albeit an irresistible one. The ideal lesbian bar is a one-stop shop where women can find love and friendship, blow off steam, live out pool-shark fantasies, bond as teammates, dress however they like, dance with whomever they like, and learn the address of the nearest Subaru dealership. One woman who had married a man after exploring the lesbian scene in the 1940s admitted that for years afterward she would call local gay bars to recapture that thrill through the phone line: "I would just hear the noise and the laughter in the background. I just wanted to be there."[67]

It seems obvious that as more lesbians are fully out to their families, employers, and coworkers, there is less need for secrecy. Even today, though, bars need to feel like a safe space for shy women just starting to explore their sexuality, for the very private, or for those who would prefer at least some of the people in their lives to assume that they are heterosexual. This explains why, historically, many queer women have felt more comfortable socializing in neighborhoods where they're unlikely to run into anyone from their "straight" life. If the bar is far from their usual stomping grounds, the only people likely to recognize them are other patrons of the queer space—people who have their own secrets to keep. Until quite recently, the ideal lesbian bar was one where everyone knew your name, but no one saw you going in.

Of course, every distant neighborhood is someone's home turf. Mac McCann shouldn't have been surprised that Black women were reluctant to patronize her bar when it was based in a Black neighborhood. While white women may have stayed away because of racially inflected "safety" concerns, women of color likely avoided the place because they lacked anonymity there. Take a city like Washington, DC. While a white woman from a high-income area of the northwest of the city may feel she's unlikely to run into an old school friend or someone her mother knows from church in the predominantly Black southeastern part of town, women who grew up in that neighborhood don't have the same expectation.

Partly because of racist attitudes in predominantly white bars, and partly because there was little Mafia involvement in predominantly Black bars, which left them vulnerable to police harassment and raids, many Black lesbians preferred to socialize at house parties. Just as with white government employees, who, keen to protect their jobs, socialized in tight circles, the invitation list for some of these gatherings was limited to groups of friends. Others, in the tradition of "rent parties" or "pay parties," took the form of unlicensed functions, advertised via flyers, where attendees would pay an admission charge, buy drinks and food, and could even check their coats.

By the 1970s, bars throughout the nation were changing. In 1973, *Lesbian Tide* singled out Butterfly West, a new Los Angeles lesbian bar that was breaking the existing mold of dimly lit, booze-sodden, "role-oriented" joints that "don't reflect our openness and pride as lesbians or women."[68] Although the owners refused to label themselves or their venue as feminist—they didn't want to turn off nonpolitical customers—they at least declared themselves willing to allow "those with fuzzy hair and work shirts" into their bar. The challenge was to get old-school patrons to understand the radical new dykes. "The older crowd is not used to seeing women with unshaven arm pits who get up and talk openly about themselves as lesbian women," one of the owners told the *Tide*. To reflect their ideological evolution, Butterfly West's owners had already taken down some of the "sexist nude-bunny-chick paintings" put up by the previous proprietors. They promised to remove the rest as soon as someone brought in posters to replace the offending images that were still covering holes in the walls.

The dingy decor that was de rigueur in lesbian bars—whether by design, as at Bonnie & Clyde, or the result of insufficient funds, as at Butterfly West—didn't make women feel good about themselves. When Leslie Cohen and her three partners set out to open Sahara, a lesbian club on New York's Upper East Side, providing a sense of luxury was very much on their minds. Cohen claimed that on Sahara's opening night in 1976, women gasped as they entered the club, "because what they were expecting was more of what they were used to, which was very little; instead, they were overwhelmed by the elegance they encountered. Depleted, minimal expectations had created a collective low self-esteem that Sahara was determined to correct."[69]

Once bars have closed, it can be hard to get a clear picture of how they were decorated and furnished. The need to protect customer privacy meant that photography was deeply discouraged, and without visual aids, few former patrons remember the interior decor. When a graduate student tracked down a longtime Crazy Nanny's bartender and one of the club's regulars and asked them to describe the joint, neither could remember anything distinctive, other than a large video screen.[70] The same cannot be said about Sahara. Cohen, who had a master's degree in art history, took great pride in the details—from the butcher-block bar to the Italian sectional couches and the paintings by women artists she hung on the walls. Although the name lacked any particular feminist resonance—Cohen wanted the bar to be "an oasis in the desert of conformity"—the logo, presented in a font that evoked swaying palm trees, became a highly visible brand, emblazoned on the outdoor awning and plastered across the large picture window, where according to long-standing tradition, it obscured the bar's interior from the eyes of passers-by.

Of course, lesbians have never socialized exclusively in lesbian bars—and thank goodness, because given their scarcity, that would be like having to eat chili for dinner every night for life. Most cities lack alternative lesbian hostelries to "graduate" to when bar-goers develop different musical tastes, can afford to socialize in more salubrious surroundings, or break up with another regular.

Ideally, we wouldn't have given the bar such a prominent role in our community. Their noise makes conversation difficult, lending outsize importance to physical signifiers, a sure-fire recipe for shallowness and superficiality. (Homosexual establishments have no monopoly there, of course.) And then there is the alcohol. Although we often describe queer bars as havens and sanctuaries, they exist to sell booze, which can be a destructive force.

As a passionate supporter of queer and lesbian spaces and culture, I hate to admit that I'm not a huge fan of the bar as an institution. Whenever I hear that old joke "the food here is terrible, and the portions are so small!" I think of the lesbian equivalent: dyke bars are awful, and there are way too few of them. OK, perhaps the "lesbian" in that last sentence is just me and my bad attitude. I rarely go to clubs anymore. I've been in a happy relationship for more than twenty-five years with someone who rarely drinks. Bars are loud, they get going too late, and they're packed with people half my age. They make me feel old.

I still feel like a traitor for abandoning them.

Since I've always had these conflicted feelings about bars—how can they be both the most exciting and the most dispiriting public spaces I know?—I remember feeling "seen" when I first read Felice Newman's essay "Why I'm Not Dancing," published in the 1978 anthology *Lavender Culture*. Newman, who was a senior at the University of Pittsburgh when she wrote the piece, was frustrated by the limited connections that were possible in such a noisy environment: "Because it is difficult, if not impossible, to develop much of a conversation in a bar setting," she wrote, "the projections of age, class, race, clothes, hair length, bodily proportions, and dexterity replace language. I did not feel that I could be known by anyone."[71] As far as Newman was concerned, the bar scene facilitated queer people's isolation rather than providing a solution to it. "We are remaindered at birth, fenced off into profitable ghettos. We are weakened by alcoholism and exploited economically."

Forty-five years after the piece was first published, I asked Newman—whom I got to know in the 1980s when we both worked in feminist publishing, she as one of the founders of Cleis Press and I as a staffer at Seal Press—to reflect on her youthful views. She remembered how the bars had made her feel intimidated, isolated, and scared and how she had desperately wanted to belong to a community but found the space that was supposed to be its home anything but welcoming. She was comfortable in intellectual contexts, talking about feminism or books, but the loud music and the way bars are organized, as a series of tight spaces that require customers to constantly push by one another, actively discouraged that kind of interaction. What Newman felt she had to offer the world— ideas, argumentation—wasn't valued in the bar.

In the 1980s, Newman found the version of community she'd been looking for in feminist bookstores, but since then she's been disappointed by our failure to build and sustain community centers. "The gay centers that we have now, they're substitutes for gay community centers. They're focused on mental health—which really needs to be addressed—or places where you can take classes. But that's not a true community center."[72]

Not everyone feels that way, of course. Actress Lea DeLaria has hosted walking tours of Manhattan's lesbian bars, and she'll sing their praises at the drop of a hat. As well as the sense of safety they provide, she values them as "one of the few places where lesbians are allowed to be sexual."[73] For DeLaria, who identifies as a feminist lothario, bars are intensely erotic spaces. "The Cubbyhole is the only lesbian bar in the world where I haven't had sex in the bathroom— and that's only because the restrooms are very small and there's always a humongous line. It would be rude," she told me.

From the 1950s onward, some women focused their efforts on creating alternatives to the lesbian bar scene. A number of these projects were led by sober dykes who wanted to socialize in an alcohol-free environment, but others simply aimed to provide a quiet space that encouraged conversation.

There's still another reason why many women didn't feel comfortable relying on bars as their primary social spaces. Today, more years have passed since the Stonewall riots set Greenwich Village alight than had elapsed between the beginning of Prohibition and the opening of Bonnie & Clyde. I mention this because I have long felt that the ambivalence many lesbians feel about the bar scene is a spiritual holdover from women's intense involvement in the temperance movement—the philosophical precursor to Prohibition— which was also inextricably linked with the fight for women's suffrage. Women spent almost as many years fighting against the very existence of saloons as they've been patronizing them in large numbers. Not until World War II did bars begin to be considered suitable venues for respectable women.

The Woman's Christian Temperance Union (WCTU), founded in 1874, was the largest women's organization of its day.[74] It had one aim: to close all bars. By shuttering the grog dens where men wasted on alcohol the wages needed to feed and clothe their families, WCTU members believed they would improve the lot of American women. In the 1870s, the closest most women got to a bar was taking part in the era's signature protest, in which temperance-minded women would hold vigils outside—and, when they could gain entry, inside—saloons, drugstores, and hotels.[75] There they would pray, sing hymns, and read passages from the Bible, imploring proprietors to stop peddling the demon drink. Inspired by temperance activists in Britain and Canada, WCTU members created coffee shops and temperance hotels to provide alternative gathering places to booze-sodden men-only saloons and to model sober socializing.

The echoes of those teetotal meeting places can be seen in the alternatives to the bar that lesbians built in the 1970s and beyond. Whether for reasons of physiology or propriety, there's no lesbian tradition of cruising areas—that is, sites for public sex—which gay men have historically created in parks, public restrooms, and parking lots. Still, there have often been restaurants, cafés, and coffee shops where queer people could gather, and because of the paucity of alternatives, they were particularly precious to lesbian and bisexual women.

The most important of these was the coffeehouse. In many ways, though, creating a viable coffeehouse was even more of a challenge than setting up a bar. Using a phrase that was often associated with feminist bookstores, the founders of the New York Women's Coffeehouse (NYWC), which operated between 1974 and 1978 in Greenwich Village—just a block from where Crazy Nanny's was located twenty years later—said they wanted the venue to serve as a women's center. Unfortunately, like women's centers, coffeehouses lacked a reliable income stream.

Temperance activists from a century earlier would probably claim that the New York Women's Coffeehouse offered more wholesome entertainment than could be found in a bar: concerts by feminist performers, movie screenings, open-mic nights, and evenings focused around discussions of tarot, astrology, and witchcraft.[76] It was, declared *Dyke: A Quarterly*, "the only women-owned, women-only, clean, brightly lit place [in New York City] where women [could] be together and have a good time."[77] The biggest business challenge was that without alcohol sales, it was tough to make enough money to stay in business. The NYWC's seven volunteer collective members put in long hours—at least two eight-hour shifts each week, plus a monthly collective meeting that could eat up a whole day.[78] At first, volunteers were enlisted to work as waitresses in exchange for food, but the practice was discontinued when the cost of the volunteers' meals exceeded income from paying customers.

A lack of waitstaff had made another kind of restaurant—the automat, where food was dispensed from vending machines—popular in the early part of the twentieth century. Automats were a huge hit, especially after Prohibition took hold, because the inexpensive fare available there was a much-needed substitute for the free lunches that taverns used to provide. Automats were particularly popular with gay people, because customers selected their own food from vending machines and then carried their choices to whichever table was available, which meant there were no waiters around to police their behavior.[79]

The anonymity of the automat was a boon for queer customers, but cafeterias of all stripes took on a lavender hue at night, after office workers and theatergoers were tucked up in bed. One antivice activist complained that sex workers and homosexuals were turning restaurants into their "resorts" after Prohibition closed down the bars.[80]

Occasionally, these after-hours hangouts turned into sites of queer resistance. In May 1959, a skirmish broke out around Cooper's Doughnuts, a shabby all-night Los Angeles coffee shop frequented by hustlers and their customers, when gays threw paper cups and doughnuts at police officers rather than submit to arbitrary arrests.[81] Similarly, in the summer of 1966, street kids, queens, and hustlers who patronized Compton's Cafeteria in San Francisco's Tenderloin district fought with cops who were trying to detain them.[82]

In *Highsmith: A Romance of the 1950s*, a memoir of her love affair with author Patricia Highsmith, Marijane Meaker shares happy memories of Greenwich Village restaurants that welcomed same-sex couples. They didn't turn away women wearing pants, and "unlike gay *bars*, which were Mafia-run and often rude to their patrons, restaurants like Aldo's, the Fedora, and the Finale gave you support," Meaker wrote. "You felt comfortable in them. You could hold hands, sit close, and enjoy being treated like any other couple."[83]

These places rarely advertised that they were gay-friendly, which meant they were only accessible to people who had already built a network of plugged-in friends. For those in the know who wanted to keep the party going after the bars closed, which in New York meant after 4 a.m., there was usually a go-to postbar destination for the gay crowd. In Greenwich Village, for many years that spot was Pam Pam's. One regular described it as "an absolute scene. Every gay person . . . wound up there at some point. It was like a bar that served coffee."[84]

In the 1970s, dining out could be an ordeal for women. According to the *New Women's Survival Catalog*, an "unescorted" woman visiting a restaurant risked being treated with condescension, stared at, leered at, and hassled. There was a decent chance that she would be "joined" by "uninvited males who regard any single women out by themselves as fair game; and insulted if she ask[ed] an intruder to take his unwanted attentions elsewhere."

A few lesbians and feminists decided to establish restaurants of their own. In Greenwich Village—where else?!—in April 1972, management consultant Jill Ward and journalist Dolores Alexander, a couple at the time, opened Mother Courage, America's first explicitly feminist restaurant, so that women would have a congenial place to dish and dine.

When Mother Courage opened, there were just three items on the menu—spaghetti and meatballs, chili, and a daily special—and though the menu soon expanded, the feminist ambience, not the food, was what drew people to the restaurant. In 1974, Ward told a reporter from the *International Herald Tribune* that in the early days, the food had been "bad," though that hadn't prevented people from coming in five nights a week to support them.[85] Ward probably felt empowered to make this harsh judgment because she had been the restaurant's first cook, despite having no culinary training or restaurant experience. Ward said she wanted Mother Courage "to be known as a feminist restaurant, not as a restaurant on West 11th where you can get Chicken Kiev for $4.95."

Alexander had been the first executive director of the National Organization for Women before being fired in an antilesbian purge.[86] (She wasn't out, even to herself, at the time.) She was proud that "a woman coming to eat here alone knows she won't feel like a freak and won't get hassled by men."[87] Ward described the restaurant as a kind of salon—a type of gathering that is usually convened in a private rather than commercial setting. She told the *International Herald Tribune*, "We're not a restaurant, we're a referral service, a check-cashing service. We'll cash anyone's check once, none have bounced yet. People come in and ask for jobs, apartments, who's a good feminist lawyer or gynecologist or plumber."

Mother Courage developed feminist food-service policies. If a man ordered for a female companion, the waitress ignored him and asked the woman what she would like. When diners ordered wine, the waitstaff always offered the first "tasting" sip to a woman, and when it was time for the check, it was always placed in the middle of the table, with no assumptions made as to who would be paying. Unfortunately, according to Alexander, women were "lousy tippers," so the restaurant imposed a 15 percent service charge for some parties so that the waitresses wouldn't be stiffed.[88]

Mother Courage closed in December 1977. Alexander was a silent partner by that point, having taken a job at *Time* magazine, and Ward became too burnt-out to continue.[89] One evening, she put a note on the door that read, "Sorry, folks, I just can't do it anymore."[90]

That was the end of Mother Courage, but on the other side of the country, Berkeley's Brick Hut Cafe was already two years into its twenty-two-year run. While the Manhattan restaurant catered to the dinner set, the lesbian-feminist-owned and lesbian-feminist-operated Brick Hut was more of a casual breakfast and lunch spot. "The morning-after place," says Joan Antonuccio, who worked at the Hut for two decades.[91] The first of the Hut's three homes had just three booths and nine more seats at a classic diner-style counter. On weekends, women waiting for a table turned the sidewalk outside the café into lesbian space. Sharon Davenport, who also worked at the Brick Hut for more than twenty years—she and Antonuccio were the final owners of record—described the crowd as including "working girls, bad boys, suburban queens, transmen, and transwomen."[92] At the height of the AIDS crisis, the restaurant, known as the Dyke Diner, the Lesbian Luncheonette, the Chick Hut, and the Brick Hug, became a clearinghouse for AIDS information. It was one of the first restaurants in the East Bay to display posters declaring, "You can't get AIDS from a glass."

The Brick Hut was fully enmeshed in the East Bay lesbian-feminist scene. Women from Seven Sisters Construction helped with carpentry and construction projects; printers and booksellers from Mama Bears, A Woman's Place, and the Women's Press Collective were regular diners; and collective members and artists from feminist recording label

Olivia Records, which was based around the corner from the café's first location, often ate there. The Hut was even used as the "set" for the cover of one of Olivia's albums. The front cover of Mary Watkins's 1978 album *Something Moving* shows her looking out from a seat at the counter, surrounded by diners who are chatting with the waitstaff.[93] The album features a song about the café called "Brick Hut," with lyrics by poet Pat Parker, another regular.

In 1995, the Brick Hut moved to its final location on a block of San Pablo Avenue known as Girl Town, thanks to the concentration of feminist businesses like sex-toy store Good Vibrations, antique emporium It's Her Business, and West Berkeley Women's Books. Here they experimented with evening opening hours and got a license to serve beer and wine—but, although there was still a line down the block on weekends, business wasn't strong enough the rest of the week to keep the place alive. Two years after their move, the Brick Hut called it quits.

Speaking with Antonuccio and Davenport in 2021, I was struck by how often they returned to topics that other interviewees who earned their living working in lesbian spaces also mentioned. Like many bar owners and booksellers, they were conscious of being working-class women who didn't have family or other resources to draw on. As was true of so many lesbian-run businesses, their restaurant was always undercapitalized. The original owner had sold the Brick Hut to a group of lesbian employees who then paid off the note at $250 a month for eight years. There was no other money available to invest in growing the business. Also as elsewhere, the worker-owners had no concerns about competition from other lesbian establishments. Antonuccio trained a woman who was planning to open another women's café just a couple of miles from the Hut. She taught her how much to order, how to make food, and how to run a line. Hadn't she been worried about competition? "The more the merrier," she still believed decades later.

Although it was undoubtedly a place of business, Brick Hut workers also viewed it as a community resource where people could stop by for information or companionship. When the café closed each day around 3 p.m., they would make the space available to social justice groups like Bay Area Women Against Rape. The creators of Black lesbian journal *Aché* met in the café for several years. During times of political turmoil, the Hut leaned into its role as a shared space. During the Iran-Contra hearings in 1987 and Clarence Thomas's Supreme Court confirmation hearings in 1991, they cranked up the volume on the café's radio and invited neighborhood people to sit and listen.

"We were great feminists; we were great socialists," said Davenport. "But we were not good capitalists. If money was the way you judge success, we weren't at all successful. But if success could be seen as contributing to your community— the whole community, not just the lesbian community—we were very successful."

The difficulty of succeeding ideologically *and* financially is a theme that will resurface throughout this book, but the challenge feels especially daunting in the worlds of hospitality and nightlife. As a community—or, more realistically, as a series of overlapping communities—we crave places that feel like home, albeit a more accepting, supportive home than many of us grew up in.

But bars aren't our homes. They are commercial enterprises whose operators must make money to stay in business. Economic theory would suggest that if dyke bars were as precious as we claim, the sector would be in a much less precarious state. It seems to me, though, that when customers become too invested in someone else's business—when they treat it not just as a place to drink and gossip but as an essential community resource—we lose sight of some fundamental realities of life under capitalism.

Queer women have high standards, especially when it comes to policing our own community. In 1977, women in Portland, Oregon, angry that Rising Moon, a lesbian-owned and lesbian-operated bar, charged fifty cents for a beer, rather than the thirty-five cents at competitors' taverns, pasted a sign on the door that read, "This Bar Exploits Women." When a local feminist publication asked Rising Moon's owners to justify their prices, they explained that as a new venture, their costs were higher than those of established bars that had already paid off their loans and purchased their equipment. The biggest challenge, though, was the bar's limited clientele. "If we had all kinds of people coming in here, we could lower the prices, and make some money," Sallie Bird explained, but their customers would only patronize the bar if it were as close to women-only as they could legally get away with.[94] The owners were also frustrated that the protesters were willing to accept poor conditions in bars operated by men. It wasn't that they didn't have issues with other local hostelries; they just didn't care enough to fly-poster their premises. We love our spaces, so we're tough on them, which often ends up hurting them.

I, too, plead guilty to this sin. A few pages ago, I made some harsh comments about lesbian bars, possibly the result of bruised feelings after a rude exchange with a person checking IDs decades ago or feeling hard-done-by when a dyke bar seemed dingier than I would have liked it to be. Have I been treated worse in straight bars? Undoubtedly! Have I seen nastier taverns than DC's Phase One in the 1980s? Repeatedly! Do I nurse grievances about those straight establishments? Not even for a minute.

The Rising Moon resentments played out nearly fifty years ago, but similar thinking contributes to the garment rending about the mass closures of lesbian bars today. Yes, the number of dyke bars has decreased dramatically in recent years, from more than two hundred in 1987 to fewer than three dozen today.[95] But that doesn't mean that our world is 80 percent smaller than it was back then. Quite the opposite. We might still *choose* to socialize in lesbian bars from time to time, but there are now infinitely more options available to us.

"We" are different now too. A movement away from separatism toward inclusion and some fundamental shifts in the way we understand gender make it impossible to compare the listings in that chunky gay guide I purchased in the early 1980s with internet search results from the 2020s.

Bars remain pretty much the same, but lesbians are very different—as are "lesbian bars." In 2023, Henrietta Hudson, located at 438 Hudson, where Elaine Romagnoli launched the Cubby Hole four decades earlier, styled itself as "a queer human space built by Lesbians."[96] May the process of reinvention never end.

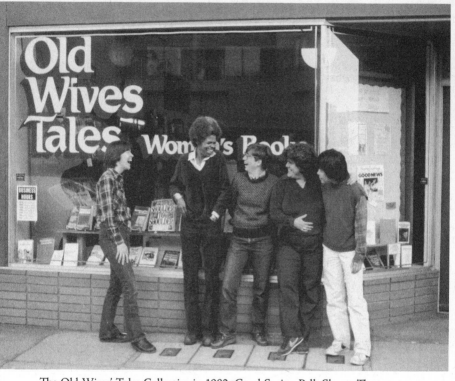

The Old Wives' Tales Collective in 1982: Carol Seajay, Pell, Sherry Thomas, Tiana Arruda, and Kit Quan. © 1982 JEB (Joan E. Biren)

TWO
FEMINIST BOOKSTORES

FOR BOOKISH LESBIANS OF THE 1970S AND 1980S, WOM-
en's bookstores were the hub of the local community—
and being without one was as isolating, and as undesirable,
as being without internet access in the twenty-first century. I
was fortunate enough to live through the halcyon days. Coming of age in the 1980s, feminist bookstores were my Google, my Craigslist, my Tinder—and, of course, my Amazon.
Among their cluttered shelves, I received an education in
politics, poetry, and feminist theory. Bookstores were a place
to meet collaborators, friends, and lovers. They shaped my
musical tastes and my reading habits, and they taught me the
importance of supporting independent lesbian businesses.
When I lived in Washington, DC, and worked part-time at
Lammas, the city's great feminist bookstore, I absorbed valuable lessons about the diversity of readers and the urgency of
their desire for lesbian books.

In the mid-1990s, about 135 feminist bookstores operated around the United States and Canada; today, around two dozen still provide resources and inspiration.[1] Bookstores weren't just the daytime equivalent of the lesbian bar, though they, too, provided a physical space for women to connect and conspire. They were open to customers of all ages and were free from the risk of exposure that accompanied a trip to a lesbian bar well into the 1970s. Indeed, they were downright respectable. During my teenage years, when my mother took me shopping in the nearest big city, she never complained about the hours I spent picking through the feminist and gay sections of Grass Roots, Manchester's radical bookstore—after all, books are educational. (No complaints—though she did wonder how I knew all the short-haired women who nodded at me across the display tables.)

Historically, books have held special importance for LGBTQ people. In her autobiographical work, Alison Bechdel has frequently depicted the personal awakenings that were catalyzed by visits to bookshops and libraries. In a 1993 cartoon, she depicts herself as a lost and lonely transfer student idly browsing the shelves of the Oberlin College bookstore.[2] What seems like minutes after coming across *Word Is Out* and inhaling the groundbreaking interviews with openly gay men and women that it contained, she realizes with life-changing clarity that she's a lesbian. "Who else has to go to a store to find out who they are?" she asked me three decades later. "But at that time in history, that's how many people figured it out."[3]

Women's bookstores were spaces of lesbian enlightenment and engines of political activism and economic experimentation. They supported artists and craftswomen by selling their wares and used their combined purchasing power to pressure male-run publishers to take a chance on new writers and republish out-of-print "classics." They taught women how to run their own businesses and gave people like me their first movement jobs—fantastic gigs that came with a perk that almost made up for the terrible pay: a sweet, sweet store discount.

When I moved to Madrid in the 1980s, the feminist bookstore network came through for me once again. My first stop upon arriving in the city was the Librería Mujeres on Calle San Cristóbal. Sure, I wanted something to read, but I also needed a place to live and to get the scoop on the social scene. I was betting that the Spanish store would have its own equivalent of Lammas's thick binders of flyers about groups, meetings, and gathering places, and sure enough, the Librería Mujeres provided connections I couldn't have found anywhere else. Days after my first visit, I moved into an apartment I had seen advertised on the shop's bulletin board—and that straight roommate introduced me to almost all the queer friends I made that year.

The stores were pillars of the community, sponsoring softball teams, distributing forests' worth of flyers, and selling tickets to concerts and fund-raising events. They hosted author readings and dedicated precious shelf space to binders of information about twelve-step meetings, affinity groups, and drum circles. It was a friendly space where you could always find lesbians and feminists and where the staff had read the books on the shelves and could advise if an author had good politics or if her sex scenes were worth reading.

To understand the importance of feminist bookstores as a physical space where women could gather, ask questions, and receive advice, where they could find books filled with hard facts about lesbian life or fantasies of romance and happily ever after, and where a few determined souls devoted their working lives to changing the ways women could access all those resources, let's look at the mother of them all, Amazon Bookstore of Minneapolis, Minnesota.

The very first women's bookstore in North America began as a ragtag collection of volumes stacked in the front parlor of a communal home. Rosina Richter and Julie Morse were antiwar activists who had created one of the Twin Cities' first feminist newsletters and had been holding consciousness-raising meetings in the Brown House commune in Minneapolis's Seward neighborhood.[4] In October 1970, they launched Amazon Bookstore. At first, the store was a casual affair without a staff or regular business hours. (Fellow commune resident Don Olson made the store's inaugural sale, since Richter and Morse were out when the first customer dropped by.)[5] But at a time when the air was thick with new ideas, it was hugely important as a central location where women could find books about feminism, along with periodicals chronicling the growing women's liberation movement.

Although it was technically a residential property, the Brown House that hosted Amazon operated as something between a private and a public space. Early patron Cheri Register remembered the commune as the center of the countercultural scene, the place you called when you wanted to know what was going on in the Twin Cities. Still, the "store" mostly attracted the attention of people who were already politically engaged. According to Register, "You couldn't necessarily find [Amazon] in the phone book; you had to be somewhat connected. You could find it in the alternative presses."[6]

Just two years later, Richter and Morse departed the Brown House to found a women-only karate school committed to teaching women to be "defenders of justice."[7] Morse's politics eventually shifted rightward. In 1987, she married Allen Quist, a Republican state representative and later two-time gubernatorial candidate who was a passionate opponent of abortion and gay rights. She later worked for Rep. Michele Bachmann and became an ardent supporter of President Donald Trump.[8] On the store's twenty-fifth anniversary, she told the *Minnesota Women's Press*, "I don't think it's a tremendous accomplishment."[9] As shocking as it is to see the founder of such an august institution renounce its ideological underpinnings, it's a useful reminder that being comfortable living an identity such as *feminist* or *lesbian* is partially dependent on finding a home in a community that supports and respects the values those identities represent. Many in the movement surely felt disappointed and perhaps even betrayed by Morse Quist's shifting allegiances, but her story is illustrative of the very real incentives to choose comfort over community.

The departing founders sold their inventory to Cindy Hanson and Karen Browne for $400, and the bookstore moved to the new owners' home on Cedar Avenue South.[10] It was an unprepossessing private house, but the women turned it into a semipublic space, erecting a huge sign reading, "Amazon Book Store. Feminist Literature," on the wall of the building's second floor. They also advertised. A handwritten ad in *Gold Flower*, a feminist newspaper based in Minneapolis, listed operating hours on four days—they were open for a total of seventeen hours a week, including evenings and weekends.[11] The ad touted their selection of women's self-defense manuals, poetry collections, periodicals, children's stories, and the "Liberated Woman's Appointment Calendar."

About six months later, the stock made another journey, this time to the Lesbian Resource Center in the Wedge neighborhood of South Minneapolis.[12] It was the early 1970s, but in the civic-minded Twin Cities, the Lesbian Resource Center was rarely subject to harassment or negative attention—in part because the center's sign was hung inside the building. Any women who did find the center were probably drawn there for reasons other than book shopping, however. The building was also home to a theater troupe, a softball team, and a literary magazine, and it served as a venue for rap groups and coffeehouses. The books were almost an afterthought, just a few boxes housed in the center's basement. Customers had to face cobwebs and worse if they wanted to dig through the stock. At this point, Amazon was a labor of love. The owners were volunteering their time and energies, not trying to turn a profit.

Hanson and Browne realized that Amazon would soon perish without a storefront. A regular visitor to the Lesbian Resource Center described it as "a very depressing place, couches with springs coming out. It was dark. You really felt like a pervert going there."[13] In September 1973, a quarter-page ad in *Gold Flower* updated the community about Amazon's latest moves.[14] The big news was that the store had moved into its first official storefront at 808 W. Lake Street. A newly formed working collective pledged to keep longer, more reliable hours, six days a week, and thus reach more customers. They invited new women to join them in "watching the store, ordering books, and making the daily decisions."

Amazon's first three commercial locations were on "shady" blocks or were afflicted with leaky pipes and insufficient heating.[15] In October 1974, though, the bookstore moved to a bright and airy spot on Hennepin Avenue that would be its home for the next decade.

In a movement whose myriad struggles include challenging classism, questions of safety and respectability are complicated ones to grapple with. The notion of "movin' on up," as *The Jeffersons* theme tune memorably put it, suggests leaving problems and poverty behind rather than confronting them and working for social change. But if Amazon were to have the impact that it hoped for—which the *Gold Flower* ad had summarized as being "to provide as many books and periodicals as possible to local women"—it was essential that all kinds of women should feel comfortable visiting and spending time, and money, in the store.[16]

The Hennepin Avenue location, while still underheated and saddled with yet another set of leaky pipes, was more presentable, more middle-class than the store's earlier homes. Longtime Amazon employee Diane Como described the new location with pride: "We had a lending library where you could sit and read, sit and watch women, sit and look around, get to know people … ask questions. It was safe, and that made us different."[17]

Safety was especially important, since the store often served as a doorway through which women could step from one stage of their lives into a different, more uncertain, era. Writer Ellen Hart described going into the Hennepin Avenue store "at a time in my life when I was trying to figure out who I was."[18] She had already looked for information at bookstore chain B. Dalton, but it was difficult to find books on sexuality or lesbianism there. Amazon, on the other hand, "felt very warm and very friendly. They had a dog—and I love dogs. They had music that I'd never heard before—Holly Near and people like that. It was a revelation." Later, when she was looking to publish her first mystery novel, one of the bookstore workers walked Hart around the store, assessing the strengths and weaknesses of the various feminist publishers and showing off their books. Customers trusted advice from the women of Amazon because they read the books on their shelves and they were experts on the companies that produced them.

Being a safe, comfortable place for women to meet and interact was essential, but Amazon wasn't lesbian space, according to its workers. "More than anything else, a feminist bookstore in the year 1995 functions as visible women's space.... We want to be a place where [women] come in to find everything surrounding them affirming them," store manager Barb Wieser told a reporter from *Lavender Lifestyles*.[19] Appealing only to lesbians was a financial nonstarter. "We couldn't survive as a business stuck in '70s lesbian separatism," she said.

It was during this era that Amazon professionalized. The store established credit with publishers and other suppliers, and the staff formalized the workers' collective.[20] This new structure meant that they weren't subject to a boss's whims. Still, shared decision-making wasn't easy. Here and in other stores, when bookstore work was the way women earned a living and not exclusively a form of voluntary political activism, debates over store policies, including staffing levels and wages, could become heated. During the Hennepin Avenue days, the collective went into therapy to heal the divisions that would sometimes arise.[21]

In 1985, it was time for Amazon to move again, this time to the Loring Park neighborhood.[22] The new location was more spacious, and it was attractive. "It's as beautiful (and well-heated) as our old store was funky and cold," a staffer told *Feminist Bookstore News* (*FBN*), the publication that chronicled the movement from 1976 until 2000.[23] Astonishingly, these benefits came without a rent hike. Amazon's business boomed. In the first year at Loring Park, sales increased 20 percent from the year before, and twelve months later, they were up another 8 percent.[24] Still, as early as 1986, a banal but devastating problem beset the store: traffic. A construction project meant that potential shoppers had to sit in blocks-long jams to access the store's one-way street. The delays were devastating, but the month after the traffic snarl-up was cleared, sales rose by 40 percent.[25]

As the 1990s dawned, the store got another boost when a new neighbor moved in next door. Ruby's Cafe, "a big lesbian hangout," drew huge crowds on weekends. "You could see who went home with who from the lesbian bars because of who came in for breakfast together," owner Mary Bahneman said in 2020. "It was the place for lesbians to go on Sunday to see what happened on Saturday."[26] Whether it was hash browns or gossip that drew the crowds, they sometimes spilled into Amazon, and Sunday sales doubled.[27]

Amazon rose with the tides of the feminist publishing boom of the 1980s and early 1990s, the burgeoning of women's studies programs, and the sense that writers like Dorothy Allison, Audre Lorde, and Leslie Feinberg were producing the most interesting and urgent literature of the period. At the same time, it exemplifies the ways in which both lesbian-centered spaces and independent bookstores struggled as the millennium approached.

By 1993, the new "superstores" created by Borders and Barnes & Noble—and more specifically, their discounted prices—were squeezing independent bookstores. At first, Amazon was hopeful that customer loyalty would shield them from the rapacious chains. When Borders took over a local independent bookstore and greatly expanded its inventory, Amazon told its supporters, "It's affecting the other chain stores but doesn't seem to be pulling customers from us."[28] Two years later, though, while still maintaining that they didn't feel threatened "by the invasion of the super big boys," Amazon conceded that "even a small loss of customers would have an effect on us."

Given how often Amazon used its newsletter to remind readers of the importance of shopping there, it seems clear that staffers were all too aware that they were in danger of losing customers to the chains' cheaper prices. "Before you make a decision to buy a book at one of the 'superstores' . . . please think about it," a May 1994 newsletter implored. "Books aren't coffee or clothes or furniture; when we can only buy books at chain stores controlled by huge corporations that means we can only buy the ideas that they ultimately approve of."[29]

In 1995, as one Amazon was celebrating its twenty-fifth anniversary in Minneapolis, seventeen hundred miles away, another was launched out of Seattle. It would soon present an existential threat to feminist bookstores and indeed to all brick-and-mortar retail outlets.

Not yet financially stressed about Amazon.com, Amazon-not-com was doing well. With fourteen workers, including part-timers, annual sales were in the $600,000 range[30]—up 13.5 percent from the year before, and the state of the store was strong.[31] A member of the Amazon collective told *Minnesota Women's Press*, "We attribute our health (in this time of fierce competition from the superstores) . . . to a friendly and creative staff, community outreach work, the burgeoning of restaurants on our block, and most of all, our loyal community who continue to understand the importance of supporting a feminist bookstore."[32]

Later that year, store manager Barb Wieser reluctantly acknowledged that the arrival on the block of a new Starbucks—"the Barnes & Noble of the coffee world"—was having a positive effect on the store's bottom line by drawing new people to the neighborhood. But the new caffeine source exacerbated the location's biggest drawback: "parking has become an even worse problem, if that's possible," she admitted.[33]

This was a time of experimentation and innovation, spurred by the arrival of new competitors and a mindset of investing, not scrambling.[34] To keep their existing customers and attract new ones, the store started a video-rental program, implemented a membership scheme, and operated a mail-order catalog. They increased the number of book groups and author readings and organized open-mic nights when customers could read their own writing or the work of their favorite authors. They developed an ambitious program for new readers and women for whom English was a second language, in collaboration with the Minnesota Literacy Foundation. They worked with Ruby's Cafe to try to increase traffic to both businesses by extending their hours later into the evening and building a door in the wall they shared.[35] (The experiment ended after a few months.)[36] They sold textbooks for courses at the University of Minnesota, renting a separate space near campus for the first two weeks of each semester. They threw parties, had sales, and sold books at as many as twenty-five conferences and other events per year.

Still, it wasn't enough. After 1995, Amazon's financials showed a steady decline. In 1996, summer sales dropped by 20 percent from the year before.[37] In 1999, Wieser wrote, "Month by month we watch our in-store sales drop—fewer people coming in the door buying fewer books."[38] It's difficult to gauge how bad things got, because the store that had been so talkative when it had good news to share went virtually radio silent.

By the end of the 1990s, all bookstores were losing customers to online sites that made it easy to buy discounted books without schlepping to a store. On top of that, Amazon experienced some unique problems because of the name Jeff Bezos had chosen for his website after friends told him that an earlier choice, Relentless.com, was too aggressive. (That URL still redirects to the Amazon.com site.) According to *Publishers Weekly*, once the online Amazon launched, "customers flooded the bookstore's phone lines, thinking they were speaking to Amazon.com representatives. Patrons ordered books from Amazon.com, thinking they were supporting the feminist bookseller. Vendors called to offer deep discounts, then lowered the discounts when they discovered they were not dealing with Amazon.com. Sales plummeted."[39]

During the 1998 holiday season—the biggest sales period of the year—the number of people confusing the two operations cost the feminist bookstore considerable time and money. "We were getting 20 or more phone calls a day from people thinking we were Amazon.com. They were looking for books we didn't have. They wanted to come down and get them. We fielded so many calls it felt like we were working for Amazon.com," Wieser told the *Corporate Legal Times*.[40]

It's worth remembering that the Amazon.com of the 1990s was a very different beast from the "everything store" of today. Those were the days before the company had built fulfillment centers throughout the nation, before Amazon Prime had been created, and when online payments were still somewhat clunky. A 1997 magazine story compared the ease of ordering books from brick-and-mortar bookstores (by telephone!) with the online process at Amazon.com.[41] While an independent bookstore handled the transaction in 2 minutes, 38 seconds, having to "to page through screen after screen of details about shipping charges, refund rules, and disclaimers about availability and pricing," meant that the same order took a whopping 37 minutes, 12 seconds at Amazon.com.

Still, in April 1999, the original Amazon filed a lawsuit against the dot-com upstart. The feminist bookstore claimed it was "losing the value of its trademark, its product and corporate identity, its ability to move into new markets, and control over the goodwill and reputation it has developed over the last thirty years."[42]

No one was surprised that Amazon.com contested the suit, but the company's tactics during the legal process were genuinely shocking. In a pretrial deposition, the dot-com's lawyers asked Amazon staffers, "Have you had any interest in promoting lesbian ideals in the community?"[43] and "Are you gay?" The women refused to answer the questions. Amazon.com's lawyers claimed they were attempting to establish that the website was not in the same business as the

Minneapolis store; but to me, it looks like the line of questioning was an effort to intimidate the worker-owners and
warn them that Amazon.com would resort to homophobic tactics if the case reached a courtroom. According to
a contemporaneous report in *Salon*, the dot-com claimed
it was attempting to prove that it was "catering to a 'general interest' audience, while Amazon Bookstore Collective is 'lesbian-owned and operated, catering to the lesbian
community.'"[44]

Amazon.com spokesman Bill Curry told *Salon* that it was
the lawsuit that had motivated Amazon Bookstore to start
describing itself as a "full-service feminist bookstore for all
girls, women and their friends" rather than as an exclusively
lesbian bookstore. "They're trying to be more like us for the
sake of their legal case," he said. This wasn't just offensive;
it was also flat-out inaccurate. The online store sold its first
book in July 1995.[45] In September of that same year, *Lavender Lifestyles* had published the story containing Barb Wieser's explicit denial that the bookstore was lesbian space.[46]

In November 1999, a month before Jeff Bezos was
declared *Time* magazine's person of the year and after six
months of "lawsuit hell" for the Minneapolis store, Amazon
reached an out-of-court settlement with its younger dot-com
namesake. "The lawyers' fees were killing us," Amazon co-op
member Kathy Sharp later told *Publishers Weekly*. "We could
not run a business and deal with the lawsuit at the same time.
So we settled."[47]

The financial terms were not made public—though
in 2003, Sharp told *Publishers Weekly* it was not "a ton of

money." The agreement contained a provision that the then thirty-year-old bookstore must thereafter refer to itself as Amazon Bookstore Cooperative (it had restructured from a collective to a workers' co-op in 1995)[48] to distinguish itself from Amazon.com. *Feminist Bookstore News* likened this demand to being compelled to refer to your sister by her full, married name—Mary Patricia McCarthy-Rabinowitz instead of just Mary.[49]

Three months later, Amazon Patricia McCarthy-Rabinowitz moved once again—this time to an airy space with twice the square footage of its previous location, on the ground floor of the Chrysalis Women's Center.[50] The lack of parking at Loring Park had gotten worse as the neighborhood gentrified, discouraging potential customers from even trying to shop at Amazon. Although she preferred the charm of the Loring Park store, Ellen Hart called the Chrysalis location "a huge step up" as far as facilities like parking and space were concerned. "It looked like a real bookstore. It was legit."[51] The digs were cushy, but the move was another hassle for the struggling store, which again needed to educate customers about a change of address, knowing that many would never make the effort to seek out the new location.

Between the chains and online competition, it became harder and harder for any independent bookstore to survive in the 2000s. When Amazon saw a 15 percent drop in sales after the attacks of September 11, 2001, and received an unexpected property tax bill a few months later, the worker-owners concluded that they would have to close the store in 2002.[52] They narrowly escaped that fate only after a national fund-raising campaign generated $30,000 to cover the losses.

If the store's supporters had assumed that the Amazon .com settlement had put the store on a solid financial footing, the appeal disabused them of that notion. The overwhelming public response, which demonstrated how much the wider community cared about Amazon's continued existence, renewed the collective's commitment. In October 2003 Wieser told *Publishers Weekly*, "I am more hopeful than before that we will remain open."[53]

Five years later, however, that optimism was spent, and in June 2008 Amazon Bookstore Cooperative announced that it was closing.[54] Nearly thirty-eight years after its founding, the worker-owners, many of whom had spent more than a decade at the store, decided that the economic challenges were too formidable. Wieser, who worked at Amazon for twenty-one years, told *MinnPost*, "It's just too risky these days. Pretty much, bookstores are owned by people with money. Young people don't see a future in it. If the most you're ever going to make is $30,000 a year, well, that's OK when you are young, but if that's your career? People looking at it realize you won't be able to support kids, a life."

As it happened, that wasn't quite the end of Amazon's story. In the final days of the going-out-of-business sale, Ruta Skujins, a newly out lesbian booklover who had taken early retirement after thirty-four years in a corporate job, stepped in to purchase the store with funds from her IRA.[55] Under the terms of the settlement with Amazon.com, a change of ownership meant the store must change its name. Amazon

Bookstore Cooperative became True Colors—and it struggled from the start.

Looking at the local press coverage at the time of the purchase, True Colors appeared destined for failure. Seemingly unaware of all the sales-generating tactics the women of Amazon had tried over the years, Skujins talked vaguely about doing more marketing outreach and promised to give the bookstore "a more visible Internet presence with Facebook and MySpace." She had plans to reach out to young women in the Twin Cities community, many of whom, she said, had never heard of the store. It was a noble goal, but it didn't work out.

Four years later, Skujins was the subject of another Twin Cities newspaper article. This time she was profiled not as the savior of a beloved local institution but as someone who had made a financial gamble and lost everything. Skujins told the *Pioneer Press* she had sunk her entire $250,000 retirement savings into the store—and she was still receiving calls from bill collectors trying to recoup the $100,000 she owed even after closing True Colors in February 2012.[56] Forty-two years after Rosina Richter and Julie Morse turned a parlor into a bookstore, what remained of the inventory was back in cardboard boxes.

No one could accuse Amazon of having gone gentle into that good night. A long line of women, from the founders through early volunteers and dozens of collective and cooperative members, worked diligently, creatively, and doggedly to keep the store alive. In the end, though, hard work wasn't enough. Back in 2000, *FBN* editor Carol Seajay traveled from

San Francisco to Minneapolis to attend the "hooray the law-suit is over" party that marked the settlement with Amazon .com. She reported that the Amazon women were "proud of having fought the good fight [but] they are painfully wiser about the financial impossibility of defending oneself against deep-pocketed corporations and about the unlikelihood of justice being served when it's independent vs. corporation."[57] It was a bracing reminder that in the long run, Goliath usually comes out on top.

It would be wrong to think of Amazon—or other feminist bookstores—as having failed because their owners made poor choices. The economics of bookselling are daunting for anyone brave, or foolish, enough to go into the business.

Whatever its intention or orientation, a bookstore's success is based in large part on its inventory. Customers must find the books they want to purchase in stock, which requires the store's buyer to predict with a high degree of accuracy what customers are going to be looking for. The store must pay for those books within thirty days of ordering and hope they don't spend too much time gathering dust before the right customer comes through the door to purchase them. This means stores must invest many thousands of dollars to acquire the most basic inventory.

With a few exceptions, the product on offer is a mass-produced commodity available to any outlet that cares to make an order. Most books have their price printed on the cover—so while sellers can reduce that price, there's a top limit on how much they can charge. Bookstores receive a 40 percent discount on most orders, and assuming they sell at full price, that 40 percent markup must cover rent, worker salaries, utilities, taxes, advertising, and losses to theft, all the costs of doing business.

An already challenging pursuit was even more complicated for feminist bookstores. Because of gender disparities in capital accumulation, pretty much every feminist bookstore was undercapitalized. Remember that when the very first stores opened in the 1970s, women-owned businesses were thin on the ground, in large part because women were often denied credit; it was only in 1974 that women gained the right to obtain credit cards independently of their husbands.[58] (Don't even ask about women without male partners.)

The chronic shortage of funds caused stress for owners and workers—there was no margin for error. Many of the women in charge of paying bookstore bills worked out a complicated system for sequencing overdue invoices so that they could stay in the good graces of their most important vendors. But dealing with creditors' phone calls inevitably took a toll on workers' mental health.

In one of the publishing industry's oddest business practices, books are returnable for full credit—in theory, stores can pull from the shelves titles that aren't selling, send them back to the publisher, and get their money back. This mitigates the risk of the initial ordering gamble, though repackaging and returning unsold items isn't always the best use of staff time. Until bookstores shifted their inventory records to early computer systems in the 1980s, this process was much easier said than done.

Even back then, feminist booksellers were much less likely than other stores to reduce their debt by returning books. Many bookwomen considered their true vocation to be compiling lists of essential titles in key subject areas, which naturally affected how they curated the selection of books on offer in the store. Every section, from lesbian romance novels to titles on recovery or spirituality, feminist theory or poetry, disability rights or international fiction, was stocked with books they felt women in their community needed. They wanted to have those titles on hand at all times, even if they only sold one or two copies per year.

Feminist bookstore owners had conviction to spare. They were driven by a desire to get feminist texts into the hands of as many people as possible, and their beliefs shaped their business practices. In many ways, the events of the thirty or so years that passed between the founding of the Amazon women's bookstore and the rise of Amazon.com could be seen as a test of whether independent stores that were devoted to building a loyal clientele based on shared values could compete with businesses maximized for profit. The answer to that question depends on how you define *compete*. Feminist bookstores may not have been able to triumph on the battlefield of big business, but they did (and still do) get feminist literature into readers' hands, build community, and enrich the literary landscape.

Indeed, Amazon wasn't the only bookstore fighting that good fight. In the 1970s, it was as if there were something in the air. In 1973, when Kirsten Grimstad and Susan Rennie published the *New Woman's Survival Catalog*, their report on the new feminist projects cropping up around the country, they were particularly taken by the bookshops, listing eleven and publishing photographs of several shabby but undeniably appealing stores. They even offered career advice. "For women who love books, who are feminists, and who want to integrate their lives with their political values," they wrote, "we can think of no better solution than getting together with like-minded women and launching a bookstore."[59]

Linda Bryant, a founder of Atlanta's Charis Books & More, was working for a social-justice-oriented Christian youth group when she joined the book trade in 1974. Years later, she wrote, "We were full of faith, but not too much business sense. We didn't have a business plan.... We just knew that we wanted to sell books by and about women, spiritual books that were challenging and opening, and children's books that were anti-sexist and anti-racist."[60] Ann Christophersen and Linda Bubon, who met in graduate school, thought a bookstore seemed like a better career option than academia, so they launched Chicago's Women and Children First in 1979.[61] Writer Dorothy Allison, who cofounded Herstore in 1974 while doing graduate work at Florida State University, wanted to build a feminist intellectual center independent of the college, whose gravitational pull dominated Tallahassee.[62] Edie Daly and Doreen Brand opened the Well of Happiness in Saint Petersburg, Florida, because they were looking for community after relocating from New York. "We wanted to find the Lesbians," Daly said. "So we had this idea that we would open a Women's Bookstore, and the Lesbians would find us."[63]

In DC, Lammas, the store that changed my life, was founded because two women couldn't stand to work "straight jobs" anymore. Sick of being treated as a "cross between a trained animal and an untrained child" while working as a waitress and secretary, Leslie Reeves taught herself silversmithing from books borrowed from the public library.[64] Her business partner, Judy Winsett, had, in the words of the *New Woman's Survival Catalog*, "worked as the only woman technician in a laboratory where everyone else was afraid of the rats"—but when her male coworkers became unbearable, she, too, chose self-employment and learned to work with silver. Reeves and Winsett started out as street vendors, selling their jewelry in Georgetown, but they eventually opened a store in DC's Eastern Market on Capitol Hill. Back then it was Lammas Women's Shop, and they didn't shy away from the other L-word. An early ad shows a photo of five smiling DC dykes, including then manager Mary Farmer, arrayed on the store's stoop, proudly displaying some of the "gay gifts" available for sale.[65] A line of type at the bottom reads, "Owned and Operated by Your Friendly Neighborhood Lesbians." Being unbossed freed the silversmiths from having to pull punches. "We'd rather lose a sale than put up with any shit," they said. "This is what our sales reps do, too—tell obnoxious men to fuck off."[66]

Mary Farmer became manager of Lammas in the ultimate lesbian setting—she was offered the job at the end of a softball game.[67] Reeves and Winsett didn't enjoy the social

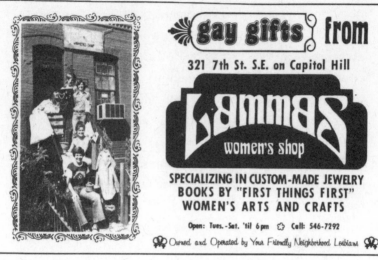

Lammas founders Leslie Reeves (in black) and Judy Winsett stand at the top of the steps. Sue Brennan stands to their left, and Beth Crimi sits below them, both friends and supporters of the store. Mary Farmer, wearing a Lammas T-shirt, sits on the stairs. (Originally published in *Just Us: A Directory of the Washington Gay Community, 1975 Edition. Source:* Lesbian Herstory Archives.)

aspects of retail, preferring to hole up in their studio and make jewelry. Farmer, though, was the ultimate schmoozer: friendly, warm, exuding butch confidence. People gravitated toward her and loved to hang out with her. When the founders decided to sell in 1976, Farmer was in love with the place, and with the help of an ex-lover who cosigned the loan agreement, she became its new owner. Knowing the business well by then, she had no expectation that she'd ever make more than minimum wage, but she was willing to risk it—she had an old clunker of a car, and her housing situation was stable.

Looking back forty-five years later, Farmer makes Lammas's evolution from a women's craft store to a feminist bookstore seem like an organic process: "I was reacting to what was happening in the Washington-area feminist community." DC was a happening place where women were building all kinds of alternative institutions—a credit union, a garage, a feminist bakery, a women's center, to name just a few. There was an almost unquenchable thirst for the feminist books that were starting to be published. A few blocks away from Lammas, Sue Sojourner, who ran a "fe-mail order house" called First Things First, was "mailing books out like a maniac."[68] Eventually, books and records edged out the pottery and jewelry on Lammas's shelves.

The shift into a de facto community center was also unplanned, according to Farmer:

> The store was run by known lesbians. People felt comfortable going there and being themselves. It didn't take long before there were some concert flyers and book-group flyers pasted on the wall. People called constantly: Did we know about any housing, did we know about child care? Did we know how they could find a doctor who wouldn't mistreat them? We started putting together resource binders. At that point, we sort of fell into a community-center function. Did we design it that way? No. But people needed things.

Selling the store, which Farmer did in 1993, is still a cause for regret, but everyone reaches their limit when faced with the rising cost of living. "If I could've made a decent salary, I'd still be there, but I just couldn't make it any longer," she told me in 2021.

And why did women want to *work* in feminist bookstores? Because they wanted to spend their lives surrounded by feminists and books more than they wanted money. As anyone who works in publishing will attest, a love of books can be as destructive to one's bank account as a drug habit.

Deb Morris got her first job at Lammas by persuading Mary Farmer to let her open and run the store on Sundays in exchange for books.[69] She had a full-time job she hated at the phone company, but she happily volunteered to take on more work "because I was in the place that I loved. I knew a lot about different authors, particularly Black authors and authors of color, and it was important for me to share that information. I didn't mind being there on Sundays—it wasn't like people were beating down the door, although we did have customers, and phone calls."

Ah, yes, the phone calls. It might seem strange to dial up a bookstore when you're worried about the way a sibling is raising their daughter or need a new doctor, but women's bookstores were often the only feminist locations people could find to reach out to. (In Britain, the feminist magazine *Spare Rib* tried to solve this "who you gonna call" problem by paying for phone book listings under "Women's Liberation.")[70] According to Sara Look, a co-owner of Atlanta's Charis Books & More who first worked in the store in the pre-internet age, there are now fewer of those calls—but people do still reach out.[71] Today, most of the calls Charis receives are about trans issues. There's a lot of information on the web, but people want to talk through their concerns with another human being, and the Charis website is one of the few resources they can find that provides a phone number.

In 1983, Susanna Sturgis, then Lammas's book buyer, described running a feminist bookstore as being "something like kindling a fire in high winds and a torrential downpour: it can't be done, but all around the world we're doing it."[72] Thanks to hard work and low pay, Lammas thrived for years, for a while operating two branches in DC and eventually expanding into Baltimore. When reporting on the store's last day in business in September 2000, the *Washington City Paper* described detritus being tossed out of a second-floor window, including a hand-made sign that had hung behind the cash register for years. It read, "Lammas. More Than a Bookstore. A Movement."[73]

Ultimately, Lammas fell prey to the same forces that killed Amazon and its sisters. Between the massive increase in commercial rents, corporate consolidation, especially in the book industry, and the rise of the internet, Mary Farmer says it's hard for any small business to survive—"whether you're selling marshmallows, diapers, or books, the economics are tough." But she's proud of the work Lammas did. "Getting people together, inspiring people, being a safe place for decades—that was reason enough for the store. Lammas made a difference in the lives of many, many people."

Feminist bookstores not only transformed the lives of the people who worked at and patronized them; they also left their mark on the publishing industry. Feminist booksellers were activists by nature, so they organized and cooperated.

They shared tips and warnings in the pages of *Feminist Bookstore News*, coordinated gatherings and workshops at events like the annual American Booksellers Association convention (then known as "the ABA," though it later rebranded as BookExpo), and distributed the products of their labor. Stores with particular subject matter expertise circulated the lists they had compiled on those topics. They also used their knowledge to alert other feminist booksellers to titles they should avoid ordering.

The booksellers understood their collective power and used it to fight for the titles and authors they believed in. They knew that as individual stores they had no pull with the mainstream presses—"the boys on Publishers Row," as *Feminist Bookstore News* referred to them—but if they presented a united front, there was a chance they could have an impact.[74]

When publishers' sales representatives visited their stores or when the feminist bookwomen met with publishers at the ABA, they would advocate for titles they felt were being mistreated. "It took only two trips to the new merged Fawcett/Ballentine [*sic*] booth at ABA and three follow-up calls from a committed sales rep to find out what happened to that best-selling lesbian classic *Patience and Sarah*," reported Carol Seajay, *FBN*'s founder-editor, in the September 1983 issue of the magazine.[75] The book was back in stock within months.

Was the inventory at feminist bookstores really all that different from what filled the shelves of "straight" stores? One thing is certain: they stocked and sold a lot more books by women. On the fiction side, lesbian novels were the big movers. In October 1987, Seajay estimated that lesbian books "routinely generate 30–35% of feminist bookstores' sales out of 10–15% of total inventory."[76] I used to mock the predictable lesbian romances published by the now defunct Naiad Press—but, of course, readers were drawn to those novels for the happy endings that real life didn't always deliver. The truth is that lesbian romances kept a lot of bookstores in business. Some Lammas customers would purchase an armful of Naiads on Friday night then come back for more a week later.

So, were feminist bookstores lesbian spaces—and should they have declared themselves as such? Or was Amazon's Barb Wieser right to emphasize the financial imperative of appealing to as broad a customer base as possible? Everyone benefited from feminist bookstores' coyness. From a cold-eyed dollars-and-cents perspective, it is foolish to target a business—especially an enterprise whose products are not essential, in the way that food or clothes are—at a group that represents perhaps 5 percent of the population. Besides, visiting a "women's bookstore" provided plausible deniability for closeted shoppers in a way that a trip to a "lesbian bookshop" would not.

This surely explains why so many feminist bookstores chose obscure names referencing women warriors from antiquity, figures from Greek mythology, or pagan holidays. Those in the know—women thirsty for information about lesbian history and culture—could easily crack the code. But to outsiders, the names just seemed cultured and a little mysterious. Being "caught" in a bookstore with a name like Amazon,

Antigone, or Lammas was much less compromising than being spotted in a drinking establishment called Fannie's, Girlbar, or Don't Tell Anyone.

It's true that most of the women who worked in women's bookstores were lesbians, as were many of their customers—but by no means all of them. And if Carol Seajay was correct when she estimated that 10 to 15 percent of feminist bookstores' inventory and 30 to 35 percent of sales came from lesbian books, it follows that as much as 90 percent of inventory and 70 percent of sales came from nonlesbian titles. Feminist bookstores were always intended for all women, but because there were so few places where lesbians were welcomed, much less celebrated, they were particularly precious spaces to us. Feminist bookstores were maps of the lesbian world. Their books took lesbians to places they couldn't yet visit, and the flyers, magazines, and binders showed them where they were already welcome.

Still, by the 1990s, when chain stores were offering discounts on popular titles, a book that cost $8.95 at Lammas could likely be had for $6.27 at the Crown Books five blocks away. Toward the end of that decade, even including Amazon .com's shipping fee in the pre-Prime era, the e-tailer could put a book in a woman's hand for the same price as Lammas, without her having to deal with bus schedules, traffic, parking, or sales tax. In other words, customers who gave women's bookstores their business were paying a premium to obtain the exact same item they could get elsewhere for less money and effort. For a while at least, women willingly paid that premium. Women wanted to shop at businesses that shared their values, and they knew that where they chose to spend their money made a difference.

Feminist bookstores weren't islands of individual entrepreneurship but interconnected elements in a complex ecosystem of like-minded projects. Making a purchase at a local bookstore provided concrete support to writers, publishers, musicians, and women working in production and distribution all over the country. Buying a lesbian novel at a feminist store allowed its author to spend more time writing and fewer hours at her "straight job," made it possible for her publisher to send more work by new authors into the world, paid the wages of the butch bookseller who no longer had to deal with homophobia in a heterosexual workplace, and kept the store in business so it was open when a young woman started to question the misogynist misinformation she'd been fed by her family since childhood. Every transaction was a link in a chain that might affect thousands, or hundreds of thousands, of women.

And then something changed.

In the fall of 1993, Judith's Room, a feminist bookstore on the western edge of Greenwich Village, used its newsletter to inform customers that the store was in trouble: "Simply put, we don't have enough customers," the women of Judith's Room stated with brutal clarity.[77] They wondered if the need for specialty stores had disappeared. "If you are getting what you are looking for at mainstream bookstores in Manhattan, then there is no need. In fact, it would be senseless for us to struggle on." Nevertheless, they made it very clear that they really wanted to struggle on. "The womanspace in this city is limited," they wrote. "We hope you do not want to lose one square foot of it, let alone the 1,000 square feet that is Judith's Room. Women have always had the responsibility of struggling to keep what is theirs. It is sometimes a burdensome responsibility; but, if not you, then who?"

Who indeed? When Judith's Room finally shut its doors in January 1995, local lesbian newspaper *Sappho's Isle* blamed the community. "Hardcore feminist doctrine has been seemingly replaced with apathy, or with activism focused on other issues such as gay rights," an editorial declared.[78] Those early bookstores were precious havens, and women enthusiastically headed there for meetings, readings, and discussion groups. Unfortunately, though, they gradually stopped *shopping* there.

I, too, eventually abandoned my favorite feminist businesses, at least for my day-to-day shopping. It's hard to pinpoint exactly why. Chain stores meant that I no longer had to go to a feminist bookstore to find feminist books, and improvements in Amazon.com's service made ordering there more convenient than anyone had thought possible. But part of it was even simpler: around this time I switched from movement jobs to a professional career and found that I didn't have the extra time to make the trek to a feminist bookstore. (In the changing economic and political times of the mid-1990s, I suspect I wasn't the only young lesbian to undergo this process of bourgeoisification.)

Many bookwomen were disheartened to see how quickly their customers defected to the chains. Theresa Corrigan, who owned and operated a women's bookstore in

Sacramento, California, tried to persuade feminists to stand by their local stores by sharing a parable from her past. Back in the 1970s, she wrote in *Womyn's Press*, Sacramento had been served by a single women's bar. It was "huge, grungy, and owned by a man," but the lesbian community made a home there.[79] A few years later, a new, much fancier bar opened about a mile away. The original bar closed when women shifted their loyalties, and shortly after that, the operators of the new bar announced policies that aggressively discouraged women from patronizing the place. Among other things, the bar employed a familiar tactic, putting a sign on the door that read, "Men welcome. Women will be tolerated with three forms of ID." Lesbians were no longer comfortable at the new place, but they had nowhere else to go. "This experience taught me a valuable lesson about loyalty," Corrigan concluded, "not necessarily to a particular person or place, but to an alternative that I, as part of a community, had created." If women abandoned the feminist bookstores for cheaper prices, Corrigan implied, they should once again be prepared to lose essential community resources.

Of course, feminist bookstores sold more than books. Indeed, offering other items was an explicit part of their mission—and potentially a financial lifeline.

Sidelines—T-shirts, calendars, buttons, cards, music, crafts, jewelry, and, in some stores, erotic toys—were one of the attractions that distinguished women's and gay bookshops from other, nonspecialist stores. "Literacy is a women's issue, too," Carol Seajay wrote in *Feminist Bookstore News*, "and a poster or a button or a t-shirt is a lot more accessible to many women than books. One button worn in the right situation may be worth a thousand words."[80]

In 1982, when I was at graduate school in Delaware, I made my first solo visit to Washington, DC. The place I most wanted to visit in the nation's capital wasn't the Lincoln Memorial or a Smithsonian museum; it was Lambda Rising, the gay bookstore that seemed to advertise in every feminist and queer publication in America.

The feeling of abundance was almost overwhelming—there were so many books (and so much gay porn)—but I'm pretty sure that after hours of awestruck shopping, I left the store without a single book. Instead, I bought stickers, buttons, and a pair of socks with a lambda symbol on the calf. (Back then, the rainbow flag was mostly a West Coast symbol. For East Coasters, lambdas and pink triangles were the gay signifiers of choice—along with labryses, the Amazons' double-headed ax, for lesbians.)

No other store offered as many LGBTQ-themed books as Lambda Rising. Nevertheless, it was its sidelines that were truly unique. I could ask my local mall bookstore to order a copy of *Sappho Was a Right-On Woman*—but I would never find queer tchotchkes at B. Dalton.

It would be wrong to dismiss sidelines as mere souvenirs, though. Before the internet, the magazine section of the women's bookstore was the movement's newsstand. Being informed required reading the national gay and lesbian press. Coverage of national political debates, news reports, music and book reviews, and lesbian-focused creative writing came in publications like *off our backs*—whose collective I was part of for several years in the late 1980s—or Boston-based *Sojourner*; journals like *Sinister Wisdom, Conditions,* or *Common Lives/Lesbian Lives*; review-oriented periodicals like *Women's Review of Books* or *Belles Lettres*; sexually explicit publications like *On Our Backs* and *Bad Attitude*; and eventually glossy lifestyle magazines like *Curve* (originally *Deneuve*).

The musical genre known as "women's music" grew in parallel with the women-in-print movement. Perhaps because it's no longer possible to go into a store and hear the records playing, people who weren't around in the 1970s and 1980s seem to have a different impression of the genre from those of us who were. The enduring image is of white folkies belting out earnest love songs. Certainly, white artists like Cris Williamson, Holly Near, and Meg Christian did play acoustic guitars and sing about loving women, but their work was also political, poetic, sexy, and funny. The record bins at Lammas were full of albums by women of color, performing in all genres—Sweet Honey in the Rock, Casselberry-DuPreé, Linda Tillery, Deidre McCalla, Mary Watkins, Gwen Avery, and many more. Lammas's downtown branch was managed by jazz aficionado Deb Morris, so while the store stereo only played women's voices (between hours of NPR), the rotation was heavy on jazz and world music (the only musical genre with a worse name than *women's music*).

In the days before music streaming and online ticket buying, feminist bookstores were at the very center of the women's music ecosystem. They played and sold the records, and when artists went on tour, they sold the concert tickets.

Those shows were the place to see and be seen. At one memorable Sweet Honey in the Rock performance in the 1980s, I sat in the same row as my girlfriend, two exes, and my therapist.

I was one of those unsubtle people who for decades always wore what one stylish straight roommate liked to call "T-shirts with things written on them." Political slogans, queer symbols, festival and Pride souvenirs, the logos of obscure publications—if it could serve as the equivalent of a flashing neon sign screaming "lesbian-feminist," I'd wear it. Still, for feminist bookstores, clothing wasn't an ideal sideline. Having a range of sizes on hand meant investing in inventory—and hoping that the sizes left unsold matched the size of the customers who came in wanting to buy them.

Jewelry—usually on consignment from local craftswomen—was always the sappiest section of a store. It's hard to imagine queer couples feeling comfortable shopping for rings in a mall store four decades ago. In feminist bookstores, though, women could try on rings without having to pretend that one was a platonic friend there to provide supportive company for the other. And high-street jewelry stores certainly didn't sell labrys pendants or earrings featuring double women's symbols. This sense of openness and safety also explains why, at a time when few cities had their own feminist sex-toy stores, some women's bookstores also sold vibrators, dildos, and lube.

Another important reason for feminist bookstores' gradual rebalancing of the books-to-sidelines ratio was money. Manufacturers don't print prices on sex toys, rings, and labrys-shaped mousepads. Most retailers "keystone" their merchandise: they set the price by doubling the amount they paid for the items. The increased profit margin from sidelines made a huge difference to cash-strapped bookstores. In 1985, *FBN* reported that sidelines accounted for as much as 35 percent of stores' total sales, sometimes reaching more than 40 percent in the December holiday period.[81] (It also explains why the surviving brick-and-mortar bookstores devote so much real estate to gift items.)

I suspect that one of the reasons feminist bookstores felt so significant to me—quite aside from the products on their shelves—was that they represented a reversal of a usual pattern. For once, queer women's institutions outnumbered gay men's, with a total of around two hundred feminist bookstores existing over the years, compared with twenty or so gay bookstores, which were typically founded and owned by men.[82] This was in sharp contrast with the world of nightlife, where men's bars were (and are) more numerous.

This is not to discount the importance of gay bookstores, which distinguished themselves from bars by making space for a variety of identities. Whereas at gay men's bars female customers were often barely tolerated or were invited to take over a club just one night per week or per month, generally speaking, gay bookshops extended a warm welcome to women.

Still, at least in the ones I visited, products aimed at men dominated their shelves. They sounded different—I never heard Cris Williamson or Sweet Honey in the Rock playing in a gay store. Most significantly, they looked a little different from standard bookstores, because most were laid out in a way that permitted the creation of a side room designated for adults only—the place where they stashed the porn. To be clear, these were not "adult bookstores," where pornographic magazines and videos made up the bulk of the inventory, but rather shops where customers could pick up the latest literary novel, a copy of *Gay Community News*, and a selection of queer skin mags. This high-profit-margin, customer magnet of a product category was essential to the economics of most gay bookstores, but it was just one part of the mix.

Only a few large cities were home to both a feminist bookstore and a gay bookstore, but a small number of lesbians spent time working in both. Linda Semple is one such person, having spent several years at Gay's the Word, Britain's oldest LGBTQ bookstore, before heading to Silver Moon, a women's bookshop located at 68 Charing Cross Road in the traditional heart of the London book trade. If only because of its name and unambiguously queer identity, Gay's the Word was in some ways the more political space. Although Silver Moon was undoubtedly a feminist enterprise, it provided cover for closeted customers. Gay's the Word was founded and originally run by gay men, but they quickly hired a lesbian manager and appointed women to their board. The store always contained an extensive women's section alongside the men's books, and the Wednesday night Lesbian Discussion Group was legendary. "Any lesbian who spent time in London between about 1982 and 1990 went through that discussion group—and the people in it—at some point," says Semple.[83] Silver Moon, meanwhile, sold only books written by women—with five exceptions. They were contractually obliged to stock the entire Virago Modern Classics list, which included four titles written by men. As a matter of principle, they added *The Satanic Verses* to the inventory when Ayatollah Ruhollah Khomeini issued a fatwa against author Salman Rushdie and his publishers. (They later permitted nonfiction by men—but only if the books were about women.)

Semple's strongest memory of working at Silver Moon was of how "desperate" she was to get to work every morning. "I loved switching on the lights and smelling the books and knowing we were going to have wonderful people coming through. I know customers loved the fact that they got very personal service from us." Gay's the Word, meanwhile, "had even more of a social side. We had a coffee machine at the back, and people would come and sit and chat." There was a famous noticeboard where people would make all kinds of requests, including, in the days before same-sex relationships had legal status, from people who needed to make a marriage of convenience so they could stay in the country with a partner the authorities didn't recognize as kin. Silver Moon focused more on the business: "We did have a small board where people could put leaflets, and a list of telephone numbers that we would point people to if they needed help, but that wasn't our primary purpose. It felt important to have a serious women's bookshop on the street that the world knows from *84 Charing Cross Road*," Semple said.

Skyrocketing Central London rents, competition from chain stores that could offer steep discounts, and Amazon

.co.uk's launch in 1998 led to the closure of Silver Moon in 2001. More than twenty years later, Gay's the Word is still thriving. When I asked Semple why she thinks it has survived, she offered a few theories. First, it's "the original and best"—by now the store is woven into queer British history, making a cameo in all manner of biographies and memoirs. Gay's the Word also got a boost from the emotional 2014 movie *Pride*, which chronicled its role as the informal headquarters of a 1984 campaign to provide gay and lesbian support to striking Welsh miners. Let me add another theory to that list: because pornography is more tightly regulated in Britain than in the United States, Gay's the Word never sold it. Therefore, unlike gay bookstores in the United States, they didn't lose a key revenue stream when smut, gay and straight, shifted to the internet.

One gay man in particular provided an inspiring example of the potential for bookstores to be transformative gathering places. Craig Rodwell, who opened the Oscar Wilde Memorial Bookshop in 1967, two years before Stonewall and three years before Amazon was dreamed into existence in Minneapolis, had an explicitly political agenda. He saw a store as a place to grow the gay and lesbian civil rights movement and to make queers feel better about themselves. "My commercial interests were not as strong as my desire to carry books, pamphlets, periodicals, etc., all with a positive gay theme to help raise the self-image of gay people," he wrote in 1971.[84] Frustrated with homophile groups that seemed out of touch with rank-and-file gay men and lesbians, he had pushed the New York branch of the Mattachine Society, the gay rights group of which he was vice president, to rent a storefront. He wanted to see politicians and organizers mixing with gay people rather than hiding away indoors. His vision was of a combination bookstore, counseling service, fund-raising headquarters, and office, but "the main thing was to be out on the street."[85]

Quickly realizing that the other Mattachine officers didn't share his desire to rub shoulders with the hoi polloi, Rodwell decided to go it alone. He worked two summers at a bar on Fire Island to save money, and having accumulated a little over $1,000, he found a rental space on Mercer Street in Greenwich Village for $115 a month.[86] He opened the day after Thanksgiving, serving free coffee and cookies to anyone who stopped by to check out the twenty-five titles displayed on a dozen shelves.[87]

Rodwell had attended a Christian Science boarding school and was a loose adherent of church founder Mary Baker Eddy's ideas. He wasn't particularly observant and certainly wasn't unquestioning—indeed, he spent decades protesting the church's homophobia—but some of its practices stuck with him, like the benefits of the Christian Science Reading Room. Mary Baker Eddy herself had ordered the first reading room to be established "in that part of the city where people will be most apt to go to it."[88] Today there are around 785 reading rooms across the United States, and they are open to everyone, regardless of denomination.[89] They provide Christian Science texts for purchase or consultation, but ultimately their intent is to proselytize for the church by showing that its followers are friendly and approachable.

The physical space that became the Oscar Wilde Memorial Bookshop had a similar purpose beyond the books it offered for sale. Rodwell sold buttons and stickers slathered with slogans like "Think Straight, Be Gay" and "How Dare You Presume I'm Heterosexual," and he placed positive messages all over the store.[90] A sign in the window read, "Gay Is Good," repeatedly confronting passers-by with a concept that at the time represented a decidedly minority view. Rodwell was extremely selective about the store's inventory. He initially refused to sell pornographic material—and while he eventually relented, he was always picky. He wanted to stock books that "depict homosexuality as basically good."

The Oscar Wilde Memorial Bookshop moved to Christopher Street in 1973.[91] It quickly became the activist drop-in center Rodwell dreamed of—or, as a bitchy Mattachine Society memo from 1969 described it, "general field headquarters for every revolutionary gay in the New York area."[92] It was a beacon constantly transmitting signals to would-be activists looking to connect with a cause. Rodwell died in 1993, but the bookstore stayed in business until 2009.

One of Rodwell's ex-boyfriends also recognized the community-building potential of retail locations. When Harvey Milk moved from New York to San Francisco, he opened a store of his own.

Once on the West Coast, knowing very little about film or cameras didn't stop Harvey Milk and his lover, Scott Smith, from launching Castro Camera. Milk's father and grandparents had been shopkeepers, and he wanted to be an active participant in the life of the booming Castro neighborhood. The couple were down to their last $1,000, but that was enough for some basic equipment and the lease on a twenty-five-hundred-square-foot store that came with an apartment upstairs.[93] When business was slow, as it often was, Milk paid calls on the other stores on the Castro strip, building relationships but rarely trying to generate business. In contrast to the women who worked in feminist bookstores, who really did want to sell books, Milk doesn't seem to have been all that interested in developing photos. The store became his informal campaign headquarters, and after he was elected to the San Francisco Board of Supervisors, it wasn't needed anymore. It was scheduled to close on December 1, 1978.[94] On November 27 of that year, Milk and Mayor George Moscone were shot and killed by Dan White in San Francisco's City Hall.

Between 2010 and 2021, the LGBTQ rights group Human Rights Campaign (HRC) operated a store in the Castro Camera space.[95] HRC has run similar emporia in queer tourist destinations like Provincetown, Fire Island, and Palm Springs since 1993, when the organization ran its first pop-up shop at that year's March on Washington for Lesbian, Gay, and Bi Equal Rights and Liberation. According to HRC's Don Kiser, the brick-and-mortar stores are a great marketing tool.[96] People are far likelier to go shopping for T-shirts than they are to seek out political literature, but since each store contains an "action center," shoppers find themselves perusing information about HRC's advocacy efforts alongside the sweatshirts and coffee mugs. In the 1970s, Harvey Milk painstakingly copied names and addresses from all the checks presented at Castro Camera and added them to his campaign mailing list; HRC's point-of-sales software ties directly into its membership database, doing the same job far more efficiently.

It's all too easy to see the mass closure of feminist bookstores as a failure, but the women who created and toiled in those stores weren't motivated by thoughts of longevity. Their goal was to establish locations that would transform the lives of the women who walked through their doors. By that measure, they were hugely successful. Queer and feminist bookstores transformed the publishing industry, had an outsized impact on the kinds of books that were published and reprinted, and shook up the staid library-like vibe of the typical mid-century bookstore.

A few pioneering feminist bookstores are still in business—and they are real community bookstores, not hipster curiosities. Chicago's Women and Children First has signage in its window declaring, "Opened in 1979. Open Today. Open Forever."[97] In 2014, the original founders sold the store to two employees, and the store remains committed to offering "a welcoming space for learning, dialogue, and reflection." In 2021, after more than forty-five years in downtown Madison, Wisconsin, a high-rise apartment development pushed A Room of One's Own to move to the city's East Side, where it is thriving.[98]

In 2019, Charis Books & More left the building it had owned and occupied for forty-five years in Little Five Points, once the epicenter of the Atlanta lesbian community, and relocated to a spot just off the campus of Agnes Scott College, a private women's school in Decatur, Georgia. The new partnership suited both parties. With students ordering their textbooks online, the Agnes Scott bookstore had been set to close, leaving students, in the words of *Atlanta* magazine, "without a convenient place to purchase school spirit swag, aspirin, and tampons."[99] Meanwhile, Charis was contending with rising property taxes and parking problems in its longtime home. In the new location, Charis stocks way more logo gear than its founders ever dreamed of, but the future is much more secure.

Cafe Con Libros, which opened in Crown Heights, Brooklyn, in December 2017, has the words "Black, Feminist & Bookish" painted on the lintel of its doorway. The mission statement that appears front and center on the store's website—"Through our choice of books, programming and great coffee, we endeavor to create a vibrant community space where everyone; specifically womxn-identified folx, feel centered, affirmed and celebrated"—proves that the need for welcoming space was just as urgent in the 2020s as it had been in the 1970s.[100]

Other founders have taken the pop-up approach that transformed the lesbian bar scene. In April 2019, Christina Pascucci-Ciampa started All She Wrote Books by taking beloved titles from her own shelves and selling them in Boston-area venues, including, memorably, a brewery. By the third or fourth event, ravenous buyers had thinned her personal stash of used books to such an extent that she had to cajole friends into clearing space on their shelves by sharing their favorites with her. When three-quarters of those volumes sold and organizations kept calling, asking Pascucci-Ciampa to roll her IKEA book cart into their markets and fairs, she realized it was time to add new books to the inventory. In 2020, she opened All She Wrote in Somerville, Massachusetts. Nowadays, sidelines include pronoun pins and cards commemorating top surgery. For Pascucci-Ciampa, the joy of a bookstore is in the human interaction it enables: "No algorithm can talk to you about the ideas that are in a book that she's read and been inspired by."[101] She's also conscious of providing an alternative to the bars: "Many of our people in the queer community are dealing with drug and alcohol dependencies, and they need spaces where they can come and not feel the itch to grab a drink."

It's clear that Pascucci-Ciampa and the other young feminist and queer booksellers opening stores in Birmingham and Montgomery, Alabama; Inglewood, California; Asheville, North Carolina; Water Valley, Mississippi; and Norfolk, Virginia, are meeting a newly urgent need for people to share physical space together.[102] What's more, people are expressing a hunger that the women from the first wave of feminist bookselling would surely recognize. In the 1970s and 1980s, booksellers fought to provide readers with titles that had been impossible to find, perspectives that had been suppressed, and authors whose work had been all but lost. Now most of *those* books have fallen out of print, and readers are still demanding to hear from populations who have never received the attention they deserve. When I asked Pascucci-Ciampa why people go to All She Wrote when feminist books are available in so many other places, she sighed. "Yes, stores have a feminist shelf, but you see the same five feminist texts, the same five queer books. It's not good enough!"

In the 1980s, I loved walking into Lammas, sure in the knowledge that I would find the newest books, the hottest music releases, the queerest T-shirts, and the best-informed, most helpful, most out-and-proud bookwomen there. Lammas may be gone, but its spirit endures. Today I live in a city of about five hundred thousand that is home to both a radical, queer bookshop and a store that "champions female authors."[103] These kinds of spaces are endangered, but they aren't yet extinct. Besides, all the items on my Lammas checklist are now easily discoverable online—along with so many of the other "sidelines" that forty years ago were only available thanks to the careful curation of feminist bookstore workers.

Yes, the internet made it possible for an inappropriately named, predatory dot-com to threaten the survival of local, independent stores everywhere, but it also provides a venue for all kinds of people to strategize, share ideas, and protest. For me, the internet is not a series of tubes but rather a collection of binders, just like the ones that used to take up so much shelf space in Lammas.[104] Like their paper predecessors, these digital resources can help young queer women find solidarity and community and discover their identities. The feminist-bookstore spirit also lives on in the crusades against unjust publishing-industry practices that regularly emerge from internet forums. (Sometimes, the people employed by those publishing houses are leading the charge.)

Of course, physical spaces still matter. In Georgia, Charis hosts regular meetings for trans youth and for parents of "gender-creative" offspring. E. R. Anderson says these programs were inspired by something Gloria Steinem said in 2006.[105] "If I could have one structural wish for the women's movement," Steinem told Marianne Schnall, "it would be that we have a kind of Alcoholics Anonymous group structure all over the world, so that wherever you go ... you can find the feminist equivalent of an AA group to ... get some support, and some help with seeing the politics of what's happening to us."[106] The early feminist bookstores stumbled into providing that kind of service. In the twenty-first century, Charis and its comrades know how much it is still needed.

Leslie Reeves at bat, with Kathy waiting for the pitch, Washington, DC, circa 1973. Teams played softball on the National Mall in sight of the Lincoln Memorial. © circa 1973 JEB (Joan E. Biren)

THREE
THE SOFTBALL DIAMOND

O NE MONDAY AFTERNOON IN THE MID-1980S, I WAS
working a shift in the Capitol Hill branch of Lammas.
It had been a quiet day—I'd seen the mailman, a UPS delivery person, and *maybe* one customer. I wish I could say that I
was doing something productive for feminist literature, but I
was almost certainly parked at the register by the door, novel
in hand, reading. At some point, the skies opened up and let
loose one of those epic DC summer storms. It seemed that the
rest of my shift would be even lonelier. Then, without warning, more than a dozen women burst through the door. They
were raucous, boisterous, and soaked to the skin—and for
some reason, they were all wearing the same T-shirt.

It was only when store owner Mary Farmer brought up the
rear of this noisy crew that I realized what was going on. This
was the Lammas softball team, and despite having worked in
the store for more than a year, I had no idea that such a thing

existed. *Of course* Lammas had a softball team! I might have had a degree in American studies, spent years living in the United States, and been in the process of conducting a pretty intense independent study of queer culture, but I had somehow missed a basic truth of American life: in just about any place where there are lesbians, there is softball.

Forty years later, I'm still embarrassed to admit to this gap in my sapphic scholarship. Apart from anything else, the Lammas softball team was one of the most famous in the land, having appeared on the cover of Willie Tyson's 1974 album *Full Count*.[1] What's more, I was no stranger to the world of women's sports: by the time I was twenty-one, I'd spent months of my life at tennis tournaments. (Britain may have lacked softball, but its condensed geography conferred *some* advantages.) Still, somehow, softball wasn't on my radar.

Softball's lesbian connection is a little like the arrow in the FedEx logo: you can spend years in blissful ignorance, but once you see it, it won't go away. The softball diamond has long been *the* place to meet other North American lesbians. It's such a given that it isn't even discussed.

Tacit though it may be, the association is so strong that it's been used to question the sexuality of anyone who so much as picks up a softball bat. In May 2010, the *Wall Street Journal* ran a seventeen-year-old photo of then Supreme Court nominee Elena Kagan headlined "Court Nominee Comes to the Plate."[2] There was no story attached, just a two-sentence caption. But the photo, which took up two-thirds of the paper's front page, showed the nominee dressed casually—jeans, sneakers, T-shirt, an unbuttoned overshirt—with her short

Never mind standing; how's the nominee's batting stance?
The front page of the May 11, 2010, *Wall Street Journal*.

hair blown back by the wind, waiting for a pitch. She seemed to know her way around the batter's box, and her broad smile suggested she was having fun.

The *Journal* insisted that no innuendo had been intended. Asked if the paper was trying to send some kind of coded signal, a spokeswoman pretentiously deadpanned, "If you turn the photo upside down, reverse the pixilation and simultaneously listen to *Abbey Road* backwards, while reading Roland Barthes, you will indeed find a very subtle hidden message."[3] So, no, I guess? To be fair, front-page editors do enjoy a chance to pun, and they often select unusual images to facilitate a droll headline, but the *Journal*'s denial—dutifully quoted in the dozens of stories it spawned—was both disingenuous and inevitable. The *Journal* would never admit to intentionally suggesting the future justice might be a lesbian, but hacks at many other publications gleefully seized the opportunity to chew over a fifty-year-old woman's clothing choices, hair style, and distinct lack of a husband. (Lest it need saying, other than the photographic evidence that she has held a softball bat, there is no reason to believe that Kagan is gay.)

Softball is so powerfully associated with lesbianism that even a vague connection to the game could be weaponized against women. In 1975, feminist newsjournal *off our backs* reported on the case of Cathy, a Chicago woman who, like many others in that era, lost custody of her children simply because a judge accepted an estranged husband's claim that she was a lesbian, which therefore rendered her an "unfit mother."[4] The "condemning evidence" provided by Cathy's husband was that she "played in an all-girls' bowling league and an all-girls' softball league." Fifteen years later in Oregon, Sue Carney and Patricia O'Scannell, who had been hired to teach an elementary school class about Renaissance music, had their contract canceled because Carney had served as composer and musical director for Carolyn Gage's *Amazon All-Stars*, a musical about the lives and loves of the Desert Hearts softball team. The American Civil Liberties Union filed a First Amendment lawsuit claiming that the musicians had been discriminated against "because the people they associate with are perceived as being lesbians."[5] State officials had been so sure that softball was coded lesbian, and that this in turn was beyond the pale, that they explicitly told the women it was Carney's association with the musical that made them unfit to teach young Oregonians. Nevertheless, they eventually settled out of court, with the musicians receiving $25,000 in damages and having their teaching contract reinstated.[6]

It's hard to imagine any other sport having such an immediate association with queerness. There's no canonical explanation for how softball became the unofficial sport of North American lesbians, but its emergence as an "industrial" recreation, when employers sometimes begrudgingly organized company sports teams to provide relief from the dreadful working conditions in factories, is surely relevant. Since women who worked outside the home before World War II were more likely to be unmarried, the women who turned out for factory teams were also disproportionately lesbian. And like soccer, that most democratic of sports, which is probably the global equivalent of softball in being a magnet for sporty women, trans, and nonbinary people, it is cheap to play. All that's needed are a ball, a bat, something to mark the bases, and preferably a mitt for each player.

Softball is also a sport that needs to be played outdoors in the fresh air, which made it appealing to women who felt stifled by the boozy smells of bars' not-always-cozy confines, and later for those who were ill at ease in the cerebral atmosphere of the feminist bookstore. For all its baggage, softball's setting in public parks makes it simultaneously unthreatening and accessible. Lesbian and bisexual women seeking evidence that they weren't alone in the world, anyone starting to suspect that they might be queer and wanting to catch a glimpse of dyke culture, and even supportive types who had learned that friends or family members were lesbian or bi could head to the park to check out the action. Similarly, women who weren't ready to come out could convincingly claim to be unaware of softball's reputation. Outsiders in 1970s courtrooms or school district offices saw nefarious connections between softball and lesbianism. Out on the field, women engaging in healthy exercise could legitimately dismiss those claims as an association fallacy. Even if it were true that many softball players were lesbians, lots of straight jocks also played the game.

Softball enables easy sociability in an often lonely world. Show up on tryout day as a stranger, and within weeks, you'll be part of a crew. You're guaranteed to see your teammates every week throughout the season, and unlike at the bars, there's no chance they'll ignore you—in fact, they'll shout your name lovingly at the slightest provocation. When they're not cheering you on, the dugout will be quiet enough that you can hear each other speak. A team is like a family—albeit one that can be rent asunder when relationships end. (In this sense, queer softball teams are more vulnerable than straight ones.) It's a source of pride.

The softball field also provides a venue for women to show off their physical prowess. A community that appreciates and celebrates women's strength is one that enjoys observing the hard, accurate throws players spend years perfecting, their talent for landing a ball into the pocket of a mitt or driving a well-pitched ball over the heads of the outfielders. The fact that these acts can be performed in an explicitly queer way—by athletes who subvert gendered grooming conventions, who shout their love for their teammates without embarrassment, and who proudly declare their dykehood—in a public space, as neighbors walk their dogs, children frolic, and locals take a shortcut through the park, makes an important statement. Lesbianism isn't something that needs to be hidden away in a distant neighborhood. You don't need to be half drunk to do it. It isn't just for intellectuals. It doesn't have to be solemn and serious. It can be fun and healthy and loud and sweaty and untamed.

Softball extends the geography of lesbian possibility to a space that isn't subject to a landlord's capacity to ignore neighbors' complaints or the ability of a business to survive market forces. Bars and bookstores close, neighborhoods are transformed by gentrification and urban planning, but parks endure. The sport also brings structure to a project that can seem impossibly amorphous. Lesbian feminism is about changing the world, challenging conventions, and smashing the patriarchy. That's a little overwhelming! What a relief to have a clearly stated goal and a well-defined set of rules to follow, right down to guidelines about how to dress. There's no confusion over whom you're in competition with or what constitutes victory. If you do something remarkable, you will be cheered. Even if you aren't particularly skillful, you will still be cheered. And when it's over, the fun continues. You get to move out of the sun and the public gaze and head to a private place where you can enjoy a different sort of physical exertion—sometimes even with a woman you were competing against a couple of hours before.

Indeed, softball is so powerful, it can transform lesbian-feminist organizations.

In 1972, a group of Atlanta dykes went rogue. Frustrated with antilesbian sentiment in the Atlanta Women's Liberation group and male sexism in the Gay Liberation Front, they formed their own organization: the Atlanta Lesbian Feminist Alliance (ALFA). Its founding members were politically active—socialist feminists, northerners who had moved to the South to do civil rights work, and women who had traveled to Cuba to work with the Venceremos Brigade, toiling alongside Cuban comrades to bring in the sugarcane harvest.[7] They were committed to exploring new territory, not just politically but also in relationships and living arrangements.

By July of that year, the group houses that lesbians were forming in the Little Five Points neighborhood on the east side of Atlanta were joined by ALFA House.[8] An informal women's center, ALFA House was home to the organization's weekly meetings, consciousness-raising sessions, a library where the new feminist books and publications were available, and a hotline for information about lesbian activities and organizing in the city.

ALFA eschewed hierarchical structure, operating instead as a series of committees dedicated to specific tasks: running the library or putting out a newsletter, organizing dances and social events, welcoming new members, or maintaining the house.[9] ALFA was a membership organization, and while the original founders were intensely political, they didn't set out an ideological agenda. Rather, ALFA was intended to serve as a hub that connected the social, political, and cultural groups lesbian and bisexual women were forming in Little Five Points and beyond.

Not that ALFA was purely social. Longtime member Pici later described the group as "a place where a bunch of dykes could get together and try to come up with some lesbian feminist theories to go along with our lesbian feminist practice."[10] Members turned out in force at pro–Equal Rights Amendment marches and Pride celebrations and gathered to protest when the *Atlanta Journal-Constitution* refused to list ALFA events alongside other local meetings.[11] They organized an ambitious regional gathering, 1975's Great Southeast Lesbian Conference, and offered themselves as living representatives of lesbianism at college classes and in the media to "reeducate the non-homosexual community."[12]

Still, in 1977, when two members published an essay on the first five years of the organization's history, they conceded, "While the formation of ALFA itself, as well as its continued existence, is a political statement, the criticism has been that she tries to be all things to all women and can satisfy none. In general, ALFA has moved from a more consciously political to a more socially and athletically oriented organization."[13]

Wait. *Athletically oriented?* Yes, indeed. ALFA's most successful outreach program—and the part of its history that has been most thoroughly documented—was its "softball strategy."

The *ALFA Newsletter*'s first mention of softball came in the March 1974 issue, with a short notice that "some of us want to get together and join other teams so we can play regularly in the Atlanta Recreation League. You don't have to be a 'jock' or even experienced in order to play."[14] It was important to ALFA that there be no barriers to team membership. Anyone could join in the fun. All around the country, women were coming out. Women were eager to learn about lesbian culture and politics through consciousness raising, rap groups, and other informal settings. Softball was yet another part of this blossoming.

In April, the *ALFA Newsletter* relayed, "Our softball team has set up regular practice times . . . and at our last practice session there were 15 beautiful lesbians (of all different ability levels—to say the least!) batting, catching, throwing, and generally having a good, tiring time."[15] By May, they were choosing a name—ALFA Omegas beat out Tri-ALFA, ALFA Unicorns, and ALFA Sapphosonics. A Gay Nineties carnival was organized to raise funds for equipment and team jerseys, and by midsummer, softball scores had become a regular feature of the newsletter.

After they lost their first game, the owners of the Tower Lounge, a local lesbian bar, surprised the Omegas by presenting the team with two practice balls and some new aluminum bats.[16] From then on, team members and supporters would head to the Tower after their games, mingling with the bar's regulars. The Omegas won their last three games of the season and celebrated with an awards banquet that "afforded an opportunity for a few to get out of their uniforms and into dresses."[17] The following spring, ALFA's participation in the city recreation league expanded. Since several women had expressed a desire to move out of the stands and onto the field, the Omegas would be joined by the ALFA Amazons and the Tower Hotshots. The latter was sponsored by the Tower Lounge rather than ALFA, but it was also considered an "outfront"—that is, openly lesbian—team.

Some of the ALFA women found their time in uniform life changing. At the conclusion of the ALFA Omegas' first season, Vicki Gabriner, who had been part of the radical Weather Underground movement just a few years before, wrote, "After 32 years of thinking of myself as a non-athlete, I discovered that I could hit the ball; I could catch, I could run, and I could throw.... For me, that was incredible, seemingly beyond reach only a short while before."[18] Gabriner gushed about the "spirit that came out of genuinely enjoying each other, our bodies, and developing our Amazon prowess." She was convinced that, given her initial lack of skills, the competitive nature of a "regular" city league team would have prevented her from discovering her inner athlete.

Like many converts, Gabriner was zealous about her new passion, contributing enthusiastic essays about softball's benefits to several feminist and alternative publications. In winter 1976, she published an article in a special issue of the feminist quarterly *Quest* dedicated to organizations and strategies. Amid a raft of stories about the difficulties of reaching collective consensus and the struggle to overcome individualism, Gabriner's piece, "Come Out Slugging!" was an island of optimism, a rare success story.[19]

In *Quest*, Gabriner said that softball wasn't just a way to build strong bodies and decompress from the stress of political organizing. It also provided a solution to one of the biggest challenges the lesbian-feminist movement faced in creating new institutions and building a power base: recruiting and radicalizing women who weren't yet engaged in lesbian politics. "We need to ask ourselves: Where do lesbians hang out?" she wrote. Softball made a new kind of outreach possible. ALFA's squads were lesbian feminism made flesh. Their presence on the softball diamond introduced closeted lesbians on other teams, and even civilians in the stands, to a new kind of woman. Longtime player Pici believes that ALFA softball teams had a significant impact beyond the urban core. "We were also going to play in south Georgia and other places. When they announced the team, they didn't just say 'ALFA,' they said, 'Atlanta Lesbian Feminist Alliance.' People who were just hanging out in the park heard that."

Their identity as politically conscious, out lesbians was what made the ALFA Omegas and the other ALFA-affiliated teams different. Even though it was tacitly understood that many (or most) softball players were lesbians, earlier teams hadn't drawn attention to their sexuality—much less celebrated it, like the ALFA teams did. "We ran onto the field, most of us with our hairy legs and our hairy armpits, sweating in the sun, exercising our muscles," Gabriner wrote. Their fans also behaved differently from other spectators. They created "queer cheers" based on terms that at the time were commonly considered to be slurs: "Two bits, four bits, six bits, a dollar. All for the queers, stand up and holler." Or "Give me an A. Give me an L. Give me an F. Give me an A. Whaddya got? Dykes! Dykes! Dykes!"[20]

The team's dykey esprit de corps was infectious. "We had energy on the field. We were a team. We loved each other. We loved each other. We loved each other. And other people—other teams, spectators—saw that," says Pici. Gabriner described softball as "one of the most powerful and energizing activities of the ALFA organization." It affirmed members' lesbianism, built positive attitudes about physical achievement, provided a new way for team members to work together collectively, exposed different kinds of women to ALFA, and recruited new members. After the first season of softball, ALFA membership grew from thirty to one hundred.[21]

As has been the case since Sappho pitched her first strike, players were sometimes more than teammates: ALFA member Elizabeth Knowlton observed that while some relationships had begun on the field, others were "buried there."[22] Or as Pici put it, "By the second season, half the team was in bed with each other."[23] The softball diamond was the perfect environment for the explorations of nonmonogamy that were prevalent in the mid-1970s. "You've got a bunch of dykes in the shortest of short pants, practicing every night. If somebody made a great play, we had group hugs. We were always grabbing at each other. It was great fun," says Pici. Occasionally, though, play was disrupted when squabbling lovers dropped their mitts and went to finish their argument off the field.

Still, as an organization, ALFA didn't shy away from self-criticism. In a 1977 essay titled "How to Start a Lesbian

Organisation," Gabriner and Susan Wells observed, "One of the energy patterns which has plagued ALFA, as it has other groups, is the unequal distribution of womanpower: only a few of the 115 members do actual work."[24] The women who were drawn to ALFA by softball didn't share the founders' deep commitment to activism; nor could they match the hands-on experience of socialists who harvested sugarcane in Cuba and moved to the American South to do civil rights work. With seeming inevitability, this dynamic led the women who did the bulk of the labor to burn out—and sometimes even to drop out of ALFA altogether. Largely left unexplored was the impact that softball had on ALFA's energy patterns. Twice a week, somewhere between fifteen and forty members were busy practicing or playing softball— time they couldn't spend in meetings, raising funds, or organizing activities. And it wasn't just players whose schedules the game ravaged. In the July 1976 newsletter, Elizabeth Knowlton described spending months watching friends on three softball teams, "which may necessitate leaving one field 5 minutes before a certain victory and battling the traffic across town in time to catch the 2nd inning at another."[25]

The sporting life didn't always run smooth. In 1975, Knowlton acknowledged that the two ALFA teams had gone through "interminable discussions" over whether to maintain the original season's emphasis on skill building and team unity over cutthroat competition. The Tower Hotshots had also endured a two-season-long dispute over "coaching style." The sporting calendar brings structure—the season lasts from the first practice until the last playoff game and then becomes an entry in the record books—but the disputes didn't end with 1975's final out. Knowlton reported, "The strain over funding new ALFA teams began in January and went on for months, nearly tearing the community apart." It was decided that in 1976 there would be two teams, though neither would carry the ALFA name. The Southern Fury would be very competitive "both internally & externally," while the Atalantas would be "less internally competitive." Taking ALFA out of the team names also meant that the words *lesbian feminist* were no longer part of the on-field announcements. As the teams' lesbianism went back to being unspoken and deniable, the players' out-and-proud queerness faded too.

De-emphasizing competitiveness had been central to ALFA's initial softball strategy. As Pici explained, "What that meant was that if you came to the practices, you played in the games, regardless of experience, regardless of athletic ability, regardless of whether it was a close game in the bottom of the late innings, with a runner in scoring position, and one out." Why? Because "our goal was not to win. Our goal was to showcase some of the lesbian feminist values that we were trying to incorporate into our lives and our belief systems."[26]

The ties connecting lesbian feminism and softball started to loosen as the player pool expanded. As more openly lesbian squads were formed, players felt extra motivation when matched up against one another, ramping up the competitiveness and reducing the urge to showcase lesbian-feminist values. By 1977, things had changed so much that the Tower Hotshots, despite being sponsored by a lesbian bar, were effectively closeted. Concerns about job security led to a team vote over the acceptability of public displays of affection on the field, and a majority decided that there should be no PDA at games or practice, at least until players reached their cars. One correspondent to *Atalanta*, as the *ALFA Newsletter* came to be known, noted the irony of a Hotshots fund-raiser program containing "a team herstory" that attributed an early softball benefit to "the R.D.T. Theater collective" rather than the name this group had always been known by: Red Dyke Theater.[27]

After dominating the *ALFA Newsletter* for three years, softball almost completely disappeared from its pages after 1976. According to Vicki Gabriner, by that point "the functioning of the softball teams was severely impaired by the painful re-shuffling of several lover relationships."[28] And for all its benefits, time devoted to softball was time that wasn't available for political organizing, and money contributed for uniforms, equipment, and rec-league fees meant that more efforts had to be made to gather the funds needed to operate ALFA House, the group's spiritual and literal home.

Still, in attracting new members, many of whom were apolitical or had little or no previous exposure to lesbian politics when they joined ALFA, softball changed the nature of the organization—and the nature of "outfront" lesbian softball teams. ALFA continued to operate until 1994, but its formal affiliation with softball ended after the 1975 season.

ALFA's clashes around competitiveness were by no means unique in the world of feminist softball. The players in *The Amazon All-Stars*, the musical that led to a First Amendment lawsuit in Oregon, debate the issue in a locker-room scene. A defender of participation for all declares, "That's what the whole straight world is about—winning. Isn't there a place where people can just do what they do and enjoy it, without always getting criticized and judged about it?"[29]

In 1976, in the Pioneer Valley of western Massachusetts, a group of women formed what would later become the Mary Vazquez Women's Softball League.[30] The emphasis was on providing women who had no softball experience with an opportunity to develop skills in a supportive environment. Team names, like Hot Flashes, Womenrising, Womynfire, and Common Womon—the last named for a local feminist restaurant whose name was in turn inspired by Judy Grahn's *The Common Women Poems*—indicate the influence of academics from the dozen or so colleges in the area. The founding organizers wanted to find a different way to frame the struggle between teams, de-emphasizing competition in favor of collaboration.

Everyone got a chance to play in every game, and league rules stated that batters who were struggling to get a hit could ask the opposing pitcher to decrease her velocity. Players whose on-field behavior was deemed to be diverging from the egalitarian spirit of the league would be sent to cool down in the parking lot, which was across the street from the usual venue. This long-held custom doesn't mean that everyone was happy with the emphasis on noncompetitive play. One frustrated player fretted that prioritizing the participation of inexperienced or unskilled players seemed like "the old kind of feminism where everything was a chore."[31]

Still in existence today, the league has never kept standings. The arrival of players who grew up in the age of Title IX and were thus more likely to have received sports coaching and encouragement in school meant that the standard of play gradually improved, and a little more focus on winning and losing emerged. Nevertheless, the league rules still state, "The main goal of this league is to give women a chance to enjoy women's softball. It should be something to look forward to each summer as fun."[32] The bylaws instruct players, "Watch your attitude" and "Be encouraging," and ask victors to "have gracious sensitivity toward the losing team." Most uniquely, in a holdover from a time when players distressed some spectators by shedding their shirts on a warm day, the rules also demand, "Clothes must be worn on playing fields at all times."

The great lesbian debate over competition was key in the formation of another politically motivated team in the 1970s. Here, the issue was that women of color didn't want to compete against other women of color—or Third World women, to use the nomenclature of the time. Nor were they particularly motivated to get invested in rivalries among the bars that sponsored teams, since they were often treated poorly in those places. Vicki Gabriner recollects the discomfort she felt watching the Rebels, a lesbian softball team sponsored by a women's bar. "Their uniforms were the colors of the Confederacy. And I remember the uproar when some members of the team hung up a Confederate flag in that bar not consciously intending a racial slur, but making one nonetheless.

After several conversations with team members and the bar owners, the flag came down."

In Northern California, queer women of color formed Gente, an independent squad that joined nine bar-sponsored teams in the Bay Area Women's Softball League. In a 1974 profile, *Lesbian Tide* described Gente as "a spirited, united group of twenty-five Third World sisters," a "mixture of folks from factory teams and folks with degrees."[33]

A decade after the *Lesbian Tide* article appeared, poet Pat Parker, who had been active in Gente, provided more background on why the team was formed. She revealed that while playing in a bar-league-sponsored basketball game, one of her teammates had used a racial slur against a woman on a rival team. "Now that didn't make me feel very good," Parker told Yvonne Zipter.[34] "And of course, it didn't make the woman on the other team feel O.K. either." They met afterward and discussed what to do: "Here we are, playing our hearts out with these people, and we can't be sure of them." Gente was their solution. For Gente players, standing side by side on the softball field was a "blatant statement ... a consciousness-raising thing."[35]

Establishing their own queer team solved some problems and created others. Several Gente members who had previously played on city league or industrial league softball teams reported having experienced issues with straight women feeling intimidated by out lesbian teammates. However, playing on a lesbian team meant affiliating with queer bars, which could promote friendships and bonding but also involved women of color putting their money into the pockets of white bar owners, who didn't always make them feel welcome. The bars supported softball teams not out of altruism, after all, but to make a profit. "It's not just the team that goes to a bar. It's us and our lovers and our friends and people who just want to do something on Sunday afternoon after the games.... It's a nice way for the bars to attract people," one Gente player told *Lesbian Tide*.[36] And because Gente wasn't affiliated with a bar, they faced extra expenses. "We have to go to [our opponents'] bar, instead.... That's one of the main drains on our money. It comes to quite a bit.... Win or lose, we gotta buy drinks."

Seeing how poorly bars—including white-owned lesbian and gay bars—treated majority-women-of-color squads occasionally spurred softball teams to take action. The politically conscious Avantis, a majority-white squad from Minneapolis, were highly influenced by the Motown Soul Sisters, a Black team from Detroit. In 1975, a Minnesota bar, where squads were socializing after a tournament, refused to serve the Soul Sisters.[37] The Avantis, along with all the other teams drinking in the packed bar, walked out in disgust, never to return.

Some bar sponsors do seem to have been genuinely committed to softball. According to writer Yvonne Zipter, one of the owners of Piggens Pub in Chicago was so supportive of the team the bar sponsored—attending every game, keeping score, providing Gatorade, and hosting barbecues—that players took to drinking there.[38] They adopted the place with such enthusiasm that what was once a men's bar effectively became a mixed bar, especially on weekends during the softball season.

Softball provided the Gente community with structure and sociability. Even women who weren't interested in playing could consult a league schedule to learn when and where they could find other politically conscious lesbians of color in a healthy outdoor setting. Sports gave people something to cheer for. And it felt good to hear those cheers.

As with the ALFA Omegas, softball was just one part of a larger vision for Gente. The ultimate goal was to set up "a nice place where people can come, that's not a bar scene." Gente didn't manage to establish a women's center, though the group remained active for several years. In addition to building solidarity around sports teams, Olivia Records recording artist Linda Tillery directed a Gente-affiliated a cappella singing group known as the Gente Gospelaires, which performed benefit shows to raise money for lesbian-of-color causes.[39]

Softball provided West Coast lesbians of color with a setting where they could create a tight-knit group, apart from, but also within, a de facto white lesbian institution. They were still subject to bigoted responses—white women accused team members of reverse racism and one asked a Gente player, "Haven't we been treating you nice?"[40] Still, forming a team allowed them to connect with other lesbians of color, a crucial development. "We're not supposed to be together," one player told *Lesbian Tide*. It made some white women uncomfortable, but forming a team exclusively for lesbians of color was affirming and productive for the women of Gente.

Softball has a lot to offer lesbians, even if they don't or can't take to the field themselves. The thrill of visceral self-recognition is one benefit. As numerous lesbian memoirs attest, many young women feel an instinctive connection with softball and softball players in the early years of their tomboyhood. In the introduction to *When Women Played Hardball*, her 1994 history of the All-American Girls Baseball League, Susan E. Johnson remembers her ten-year-old self watching the Rockford Peaches "with wonder and an excitement that was close to erotic."[41] Meanwhile, in North Dakota, preadolescent Dianna Hunter would walk a mile to the park where a women's softball team played. Although Hunter didn't recognize her feelings for her favorite players—"a wiry, boyish girl" and a pair of sisters with "trim, athletic bodies"—as sexual attraction, she asked her father to make a pen-and-ink sketch of the sisters, which she placed on her dresser.[42] Hunter's mother, who was aware of the sport's reputation, warned her to be "careful," since she'd heard that some of the players were "queers." With hindsight, Hunter notes, "The next ten years might have been so much easier if I had been alerted to some inner truth right then, but perhaps just knowing there were girls like that was enough."[43]

If anyone should know that the benefits of sport are also available to those who merely sit and watch, it's me. After all, I found my first queer community at tennis tournaments. As a teenager I was obsessed with women's tennis in the same way that I was obsessed with music, television, and the Patty Hearst story—not as a participant but as an extremely engaged observer possessed with a compulsion to track down every obtainable nugget of information. I consumed those facts and figures with such intensity that I could recite huge chunks by heart. Tennis was different from my other passions, though, because it involved women performing feats of strength and athleticism. A kind of homing instinct told me that if I could get to a tournament, I could also satisfy my other great hunger: an intense desire to meet other lesbians, which didn't seem possible on my home turf.

Looking back, I'm astonished that I pulled it off. The heist-level scheming and planning required to find a way to spend a week in Eastbourne, the home of the traditional women's pre-Wimbledon grass-court warmup tournament, now makes me suspect that I may have had superpowers back then. (Cheap train fares, inexpensive accommodation in seaside towns that had been abandoned as holidaymakers headed to sunny destinations abroad, and the more robust British welfare state of the time helped too.)

Tennis is a very uptight sport, but in the lightly attended early rounds, it's possible to converse quietly. I quickly found my people. We had things in common: a fanatical interest in women's tennis and, it turned out, queerness. On the first day of the 1979 Eastbourne tournament, when the British tabloid newspapers splashed the scoop that Wimbledon favorite Martina Navratilova was dating lesbian novelist Rita Mae Brown, it transpired that almost everyone in Devonshire Park had read *Rubyfruit Jungle*, even though the book was hard to find in Britain at the time. Not everyone in attendance was gay, of course, but back then the closet was so deep you couldn't always believe people's declarations of heterosexuality. (What a shock it was when an American who had spent a good chunk of the morning taking great pains to establish that he definitely wasn't gay showed up in the obscure, back-street gay pub it had required advanced navigational skills to locate.)

I don't want to suggest that the tennis itself was incidental. I loved it, and I got to know several players, thanks in large part to all those facts I'd committed to memory. But when I look back, only a few of my memories involve on-court triumphs and disasters. Far stronger are recollections of my first visit to a gay bar and of how the friendships I made that week and at the dozens of tournaments I attended in the next five or six years became key nodes in my queer network.

Those weeks "at the tennis" led to crushes, manic spurts of letter writing, evenings in bars all over the world, and eventually to my returning at least some of the hospitality I received. You don't have to play to enjoy the social advantages of sports.

Softball is still an integral part of the North American queer social landscape. In New York, the Big Apple Softball League (BASL) has been providing a place for lesbian, gay, bisexual, and transgender adults to "play softball in a safe environment of friendly competition" since 1977.[44]

That isn't to say that softball hasn't changed over the decades. What was once the women's division of BASL is now called "women+" and welcomes all but cisgender men to participate. Integrating trans and nonbinary players into the game wasn't without a few hiccups. Former Houston mayor (and feminist bookstore co-owner) Annise Parker told me that when she introduced trans jock Phyllis Frye to the lesbian softball team she coached in the 1980s, some players "freaked out."[45] She told them, "She's not welcome anywhere else. One of the reasons we started this league in the first place was so we would always be welcome." Once the objections were withdrawn, Frye became the heart and soul of the team. "It mattered so much to her," said Parker.

One BASL player told me that the presence of many nonbinary and trans people was what drew her to the league.[46] She jokingly noted, "My team probably has the most top surgeries. Some of our best players are sitting out right now because they're getting surgery. It's like, 'I'm happy for you, but we need our shortstop. Do it in the offseason!'" The league switched to a new provider of umpires in 2022. Players told me the previous crew refused to stop using "ladies" as the default term of address when making announcements.

Women+ teams are divided into two subdivisions, one "more competitive" and the other "more recreational"—or as player Alina Butareva described it to me, "a bit more chill."[47] Ultimately, though, the underlying purpose is the same as it was in the 1970s and before—to compete, socialize, and flirt, not necessarily in that order. Certain verities endure, such as relationship drama: Butareva's team, Resting Pitch Face (RPF), was originally formed after a breakup also broke up the former couple's softball squad. (In the spring 2022 season, Resting Pitch Face's lineup included 6.5 couples. The .5 recognizes that one half of one couple technically played for another team, but as long as her side wasn't required on another field at the same time, she was sure to be found in the Resting Pitch Face dugout.)

In June 2022, I headed out to Randalls Island, across the East River from Harlem, to watch Resting Pitch Face play

three games. The competition started at 9 a.m. on a Saturday morning in Pride month, which spoke volumes about
the players' commitment. One woman told me she'd had
two hours' sleep the night before, and I'm confident she was
rounding up. She still arrived in time to join her teammates
in setting up the dugout before taking to the field, where she
played with the casual confidence of a natural jock.

Randalls Island is sufficiently remote (and New York City
sufficiently suffused in queerness) that it's unlikely to be
casual spectators' first exposure to rainbow flags and nonbinary people. Still, BASL's presence among youth teams and
corporate rivalries felt radical. The names printed on the
backs of the players' uniform shirts made statements about
gender ("Trixie's Dad," "Smol Papi") or sexuality ("No Het-
ero"), along with playful riffs on player names, as in Alina's
"Bootyreva."

The spirit of camaraderie that Pici identified in 1975 was
on display nearly fifty years later. Not only did Resting Pitch
Face players support their teammates with encouraging
words and proud shoulder pats, but they also applauded fine
plays by rival players. Their opponent for the first two games
of the day was a newly formed squad that hadn't yet found
much success. RPF wanted the win, but once that outcome
was assured, they eased off the throttle. From my position in
the dugout, I could hear players suggest to teammates that
they might take their time running the bases to minimize the
misery of their still-winless rivals. (That said, some runners
had a hard time hitting the brakes once the ball was in play.
They might have been playing in the chill league, but people

who schlep to an island off the Bronx early on a weekend morning possess more hustle than the average human.)

Softball is a social game, and several players told me they had been drawn to the Big Apple Softball League out of a desire to meet other queer people. Between innings and games and when the other team was fielding, players would kibbitz in the dugout. Though they hailed from all over the city and beyond, teammates made plans to connect at Brooklyn Pride later that day, and pains were taken to coordinate outfits for Manhattan Pride a couple of weeks later. (This was the summer of mesh.) Just as it was for the ALFA Omegas in 1975, so it was for Resting Pitch Face in 2022: softball is a great queer hang. Butareva told me, "It's really hard to make friends as an adult. Some of my college friends only speak to people they went to college with and maybe a stray coworker. I've made so many friends as an adult through sports. Most of my core social group are people I play softball with."

This easy sociability isn't the only explanation for softball's enduring appeal. Unlike most of the spaces where lesbians have traditionally gone to find one another, on the field there are no business imperatives at play. Most leagues require players to pay a small annual fee to cover league expenses— field rental, umpires, and so forth—some of which may be subsidized by a sponsor, but otherwise there's no pressure to squeeze the square peg of lesbian culture into the round hole of for-profit capitalism.

While the wider world of sports might thrive on cutthroat competition, lesbian softball is pleasantly light on drama related to the actual game. Women "retire" from playing when their bodies feel the physical strain, drifting away of their own accord. Younger women take the old-timers' spots on the roster, and the cycle of softball life continues. And while I'm conscious that softball lore seems heavy on tales of breakups and on-field bickering, the stories I heard were recounted in a playful tone. The softball field provided a rare venue where women could openly flaunt their romantic partnerships. They were sometimes obliged to acknowledge their breakups there too.

Softball has also escaped the attention of cis-het men. While lesbian bar owners had to strategize and scheme to keep cisgender men out of their clubs, softball's butch aesthetics, coupled perhaps with its lack of secrecy and concealment, kept gawkers away. (I understand why old-school lesbian bars didn't try this tactic, but telling straight, cis guys they're welcome seems to cause many of them to lose interest in infiltrating queer spaces.) With no money to be made, outsiders tend to steer clear.

The stories of ALFA and Gente show that, at some points in recent history, the softball field has been an unexpected venue for political organizing. Today, for most players, softball is a distraction from everyday life, providing a place for apolitical women to get together and offering activists a sanctuary from stress. Charis bookstore's E. R. Anderson, who spent years playing softball before and after transitioning, loved that the game exposed him to people he would never otherwise have spent time with. Charis had a team—the Charis Prose—for three seasons, but none of the softball players spent much, if any, time in the store. In the early 2010s, E. R. played in a rec-league team organized by an Atlanta butch with a rainbow-bedecked Mini Cooper. It was just the breath of fresh air he needed. "My life and work at Charis is so political," he told me. "Every single one of my friends has very thought-out opinions. This was a kind of queerness that had nothing to do with politics. It was really fun."[48]

Fun. What a concept!

Cooling down at OWL Farm, Roseburg, Oregon, 1977. © 1977 JEB (Joan E. Biren)

FOUR

LESBIAN LAND

IN THE SUMMER OF 1973, THREE WOMEN PACKED THEIR belongings into a car, left Montreal, and headed west. As they wrote in a book published three years later, they were "sick of the countless evidences of the patriarchy" that surrounded them in the city.[1] Instead, they wanted to live and work exclusively with feminists amid the healing beauty of nature. The western United States, already home to several rural lesbian communities, seemed most likely to provide a safe space where they could create a new and separate lesbian-feminist culture.

As determined as they were to find this promised land, the journey was challenging. Dian Wagner, Carol Newhouse, and Billie Miracle formed an "emotional triangle," but Carol and Billie were lovers, and the group's single vehicle could barely contain the "tears, hysteria, and recriminations" that surfaced while they were on the road.[2] One day, after thousands of miles of driving through the United States and Mexico, Billie declared that she was done with traveling, so they stopped and looked for a place to live in southern Oregon.

Within a week, they found twenty-three acres, featuring a beautiful view of the surrounding mountains, eight miles outside Grants Pass.[3] The land cost $27,000, and since Dian had family money she could use for the down payment, they were able to acquire it. On April 10, 1974, WomanShare was born.

Living conditions were austere. Although there were two rundown houses on the property, they were barely habitable, and none of the women came to the land with any of the skills needed for country living. Still, for all the emotional turmoil and the physical challenges they faced, they were committed to the move. In 2022, reflecting on their original motivations, WomanShare cofounder Carol Newhouse said, "We didn't feel like we were giving up that much. We were just done."[4] They felt certain that mainstream society was harming them physically, mentally, and spiritually. However unsure they might be about what exactly they were going to build together, "we knew it was going to be better."

Nobody knows how many lesbians rejected queer urban culture and moved to the countryside to create a separate woman-centered world starting in the 1970s. Known in the 1970s as the women's-land movement and in the 1980s as the lesbian-land movement, in the 1990s they adopted the term *landdykes*, because, according to one scholar, this designation "links lesbians to the land in a way that even a hyphenated name could not."[5] (Some "landykes" spell the term with one *d*, because "it makes it hard to separate the land from the dykes.")[6] Landdykes' detachment from mainstream America was so complete that they tended to communicate with each other through the DIY magazines that emerged to chronicle and counsel the transplants, rather than with the wider world of lesbians, much less with society at large. Since most of their communities were situated in remote rural areas, they avoided publicity. Consequently, there is no comprehensive catalog of their numbers, though the consensus is that at least 150 women's lands existed at the movement's peak in the 1970s and 1980s.[7] In the early 2020s, around seventy remained, though most have shrunk dramatically as the original founders have aged or passed away and interest in separatism has waned.[8]

Women who relocated to rural communities came from all over the country, but most had a few things in common. Almost all were white.[9] Most were highly educated: in 1975, only around 10.6 percent of women had completed a four-year degree; yet almost all the transplants were college graduates, and several had done postgraduate study.[10] Most had been involved in the progressive political movements of the 1970s, abandoning them when the sexism and homophobia that emerged became insupportable. Some moved directly from the city to lesbian land, while others began their rural journey in mixed-gender communes—some of which, like Oregon's Cabbage Lane and Golden, later evolved into women-only communities.[11]

Lesbian-land groups sprang up all over the United States, though the affordable prices and availability of beautiful (if agriculturally disadvantaged) land led to concentrations in southern Oregon and, to a lesser extent, the Ozarks, New Mexico, upstate New York, and Vermont. Although communities were staunchly independent, women in areas that were home to several lesbian-land groups regularly organized gatherings to celebrate pagan holy days, solstices, and full moons; hold croning ceremonies, marking the end of menopause; and participate in other neopagan rituals related to goddess worship. The women of Oregon were particularly productive. The state was the creative crucible of landdyke publications such as *WomanSpirit*, the We'Moon almanacs, and *The Blatant Image*, a groundbreaking lesbian photography magazine. The stretch of I-5 between Eugene and the California border was home to so many lesbian-land projects that it came to be known as the Amazon Trail.[12]

Why was all this happening now? In the 1970s, the possibilities for the ways a woman's life might play out expanded beyond recognition. From the febrile interplay of women's liberation, gay liberation, the Black civil rights struggle, the antiwar movement, the New Left, and a general dissatisfaction with the status quo, brand-new options for work, family, and home life were dreamed into existence.

One of these new ideas, born out of the sense of exasperation that many women felt, provided the philosophical underpinnings of the land movement: lesbian separatism.

Across America, women were coming to consciousness as feminists and asking how they could transform the sexist society they increasingly recognized themselves to be living in. Some decided that the answer to that question was lesbianism—regardless of their sexual inclinations. (Women who identified as lesbians because they believed it was necessary for women to separate from men but who weren't sexually attracted to women were known as "political lesbians.") In its 1970 manifesto, "The Woman Identified Woman," the New York–based group Radicalesbians made the point with a bang: "A lesbian is the rage of all women condensed to the point of explosion."[13] As they saw it, any energy spent trying to fix women's connections to men, their oppressors, was wasted. If women had any hope of finding their authentic selves, they must instead prioritize relationships, including sexual relationships, with other women. "Our energies must flow toward our sisters, not backward toward our oppressors," wrote Radicalesbians.[14]

It also must be said that groups like Radicalesbians were coming into feminist consciousness purely as women—not as white women, which the vast majority of them were. Lesbian separatists focused their energies on gender-based oppression, leaving racism and to a lesser extent classism as afterthoughts. To them, the "oppressors" were men, and only men. As a result, many Black and Brown feminists disengaged from the separatist movement, unwilling to contribute to a vision of feminism built around the needs of white women.

Other separatist commentators likened men to paratrophic organisms. In 1977, philosopher Marilyn Frye described a notion, then "floating around," that "females and males generally live in a relation of parasitism, a parasitism of the male on the female.... [I]t is, generally speaking, the strength, energy, inspiration and nurturance of women that keeps men going."[15] According to this line of thinking, separating from men—denying them access to women's beds and the rest of their lives—was the only way to stop men from continuing to sap women's strength.

Given the circumstances women faced at the time, none of this strikes me as particularly radical. As they say on the plane, put your own mask on before you help others. The last part of that instruction is crucial, though. Exhausted by millennia of being consigned to the helping role, some separatists rejected, or forgot about, that second clause. How else to explain why members of a group that disengaged from their oppressors in order to build a more just society eventually developed such a significant blind spot when it comes to their own treatment of at least one marginalized segment of the population: transgender people?

Lesbian-feminists, including some separatists, saw this coming. The Furies were an (all-white) explicitly lesbian-separatist collective, but in an essay in the fall 1972 issue of *The Furies* newspaper, member Charlotte Bunch warned about the dangers of exclusionary politics. "We start with the useful strategy of working only with a particular group, x, lesbians, working class women, young women. But we slip into the purist assumption that if you aren't x, you can't be in our revolution rather than stressing the development of x-consciousness whether you are x or not."[16] Practically speaking, this is a mistake, Bunch believed, because it narrows the number of people who can join the struggle (or live on a piece of land or attend a music festival).

Timing is everything. I'm too much of a city slicker to have ever considered relocating to lesbian land, but I was a separatist in the 1980s. Although I was surrounded by what we would now call gender-nonconforming people—heck, despite not really fitting into the gender binary myself— back then, it seemed relatively easy to define *x* when it came to deciding who belonged in lesbian spaces. Now those clear definitions seem much fuzzier, and I can't support projects that exclude trans and nonbinary people. Like many other people's, my understanding and experience of gender has expanded and transformed in the last couple of decades, and what seemed like a productive strategy forty years ago now feels rude and wrong.

Still, this experiment represents an important chapter of lesbian-feminist history. My own feelings about and understanding of separatism have shifted, and I now find myself in profound disagreement with the trans-exclusionary politics of most contemporary landdykes. However, as I'll explore later in this chapter, I don't believe that this ideological development was an inevitable consequence of communal rural living. And as someone who often feels that I could do more for the movement—shouldn't politics demand sacrifice?—I still admire the commitment of women who lived out their values in these austere, isolated settings.

Lesbian separatism manifested in other ways besides the extreme variant of rural living. In the tumultuous 1970s, women all around the United States were experimenting with new kinds of living arrangements. In cities, newly minted lesbians moved out of their husbands' or parents' homes and formed group houses. On a practical level, it was much cheaper for a number of women to share the properties that became available in urban neighborhoods like Atlanta's Little Five Points as white families fled to the suburbs than it was for women to rent their own apartments. The budgetary benefits were just the beginning, though. Women felt safer living together, and shared homes were social and fun, zinging with sexual and intellectual energy and a sense that anything could happen.

In the Bay Area, poet Judy Grahn was part of what became known as the Terrace Collective, based in a four-bedroom house on Oakland's Terrace Street.[17] The home served as an informal resource center: women looking for concerts, parties, or political activities could call to learn about upcoming events, as well as the car-repair classes one resident offered. Living together made it easier for women to dream and scheme together: two of the founders of the ICI: A Woman's Place bookstore and about half of the thirteen members of the Women's Press Collective were among the approximately forty women who lived at Terrace House during Grahn's five years there. She later wrote, "I consider living there one of the greatest privileges and learning experiences of my life, because I got to participate in helping to formulate a particular kind of revolution—a women's revolution. Only a few precious times in history have women been in a position to separate from the rest of society in order to describe the world as we see it, and to change it for our needs."

Ginny Z. Berson was a member of America's most famous collective lesbian household, one of the three homes in Washington, DC, where the Furies, a twelve-woman collective of writers, artists, and troublemakers lived, met, and fomented revolution between 1971 and 1973. The row house at 219 11th Street SE became the first explicitly lesbian site added to the National Register of Historic Places in 2016.[18] After the Furies dissolved, Berson was one of the founders of the pioneering women's music label Olivia Records, which also operated as a collective, with some members living together.[19]

In 2021, I asked Berson why cohabitation was so integral to those early lesbian-feminist projects.[20] After acknowledging the financial advantages, she situated communal living as a response to the rugged individualism that is integral to the founding myth of the United States. "It was all about building community," she told me. The women of the Furies and Olivia had grown up in the 1950s and 1960s, "when there was such a societal value placed on everyone having their own house, their own car, their own washing machine. We didn't want to be part of consumer capitalism. It's not healthy, and it's just a way to keep people separated from each other." Sharing space was also about sharing privilege. "We were trying to equalize things a little bit so that the women who had more, or had privilege and so had better paying jobs, put more into the living situation." Ultimately, though, they were consumed with politics, organizing, and studying and wanted to devote every available minute to those pursuits. "We were trying to live the way we imagined the world could be," Berson said. "We always wanted to be together."

Group living didn't disappear with rotary phones and typewriters, and it isn't just for LGBTQ people. The ever-increasing cost of accommodation means that most young people who leave their family homes for college or work spend at least some time sharing living space with peers. I lived with straight friends in college and later in London and Madrid, and it was almost always an enlightening experience. Without realizing they were doing so, my roommates taught an only child the art of sharing. They also showed me how to be middle-class, revealing all kinds of hidden knowledge. I'm grateful to those exemplary housemates, but lesbian group living was different.

None of the lesbian group houses I was part of will ever be adorned with a plaque, but they were essential to my socialization as a lesbian. In Newark, Delaware, I lived in a house owned by an Asian American lesbian who ran a hot dog stand on the downtown strip. She was a grown woman renting rooms to a bunch of kids—college students or women trying to go back to school. We might have been twentysomethings, but we were all going through a delayed adolescence. Back in the 1980s, no one I knew had come out to their parents before they headed to college, so we didn't really learn how to date until we got to our new homes off campus. That house was the first place I could not only talk about being gay but actually *be* gay—share a room with my girlfriend and do all the first serious relationship things my straight schoolmates had been up to since their tween years, most of which involved maintaining constant physical contact. That house was like a twenty-four-hour drop-in center. Since my land-lady knew every dyke in town, the easiest way to meet the lesbians of Newark was to plant yourself on the beat-up recliner in the living room and prepare to greet the visitors.

Then came Washington, DC, the networking capital of the world. Every year, the city receives a fresh supply of future presidents, Pulitzer winners, and do-gooders, all desperate to meet their VPs, editors, and donors. In the 1980s, there were enough lesbian households in Mount Pleasant that every Saturday there'd be a party within easy walking distance, and someone with a car would be heading to a club like Tracks or the Hung Jury when it was over. This was where I learned that when a roommate returned from spending a month working at the Michigan Womyn's Music Festival, it would be at least another month before she wore a shirt indoors.

Through DC contacts I was later able to find a place in a council flat in Stoke Newington, London, which offered all the typical benefits of a lesbian neighborhood, including a total lack of Tube stations and a local library that boasted a larger-than-average lesbian-romance selection. The house-hold's books and records were shared, the living room always contained the latest issues of *Outwrite* and *The Pink Paper*, and someone in the house was sure to have the name and number of a lesbian carpenter, attorney, or travel agent in their address book.

For some women, though, urban life was too tangled up in the patriarchal system. Living alongside men consumed energy they would rather devote to each other—and they were willing to go to great lengths to pursue that dream.

In April 1973, Marea Sankey and Martha Benewicz published "A Country Lesbian Manifesto" in the Twin Cities feminist newspaper *So's Your Old Lady*.[21] The poetic, almost hallucinogenic essay wasn't exactly a sales pitch for country living. Rather, it was an introduction to an arduous "lifestyle in which you must keep yourself warm, fed, and clean without central heating, plumbing, or plentiful jobs." Sankey and Benewicz acknowledged the challenges of rural relocation, but any hesitations that might sprout in the minds of readers tempted to escape society would surely be offset by their concise summary of the benefits of country living: "Sometimes I think that the duck's first egg of spring sprouting tomatoe [*sic*] plants and the pasture fencing have nothing to do with lesbian liberation. But we remember the motivation, the need to be self-sufficient and that means gettin' the Man off our backs wanting his rent and food money and gasoline and taxes and cunt."

Few women outside—or even inside!—the Twin Cities saw that manifesto. Sankey and Benewicz weren't the mothers of a movement. Their words didn't ignite a revolution, but they captured a mood that was taking hold across the nation as women from Oregon to Vermont and all points in between abandoned the comforts and culture of the city and established new outposts in rural redoubts.

Although these women surely dreamed of rural self-sufficiency, only a tiny minority had any hope of achieving it—at least at the beginning of their pastoral adventure. They were founding mothers, not would-be farmers. (A European visitor to southern Oregon expressed frustration that the various communities in that region didn't coordinate their efforts: "All these women were still buying food when a lot of it could be produced on the land," she wrote. "All we need to do is organize who will grow what.")[22] This focus on process rather than produce, feelings rather than food, is evident in the way Billie Miracle described WomanShare's purpose: "Our goals for ourselves were to make a family, to learn to live together, and deal with shared responsibility and shared leadership."[23]

Living in rural communities wasn't for everyone. Conditions were brutal, and the stakes were stratospheric, but hundreds, perhaps thousands, of women were willing to face the hardships for a chance to start over in nature. Since they could only afford to purchase or rent underdeveloped parcels of land, the pioneers typically found themselves on properties that contained barely habitable shelters: crumbling farmhouses, abandoned chicken coops, and rickety shacks; superannuated school buses or aged mobile homes; flimsy tipis and tents. Some built casitas from adobe, following instructions provided in the DIY publications created by and for country dykes. Lightly used yurts were passed from woman to woman, with a crucial piece of hardware sometimes going missing along the chain of ownership. Few land-dykes had access to electricity or septic systems, never mind running water. Without proper insulation, they were often as cold or overheated and as subject to the predations of bugs and rodents in their rudimentary quarters as they would have been if they had simply rolled out a blanket and slept under the stars. They preferred property where trees or distance from rural roads provided protection from prying eyes, but that topography and remoteness made it hard to access and cultivate the land.

Many women who were drawn to the idea of lesbian land changed their minds once they sampled those primitive conditions. Oral histories recorded by early land women are full of stories of those who couldn't hack it. Two longtime landdykes told the story of another couple who partnered with them in the purchase of a piece of land.[24] On their first visit to the property, it took the new arrivals an hour to crack the ice that had formed overnight around the entrance to their tent. That freezing morning and the lack of bathing facilities convinced them they weren't cut out for country life. Another longtime denizen of lesbian land described the "rugged existence" there as "hauling wood, building houses, hauling wood, doing farming, you know, walking. Walking, walking, walking, walking, walking. . . . Every bit of it was hard." She added, "And I loved it."[25]

This was not a relocation for the fainthearted, but conviction alone couldn't clear land or dig wells. As Dark Artemis Silverowl, a resident of DW Outpost in Missouri, noted, winter was particularly trying: "Icy roads, cold winds, sub-zero temperatures, smoky stoves, and frozen waterpipes can wear even the strongest Amazon to the point of breaking," she wrote in *WomanSpirit*, a quarterly magazine created on women's land in Oregon.[26] Few landdykes arrived at their new acreage with the kinds of skills that were required there. Even those who had grown up on farms or in the country struggled to transfer that experience to the inferior land that was available to them. Most lacked even that background.

It wasn't that the particular subset of women who decamped to the countryside were unusually impractical. In the 1970s and 1980s, very few women had been taught the kinds of survival skills required in the wild outposts of the lesbian nation—tree felling, home building, plumbing, vehicle maintenance, and all the other kinds of manual labor that are required in remote locations. Beyond the borders of lesbian land, feminists were preaching the necessity for women to expand their skill sets. Coletta Reid, who went into the printing trade at feminist publisher Diana Press after the Furies collective broke up, threw down the gauntlet in a 1974 piece she wrote for *Quest*.[27] She observed that because women in the workplace had historically been restricted to support roles, few knew how to handle the basic logistical operations needed to run a business, which put them at a competitive disadvantage. Worse still, because women had traditionally worked primarily in service jobs, they didn't know how to operate and maintain machinery and hadn't been taught how to perform the physical tasks associated with other kinds of work. In short, wrote Reid, "women don't have the physical experience and machinery skills of working-class men nor do we have the organizational and administrative experience of middle-class male managers."

Why did this matter? Because a lack of practical skills had doomed earlier revolutions. "One way to keep a group down is to keep them from gaining the knowledge and expertise necessary to run things themselves," Reid wrote. In what may not be an entirely accurate representation of the historical record, she continued, "The Russian Revolution was lost when Trotsky had to return the bourgeoise to positions of power because of their skills." If feminists wanted to avoid such a fate, Reid encouraged them to shift their focus from service and retail industries to thus far unknown territory: "Women need to learn to farm, to mine, to sail, to build buildings, be machinists, etc."

A few women did indeed learn to farm, but it was an exhausting and sometimes humbling process. It also required them to discard any romantic notions about what it meant to live in nature. In *Country Lesbians*, a book the Woman-Share collective self-published in 1976,[28] Nelly, one of the first women to join the founding triad on the land, described how she had learned to love the chainsaw.[29] In her first winter at WomanShare, Nelly cut wood by hand—"a realization of my country dream of quietly, peacefully fulfilling my basic physical needs with minimal help from the decaying machine-oriented male culture." By the next year, however, the romance had worn thin, and by year three, "it was a tiresome chore. I felt that the work was always hanging over my head. I wanted my time and energy freed for other tasks." After the next thaw, the collective bought a chainsaw, but no one knew how to use it. Nelly called the forestry department and chainsaw stores and consulted the local library, all to no avail. Finally, she had to relax her separatist principles and seek help from a male logging teacher at a local community college. He set up a course, which Nelly and two other land women attended. They then passed on this heretofore occult knowledge to other landdykes in southern Oregon. Although her comfort with operating a chainsaw was hard-won, Nelly appreciated the confidence it gave her to "take power over other traditionally male-identified work. It repeatedly strengthens and renews my image of myself as a strong dyke," she wrote. (The WomanShare collective later realized that although sharing knowledge was powerful, sharing tools was "intolerable." When the chainsaw was made available to other collectives in the area, Nelly hated not knowing who had it, what condition it was in, and whether she "would get it back before the woodpile was gone.")

With so much to do, lesbian-land communities often clashed over differing attitudes to work. The residents of WomanShare spent a lot of time processing their feelings about domestic and outdoor labor, which led them to recognize that sometimes "anger about a messy kitchen is really displaced anger stemming from another cause and sometimes it is simple irritation at not being able to find a clean place to make breakfast."[30] Here, as elsewhere, tasks that were traditionally coded as women's work were particularly abhorred. The collective eventually developed a strategy to avoid resentment about unequal distribution of housework: each woman committed to doing thirty minutes of domestic labor five days per week, no more, no less.

Disputes about equitable allocation of housework also surfaced at Kvindelandet, a women's-land community in Denmark. There, tensions centered on women who had moved to the land to heal from the harms of patriarchy, which frustrated other residents who felt that this recovery time would be more usefully devoted to essential labor. Again, "feminine" tasks like cooking and cleaning were especially contentious. Shosana, an American who spent a year at Kvindelandet, overheard one resident say of another, "She only does the glamorous things round here, like plowing the fields."[31]

The valorization of physical labor over domestic chores extended even to landdykes' artistic pursuits. In the first issue of *The Blatant Image*, Ruth Mountaingrove noted that she had made more than five hundred photographs of women building cabins on the land; yet she didn't have a single image of herself or her partner preparing food, even though they produced three meals a day nearly every day of the year.[32]

It also must be said that some women liked the idea of country living more than the demanding, largely unglamorous, and usually rather muddy reality. In 1975, Merril Mushroom wrote a poem, appropriately titled "Work Ethic," about the experience of coming home to lesbian land from her job in the city to find two of her landmates lounging around with houseguests while urgent work was left undone.[33] The second stanza reads,

I see
firewood not stacked, not even split yet,
compost overflowing the bucket,
water jugs still empty,
dirty dishes piled on the counter,
chickens not yet fed,
eggs not collected,
no supper on the stove,

and
the four of you sitting on the porch
wearing your nice, clean, brand-new
overalls.

While a few landdykes might have romanticized rural life, it would be condescending and ahistorical to assume that all the women who lit out for lesbian territory were physically and psychologically unprepared for its hardships. In 1990, Jean "Shewolf" Boudreaux realized a decades-long dream and left her university job to move to Woman's World, one hundred acres "in the far away back woods" of Louisiana.[34] It was fertile, flat land; she had carpentry skills and construction experience and owned the property outright. Shewolf's dreams of building a community there led her to offer to sign over parcels of her land to other lesbians after they had lived and worked in the community for some period—her initial thought was five years. To set this process in motion, she wrote to *Maize*, a grassroots country lesbian magazine, with a generous offer. "Women who aren't afraid of hard work, living without luxury, and stretching themselves emotionally to learn to be real and loving, are encouraged to write and tell me their dreams." Nevertheless, after many years of repeating this proposition, no one moved to Woman's World permanently. "It never really worked out," Shewolf said in 2013.[35] "Most of the women that came were pretty nice gals that did a good job. But they had issues, they all had issues."

Writing from the comfort of my warm, well-lit apartment, I'm not surprised that the vast majority of lesbians decided to stay in cities and towns. The demands of rural living could overwhelm even women who were fully committed to getting stronger and developing new abilities. Sallie, one half of the couple who started Greenhope in Vermont, said, "Neither of us is very brave or very rugged, and often we are frightened together. But together we have done some surprising things: we've built a barn, dug out and drained our septic system, installed a hot water system that operates off the wood stove, cleaned our sugar woods of unwanted softwood, learned to drive and skid our 1600 pound work horse."[36] Their accomplishments were all the more impressive because they were constantly pushing the limits of their inexperience. "We don't have as many skills as we should to live a life such as this," Sallie wrote in *Lesbian Land*, a landmark 1985 anthology of stories from women's-land communities, "but together we manage, and our triumphs are greater because we struggle so hard."

Seemingly endless labor was required to maintain minimally viable living conditions, and when those conditions deteriorated, so did women's ability to take care of basic chores. According to Shosana, once the facilities at Kvindelandet declined to what in hindsight seem like dangerous conditions—a broken furnace, only one working burner on the stove, the women who had to sleep outdoors worrying about losing toes to frostbite—even essential tasks went undone. "As things broke down they would not get fixed," Shosana wrote. "The communal lifestyle disintegrated as well, until women were living quite separately or in little family units. Some women tried organizing meetings to get other women to work."[37]

Given the general shortage of rural survival skills, from a practical point of view it wasn't ideal that the land movement tended to reject rather than embrace assistance from outside the community in the name of lesbian self-sufficiency. One woman's list of self-imposed restrictions on the kind of help she was willing to accept when building a home for herself and her daughter was "no men, no power tools, no synthetic building materials, no bulldozers."[38] These constraints were still less rigid than those imposed by one group of Francophone landdykes in Quebec who rejected all technology, including the written word.[39]

Women didn't receive wages for the work they did on lesbian land, but there were still plenty of arguments about finances. Indeed, disagreements about money—who had it, who didn't, how much was needed, how little was available— were high on the list of problems that splintered communities. Separatists firmly believed that issues like classism should and could be addressed in lesbian-feminist communities, but they didn't have knowledge of mediation techniques beyond a willingness to engage and a strong desire to do better than the broader society. This was the first time most landdykes had held honest conversations about property and privilege with women from different class backgrounds, so it shouldn't come as a surprise that discussions could become heated. As one landdyke put it, "What I would consider just a terrible, destructive fight, some of the other women from a more working-class background considered talking."[40]

Given how difficult it was to generate income in remote rural areas, it's hardly surprising that the very act of moving to the land brought up intense feelings about money. In the areas surrounding lesbian-land communities, it was almost impossible to find a job that paid a middle-class income, a reality that was especially salient for first-generation college graduates who, under normal circumstances, could have expected to leverage their degrees to live a less precarious existence than their parents. WomanShare's Nelly reported that her grandparents had been "poor, politically oppressed refugees," while her mother and father had "struggled their way up the class ladder to positions of relative comfort. I, to complete the cycle, choose to live as a poor, politically oppressed woman."[41]

At the same time, the cost of living was much lower in the country, and isolation encouraged frugality. Reduced expenses allowed women to devote more of their time to creative and spiritual projects. What's more, collective ownership enabled many women who otherwise had little hope of acquiring property to have their names on a deed.

Of course, classism wasn't the only systemic issue that landdykes needed to address. Even the most partisan defender of the women's-land movement would accept that it failed to serve the needs of lesbians of color. The secluded locations that landdykes chose for their settlements could be lonely and dangerous for women of color, who, given the whiteness of the movement and its failure to tackle racial oppression alongside sexism and classism, were more likely to reject lesbian separatism. As Black lesbian Anna Lee put it, "I still feel alienated from the black male nationalist community because I am a lesbian, and yet I understand that our struggles are intimately intertwined. At the same time, I often feel alienated by the white feminist community which has the privilege to ignore and to minimize racism."[42]

Over the years, several attempts were made to establish communities specifically for lesbians of color, including La Luz de la Lucha in Northern California, Arco Iris near Fayetteville, Arkansas, and Maat Dompim in central Virginia, though none of them thrived as long-term residential spaces. The issue wasn't a lack of need, however. A group of women of color who were living at Arkansas's Sassafras in 1983 explained that they needed a separate space where they could seek refuge from both the patriarchy and the racism of white lesbian feminists. They sought "safe and sympathetic environments for women to come where they can be reasonably free of the subtle and overt racism and cultural arrogance frequently displayed in predominantly white, middle-class women's spaces," "where something other than sterile white women's culture can flourish and expand," and "where Women of Color may discover their personal inner beings and creative selves, where they may bring their children for a taste of 'free-space,' safe from the rampant racism of the larger society."[43] Many of these communities still exist in some form, but they are increasingly shifting to become retreat centers, nature sanctuaries, or short-term workshop venues rather than enduring as residential communities. After several years of dormancy, Maat Dompim has been reinstated as an active nonprofit organization.[44] Its original "unmanageable wilderness" site was sold and a smaller property and structure purchased to serve as headquarters for future initiatives.

Some older communities are now transitioning into spaces for people of color. As of early 2023, the two surviving members of the original WomanShare collective, Billie Miracle and Carol Newhouse, were in the process of gifting the property to "Native and Queer women and Two-Spirit people."[45] The new stewards, Bianca Fox Del Mar Ballara and Lycan El Lobo Coss, intend to evolve "what began as a radical project to hold safe haven for lesbian women in the woods during the 1970's . . . into a matriarchal space."[46]

Once women had decided to uproot their lives and move to the country and somehow managed to find an affordable, available piece of property, a huge question still remained: Who could live on it?

It wasn't just a matter of finding a core group of women you could get along with, forming a quasi-family unit, and avoiding fights, though that was a formidable challenge. All housemates squabble, and a perusal of the history of lesbian land suggests that groups splintered over just about any cause: diet, dress, relationship drama, sexual preferences, sexual styles, musical tastes, too many meetings, too few meetings, attitudes to drugs, pets, work, and just plain not getting along.

Conflict in undercapitalized, sweat-equity lesbian-feminist projects is often freighted with extra intensity. A friend who left a job at a feminist bookstore under difficult circumstances more than twenty-five years ago still feels so much pain and anger about her departure that she can't bear to discuss that time in her life. On lesbian land, the stakes were even higher. This parallel rural universe was so all-encompassing—it incorporated home, work, sex, family, politics, philosophy, and more—that women wanted to be sure they were living all their values.

And yet, of course, there were disagreements about whose values should prevail. Would all women be welcome, or only those who lived as lesbians? And how was *lesbian* defined? Was it enough for a woman to decide that she wanted to devote all her energies to other women, or must she be sexually *attracted* to women—or involved in a sexual relationship with a woman? Could mothers bring their children to the land? If daughters were allowed, were sons? Were adult men permitted on the land? If so, in what capacity? Could they stay overnight? What about male relatives? Juana Maria Paz, a veteran member of rural collectives and communes who often acted as a teller of difficult truths, summarized the difficulties of formulating policies: "If A has a male child and B feels oppressed by male energy, whose needs should predominate?"[47] If no one was empowered to decide, communities were left in stalemate—or worse, in conflict.

The policies that defined a feminist community were subject to change as new women moved onto the land or as residents' needs and feelings changed. For example, if a community had formulated policies that allowed residents to consume alcohol but prohibited cigarettes, women who were smokers wouldn't be tempted to move there. But what if at some point one of the founders accepted that she had an alcohol problem and no longer wanted to have booze on the property or fell in love with a woman who was a smoker and that woman wanted to join the community? Then the rules were likely to be subject to debate and potential change—and anyone who had joined based on the conditions that pertained when they arrived would be justified in feeling profoundly unsettled.

Sexual conflicts were particularly disruptive in landdyke communities. Any resident could potentially pair off with another, and some groups seemed determined to explore every possible permutation. In the 1970s, many lesbians rejected monogamy as yet another tool of the patriarchy designed to keep women isolated, but their emotions didn't always keep up with their ideology. Pelican Lee wrote that in one community "many women had several lovers on the land. It was difficult to get away from relationships one might not want to witness. Sometimes dealing with our feelings around our multiple relationships took so much energy that we had little left for anything else."[48]

Another radical experiment in nonmonogamy was carried out at Redbird, a Vermont collective of eight women and three children that was active between 1974 and 1979. Former member Joyce Cheney, who edited the landmark anthology *Lesbian Land*, used the word *purist* to describe Redbird's attitude to construction—concrete, chain saws, vehicles, and men were all outlawed (residents mostly slept in tipis)—but the term also applied to the way they chose lovers.[49] Redbird members had a tight group identity, and even though there was a "strong" lesbian community in the town eighteen miles down the road, they kept to themselves, because they believed outside relationships would "disperse energy." Since they were committed to "smashing romanticism," they decided to choose sexual partners by drawing names from a hat. Theoretically, the couples would stay together for several months, at which point they would assign themselves another partner. How did it work out? "I wouldn't recommend it," Cheney concluded. "We tried. Oh, we tried. Some combinations were just too hard, and we rearranged pairings."[50]

Relationship drama aside, the problem with getting away from it all was that it also meant getting away from other lesbians. The blossoming of urban gay and lesbian culture associated with the aftermath of the Stonewall riots of June 1969 meant that fewer people, upon realizing they were attracted to members of the same sex, feared they would thereafter be condemned to a sad lifetime of loneliness—that is, unless they voluntarily removed themselves from the gay metropolis and decamped to the wide-open spaces of the country.

Of course, their isolation was freely chosen, and some women reveled in it. In the winter 1991 issue of *Maize*, Jae Haggard praised her community's remoteness. Being two miles from the nearest neighbor, she wrote, "we never hear intruding voices, dogs, or vehicles. We are at the end of a dirt road and we keep our gate locked. This quiet insulated land is ideal for our great desire to live as separate as possible from patriarchal culture—no tv, radio, newspapers, computers. We have only wimmin's voices and energy here."[51]

Physical separation allowed women to experiment sexually, socially, and creatively. "We were so free," Carol Newhouse said in 2022, remembering her days at WomanShare. "People were really into each other. It was so intimate. Nobody was watching, and people had their clothes off. It was just a different scene."[52] The remoteness of lesbian land also permitted something landdykes valued above almost everything else: liberation from the male gaze. Beyond the range of prying eyes, women could dress—or not dress—as they pleased. Even today, very few women have access to public outdoor spaces where they can go shirtless on a warm day. In the 1980s, in the queer resort of Provincetown, Massachusetts, activist Nikki Craft was repeatedly detained by the authorities for sunbathing topless at Herring Cove Beach.[53] (Admittedly, she actively courted arrest to protest the public nudity laws she considered "unconstitutional and blatantly discriminatory" against women.)

The freedom to choose not to wear clothes outdoors was only possible on women's land, and joyfully shedding one's shirt was a standard response to crossing the property line. In a move that effectively doomed Kvindelandet's continued existence, an energy company set up a large drilling platform on a neighboring property, which enabled male employees to spy on the women next door. As a result, Kvindelandet residents had to start wearing clothes when they toiled in the fields, and once that happened, women were much less motivated to work.[54] Chopping wood or plowing the fields can feel like drudgery when clothed, but those tasks apparently become infinitely more exciting when tackled naked.

Part of the experience of rural living was learning when clothing really was required. The authors of *Country Women*, who wrote in a collective first person, stressed "the importance of wearing clothes for protection and safety," especially work boots.[55] When shod in sturdy footwear, they wrote, "I can pack down dirt, keep my balance on steep ground, roll a log out of the way, without hurting my feet. I once watched an experienced country woman chopping wood barefoot. The ax slipped and she gouged her ankle. I have learned to never use an ax, chain saw, or power tool without wearing my boots." The next sentence could be used to help a Method actor project pure terror: "From a carpenter friend, I learned not to run a chain saw or other power tool without wearing a shirt."

Thousands of women who would never consider moving to the country full-time got to experience life au naturel on a temporary basis at the Michigan Womyn's Music Festival, held every August between 1976 and 2015.[56] I attended on a couple of occasions in the 1980s, a time before the commercial internet but deep enough into the festival's history that I had heard on the lesbian grapevine how liberating the women-only, clothes-optional environment could be. Each time I went, I experienced anew a sensation that I would liken to coming around from anesthesia—a sudden, woozy realization that I was moving through the world without experiencing the usual levels of fear and shame. The surprise wasn't that I felt free from fear; rather, it was that I was suddenly aware of how much energy I expended worrying about staying safe in the "real world." The absence of cis men was shockingly clarifying.

Being naked at least some of the time allowed festie-goers to let down their guards. Unclothed, we could see each other as we really were, with all the things patriarchal society labels as imperfections proudly on display. I wasn't a stranger to the female form when I first set foot on the land, but being exposed to naked women in bulk changed my sense of "what women look like." The possibilities are endless.

Still, wherever there is nudity, there must be restrictions. Without secure gates, women don't strip down to nothing but sturdy shoes and a string slung loosely around their waists. Whenever men came onto festival property to empty the Port-a-Janes, warning cries of "men on the land" rang out. Very young boy children were allowed on the main grounds, but those between five and ten were consigned to a separate camp space, known as Brother Sun. Starting in 1991, the Michigan organizers explicitly barred anyone other than "womyn-born womyn" from the land.[57] Eventually, the decision to maintain this "intention" led to the festival's cancelation, especially after protesters established Camp Trans, an annual demonstration outside the festival gates.

Whatever the official justifications given, I will always believe that the trans-exclusionary policy was driven by a desire to provide a cast-iron guarantee that no one would ever see a penis on the land. I understand why some women—including many who had been sexually assaulted by cis men—didn't want to lose a treasured sense of security in the one place they had found it. No one asks to change a thing they love. But the rigidity that led to the festival's demise may be a preview of the fate that awaits the remaining lesbian-land communities.

Ownership has its privileges, but it also brings headaches. Women discovered that if land projects failed—when couples or friendships fractured, residents got sick, or women grew weary of the privations of lesbian land—having their name on a property deed could be a serious financial liability. For the most part, they could be held responsible for taxes due, and if they defaulted, the land could be repossessed by the state. Many communities had problems paying the mortgage—to page through back issues of *Maize* is to see repeated requests for funds. In the 1990s, Lesbian Natural Resources, a grant-making nonprofit, helped land groups make down payments, improve housing and accessibility, develop cottage industries, and pay apprentices.[58] Golden Women's Land in Oregon is probably the highest-profile community lost to foreclosure, but it was by no means the only one.[59] For many years, Maat Dompim lay unoccupied, with taxes consuming the project's remaining assets.

However worried they might be about being held financially responsible for the land, women were reluctant to simply quit their claim, because they were seldom able to find other lesbians who were interested in taking it over, and they didn't want it to fall into male or heterosexual hands. Clearing land, planting gardens, and building livable structures consumed hundreds of woman-hours of labor, and having invested sweat equity in that development, they wanted it to be available to future generations of lesbians (as long as those future generations defined *lesbian* the same way).

These concerns—personal liability and a desire to keep land in lesbian hands in perpetuity—drove a shift away from private ownership in favor of an alternative structure: land trusts, or nonprofit organizations with boards that determine policies that apply to communities under their stewardship. (Many of today's remaining lesbian-land projects operate under the auspices of such trusts.)[60]

This movement began in June 1975, when women from five of the women's-land groups in southern Oregon met together. Land trusts were an existing legal structure often used in rural areas to manage and preserve family farms and conservation areas. The Oregon lesbians' innovation lay in their vision of who might benefit. Rather than help-ing nuclear families keep land in private hands, theirs would serve "an ever-changing mobile family circle."[61] Within months, articles of incorporation had been filed for the Oregon Women's Land Trust. The founders of the trust then decided to buy a piece of property that would operate as "open land," meaning that any woman could take up res-idence there and decisions would be made collectively. They believed this would eradicate the power divisions between owners and tenants and make living on land possible for all women, regardless of income, the gender of their children, or their desire to live with a pet. By the next spring, women from the Oregon Women's Land Trust had volunteered to identify appropriate property for this open-land project.[62] A 147-acre parcel near Canyonville, including a log house, a barn, a chicken coop, and a toolshed, was found very quickly. Soon, $18,500 had been donated for a down payment, and the land was acquired. In July 1976, the first women moved onto what later became known as OWL Farm.

Open land appeared to be a solution to some of the movement's biggest challenges, helping women who lacked the means to purchase property to find a stable home with other lesbians and preventing the heartbreak and intense disruption that often ensued when land communities splintered. Women who were banished from land after disputes sometimes likened the experience to a particularly wrenching breakup—and indeed, in many cases, expulsion was precipitated by the breakdown of a romantic relationship. In 1997, Diann Bowoman described her own complex feelings after being pushed off land: "It's like mourning many deaths at once: the dream of community, finding my life-work, friendships I thought solid, the land itself, my cabin and garden, newly established daily rhythms, as well as my partner of many years. At the end I felt as a frantic hostage watching while my 'family,' home, work and values were consumed by a blazing bonfire."[63]

Right from the start, there was excitement and organizing at OWL Farm, including outreach to and workshops for women of color and working-class women. Residents pooled their money—some received welfare, unemployment, or food stamps—and learned that they could live cheaply on the land.

It wasn't "all comfrey and garlic," however.[64] Troubled individuals were often drawn to women's land, especially open land, where they didn't have to pass a vetting process. Given the lack of resources available to them in the larger world, moving to communal land was a rational choice, but even though other residents often felt a sisterly responsibility to help as much as they could, they weren't therapists or social workers, and they had their own issues to deal with. In the earliest days of OWL Farm, a pregnant woman who had been institutionalized several times refused to accept that she was about to give birth, and while residents didn't want to see her forced back into a mental health facility, they didn't feel capable of taking responsibility for the woman and her baby.[65] The experience left OWL Farm residents feeling "tired and discouraged."[66]

The issues that arose at the beginning of the OWL Farm experience consistently plagued open land: Who had the power to make decisions? If the answer was "everyone," did that effectively mean "no one"? Could women ever feel "at home" if they had little to no control over their living conditions? A woman with severe environmental illnesses explained that she couldn't live on open land because "there are too many new wimmin who don't understand how little it takes to create a situation where I'll get sick and how much it takes to make a structure accessible after animals or smoke have been in it. No one is intentionally cruel, simply unaware and uncommitted to accessibility."[67]

Reaching consensus, and the numerous meetings that were needed to achieve such a feat, could be exhausting. This was especially frustrating when a policy was agreed upon after extensive debate, only to be reopened when new women came to the land and restarted the conversation, unaware of all the processing that had gone before. It also has to be said that some women came with a bad attitude, or as Pelican Lee put it in 1992, some thought open land "meant they could do anything regardless of how it affected others."[68]

Despite its challenges, many OWL Farm residents were convinced that open land was *the* politically correct ownership model. According to Lee, this led residents to feud with other country dykes in the area. "They wanted other women to open their land, even though everyone could see how chaotic life at OWL Farm was." Still, a decade after she left, Lee said, "Many of us look back now on our years at OWL Farm as one of the most exciting and satisfying times in our lives, in spite of our difficulties and craziness. We were creating a new women's culture, living our dreams and visions, and pushing ourselves to our limits." Nevertheless, she couldn't imagine returning to open land, citing a growing need as she got older for "more stability and control in my life, more than I found possible on open land."

More than two decades after OWL Farm's founding, in January 1997 a group of twenty elders from the Oregon land-dyke community got together at WomanShare for two days of discussion. These women had lived in community for a combined total of more than two hundred years. Unfortunately, the meeting, which was otherwise productive and positive, was marred by what one attendee called "the Oregon Women's Land Trust Meeting Syndrome," which required the organization to focus "all of its attention and energy on administering its only asset and what has become its greatest failure": OWL Farm.[69]

A year and a half later, the Oregon Women's Land Trust decided to change the operating conditions of OWL Farm so that it was no longer open land. Other than caretakers, there hasn't been a resident community at OWL Farm since then. Most of the construction was completed before 1998, and it has since fallen prey to weather and vermin.[70] In many ways, the land is as it was in 1976, when it was first acquired by the trust. It's still rustic, and while solar panels now provide some power, there is no Wi-Fi, and cell service is spotty.

In 2021, after a fifteen-year struggle, the Oregon Women's Land Trust and nine other plaintiffs won a legal battle, preventing a Canadian corporation from building a methane pipeline through OWL Farm.[71] This affirmation of one of the land trust's founding principles seems to have brought new energy to OWL Farm. Although none of the buildings are currently habitable, in 2021 a new pump was installed on the well that was dug forty years earlier, and "natal women" with their own camping equipment can visit in warm-weather months.[72]

It's foolish to fixate on the longevity of lesbian institutions. When a dyke launches a new project—bar, bookstore, or outer space cruise line—the last thing on her mind should be how long it will last. But within our community there's always an open question about the practicality of passing the torch. Unlike the Shakers and other groups that died out because they rejected sexual relationships, lesbians aren't celibate. But since our identity isn't transmissible—queer people's children are statistically unlikely to be queer themselves—it's hard to fantasize about a family business surviving to provide drinks, books, and vibrators to multiple generations of gay, lesbian, bisexual, trans, nonbinary, intersex, asexual, and questioning customers. Rather than adult children fighting for control of their father's company, a lesbian version of the TV show *Succession* would involve a successful entrepreneur madly searching for someone—*anyone!*—to take over the institution she spent decades building.

When that 1997 gathering of the Oregon elders was able to focus on topics other than the travails of OWL Farm, the main agenda item was divining how lesbian lands could survive when they seemed to hold little appeal for younger women. Or as Bethroot Gwynn put it, "Am I devoting my life to create a world that no one wants to carry on?"[73] That question has only become more salient in the twenty-first century as the separatist zeal that fueled the movement in its early years has faded. The founders who lived on the land for four or five decades are gradually leaving their communities, but thanks to the land trusts they established, their policies will live on. Given how much time and energy they devoted to the land, it's hardly surprising that they're loath to let go.

While there are a few younger lesbians in the landdyke movement, it's hard to discern any widespread enthusiasm. In the 1970s, people moved to communes and intentional communities because they found mainstream society so alienating and intolerable that striking out for the unknown seemed preferable. This required both a conviction that there was no possibility of finding fulfillment in mainstream society and a belief that there was a decent chance the radical alternative would be more life enhancing. That calculation no longer pertains when it comes to women's land.

The more divisive issue, though, is that as a matter of policy, the vast majority of—though, it must be stressed, not all—lesbian-land communities still refuse access to anyone but "womyn-born womyn."[74] This excludes not just trans and nonbinary people but also cis women who find that policy offensive.

It's a kind of perverse irony that the survival of a subculture whose identity was shaped by a voluntary separation from those with power is now threatened because of its attitude toward another vulnerable group. For the most part, landdykes are impoverished, marginalized, and lack influence or allies, but their trans-exclusionary policies align them with political and religious groups who have long fought to restrict lesbians' human rights along with trans people's.

Which gender was assigned to potential new residents at birth is just one of a number of questions community members need to develop policies around. They first need to decide which policies are nonnegotiable. If a group feels completely aligned with an applicant's views on drug use, vegetarianism, BDSM, guns, and organic gardening and finds them open, cheerful, and pleasant, would their membership application be rejected if they had too much debt or a Y chromosome or because they used they/them pronouns? Policies around birth-gender assignment feel particularly inequitable because they are based on identity rather than behavior, as in the days of the lavender scare, when civil servants were targeted for dismissal because they were believed to belong to a particular group rather than because they had done anything wrong. This was also true for women with male children who were often excluded from land and other separatist projects when their sons reached a certain age. As poet Audre Lorde, the mother of a son and a daughter, wrote to the organizers of a conference she and her partner had planned to attend until they learned that boys over age ten weren't allowed, her responsibility for her son's education and welfare didn't end at that age, "any more than it does for my daughter's."[75]

I understand where the women-only policies originated and why they were so important—and I hope younger women can see why many older landdykes view the expansion of gender expression as a loss of lesbian identity, even if it doesn't feel that way to them (or to me). Fear of losing the land and its spiritual, political, and emotional power drives the founder generation to try to impose on the unknowable future a philosophy that was forged in a different era.

It also stems from landdykes' ideological concordance. In 1997, sociologist Nancy Whittier wrote about the concept of cohort replacement and how it applied to a group of feminist activists based in Columbus, Ohio.[76] In feminist groups, as in most political movements, each generation of activists constructs different identities based on the dominant ideas and prevailing conditions at the time of their joining. What's more, a cohort's initial perspective tends to endure throughout its members' time in the movement. As new generations bring their energy and efforts to a cause and earlier activists burn out, the cohorts that shape the ideology and focus are effectively replaced. Groups with less turnover experience more ideological continuity, and vice versa. (This partly explains why college campuses, where the population undergoes almost total replacement every four years or so, often appear to be on the vanguard of new ideas.)

The landdyke community is an extreme example of low turnover and high ideological continuity. Without newcomers bringing fresh ideas and personal connections, the movement has held on to the ideology that dominated in the 1970s and 1980s, even as the world has changed. Effectively, the community stagnated as it shrank.

Although the long-term survival of lesbian-land communities is uncertain at best, isolation and resilient ownership structures have helped them to survive longer than most other dyke institutions. In southern Oregon alone, at least nine extant land projects have been in existence since the 1970s—and even though most have very few residents these days, they have outlasted all the Beaver State bars, bookstores, and softball teams of a similar vintage.[77] The buildings that were constructed in the 1970s are tattered and battered, and their ideas may seem stuck in the past, but for the moment at least, they endure.

It's hard for me to see beyond the callous lack of empathy displayed by trans-exclusionary landdykes. This makes it difficult to appreciate their hard-earned self-sufficiency, the years of creative output, the myriad ways in which they have honored the land and made it possible for some cisgender women to experience the healing power of nature, their playfulness, their idealism, their inventiveness, and their joyful embrace of the erotic. It also means that their history and achievements don't get the respect and attention they deserve. My hope is that those landdykes who still engage with the world will recognize "the countless evidences of the patriarchy" in the current wave of political attacks on transgender people and fully acknowledge the breadth of our community.

It's not too late.

Good Vibrations founder Joani Blank poses with some of her merchandise in 1977. Originally published in the *Berkeley Barb*.

FIVE
FEMINIST SEX-TOY STORES

WHAT DO LESBIANS DO IN BED?" HAS BEEN AN IMPERTI-
nent inquiry since Eve left Adam for the UPS woman.
With few realistic representations of lesbian sexuality,
women were left to their own devices to figure out how to
please themselves and each other. Starting in the 1970s,
sex-positive toy stores, queer "sexperts," and a heterosexual
hippie who zealously advocated for the benefits of masturbation stepped into the fray to make orgasms a feminist issue,
along the way transforming the entire adult industry.

Women's social and economic liberation was impossible without sexual liberation, and nothing says sexual liberation quite like a vibrator. On the East Coast at least, the
feminist sex-toy movement started in a crowded conference
room, when artist Betty Dodson presented the Prelude, a
gun-shaped vibrator, and the Panabrator, a wand-style device,
to a special gathering of the National Organization for

Women in the summer of 1973.[1] The Prelude was so prone to overheating that conference-goers had to grip it with potholders. Nevertheless, Dodson sold her entire stock within thirty minutes. In the early days of women's sexual freedom, access to a sex toy was downright life changing.

Perhaps because some middle- and upper-class lesbians were able to gain acceptance into polite society in the days before gay liberation by passing as friends rather than sexual partners, lesbians have often been perceived as nonsexual creatures (unlike gay men, who were widely viewed as ravenous rutting rabbits). This may also explain why lesbian couples are regularly "mistaken" for siblings, friends, or roommates.

The porn industry fed straight male fantasies of girl-on-girl action, but those unrealistic scenarios excluded actual lesbians. And while lesbians themselves emphasized the erotic—in the 1970s and 1980s, romantic partners were usually introduced with the timeless phrase "this is my lover"—political organizing was sometimes seen as a passion killer. According to no less an authority than cofounder Susie Bright, *On Our Backs*, America's first sexually explicit magazine created by and for queer women, chose its name "to [tweak] the prudery of puritanical feminist publications like *off our backs*."[2] (As a former *off our backs* collective member, let me state for the record that we weren't at all prudish. It's true, though, that we were less libidinally focused than the women of *On Our Backs*.)

The movement that remade a multi-billion-dollar industry can be traced back to a pair of dedicated pioneers.

Anyone curious about the definition of "1970s San Francisco" would do well to read the profile of a recently opened Mission District store that appeared in a June 1977 issue of the *Berkeley Barb*.[3] The story lingered on the elements of the shop's decor—oriental carpet, piles of pillows on the floor, ferns, macrame and weavings on the walls—which seemed more appropriate to a bohemian living room than to a place of business.

Also featured in the piece was store owner Joani Blank, a thirty-nine-year-old public health educator and sex therapist. Over the course of researching and writing a woman's guide to vibrators, Blank had realized how difficult it was to acquire them. Drugstores didn't stock them, and shopping at an "adult bookstore" was both an "unconqueringly abysmal experience" and a "financial rip-off." So Blank decided to open the kind of place where she would like to shop for a vibrator, one with lots of variety and reasonable prices. The kind of battery-operated model the adult stores sold for $5 or more cost just $1.50 at her shop, Good Vibrations. She also sold crocheted "vibrator cozies." Blank considered the store to be "especially for, but not exclusively for, women." The focus was on information, consultation, and advice. There was even a tryout booth, though Blank insisted, "I don't encourage real masturbation trips here."

From those distinctly countercultural beginnings, Good Vibrations ultimately bloomed into a multi-million-dollar company that is still buzzing today, albeit under very different ownership.

After launching a mail-order catalog in 1985, Good Vibrations became a national brand.[4] Still, it maintained its hippie vibe for decades, until that version of the Bay Area was vaporized by tech-driven gentrification. Laura Miller, who worked at Good Vibrations between 1988 and 1995, remembers the store as a prime exemplar of the San Francisco of that vintage. It attracted people of all genders, orientations, and kinks, whose identity as San Franciscans transcended other identity markers. "Everybody really liked the fact that so many different people were there and that they could coexist in that space," Miller recalls.[5] Like every other employee at the time, Miller, whose main responsibilities involved marketing and publicity, was obliged to work at least one shift per week in the store, a job she likens to that of a therapist. "You had to learn how to talk to people in a particular way. Often you were dealing with someone for whom your interaction could be very formative in a way that retail usually isn't. You constantly felt how thankful people were."

More than a decade after the *Berkeley Barb* story appeared and years after the store had relocated from its original bijou premises, it remained a "soothing place," says Miller. "It smelled nice. The walls were in pastel shades. Everyone spoke with a soft voice. It was more like a spa." For Miller, Good Vibrations' sensibility was of a piece with Mission District neighbors like feminist bookstore Old Wives' Tales, women's restaurant Artemis Cafe, and the Osento women's bathhouse. "They shared an ethos. A calm, lavender-scented feeling that I associate with eighties lesbian and women's businesses."

Epitomizing the hippie Bay Area spirit, Good Vibrations was the first institution of its kind on the West Coast. Joani Blank wasn't the first woman to re-envision the sex-toy store, however. Three years before Good Vibrations opened, New Yorker Dell Williams had placed an ad in the classified section of *Ms.* magazine offering "liberating vibrators and other pleasurable things for women from a feminist-owned business."[6]

At fifty-two, Williams had worked in a variety of fields before finding success in the advertising industry, but now she was a woman on a mission. A few years earlier, she had attended one of Betty Dodson's masturbation workshops and left a true believer in the life-enhancing powers of the vibrator.[7] A humiliating experience trying to purchase a Hitachi Magic Wand at Macy's convinced Williams to open Eve's Garden, a store where women could acquire these instruments of liberation without being subjected to embarrassment and scorn—and without having to venture into the sordid world of "adult" novelty stores.[8]

After a year of running Eve's Garden as a mail-order business from her Manhattan kitchen, Williams quit her job at the advertising agency. She rented two adjoining offices in a building on 57th Street, one of which became the shipping department and the other a retail space. They were on the fourteenth floor, which allowed customers to shop "discreetly." Men weren't allowed through the doors, not, she insisted, because she was a man-hater but "to create an environment where women could be free to explore their sexuality in privacy, and safety."[9] (She later relaxed this policy, first admitting men as long as they were there with women and eventually adding an Adam's Corner to Eve's Garden.)[10]

In 1979, after five years in operation, Williams decided to open a street-level storefront. Although several landlords refused to rent to her once they learned the nature of her business, she eventually leased a ground-floor space on 52nd Street. The choices Williams made about the look and feel of her stores were hugely significant. Like Good Vibrations, they were tasteful, elegant, even pretty. Williams, who called herself the gardenkeeper, established a green and pleasant vibe. Her brother, Lorenz, a designer, covered the walls with large hand-painted murals full of pink and mauve flowers.[11]

Times Square, then a garish warren of porn shops, peep shows, and burlesque theaters, was only ten blocks from Eve's Garden, but they were worlds apart. Williams prioritized women's comfort, which wasn't a consideration in any of the mainstream adult stores in this "Girls, Girls, Girls" era. Their staffers were there to take money, not to give advice, though the most useful recommendation as to what to do with the cheap novelties on sale in most 1970s sex stores would probably have been "Throw it away."

Like every other business, feminist or otherwise, these new, liberated sex-toy stores had to operate profitably. Still, neither Williams nor Good Vibrations' Joani Blank prioritized that particular P-word. When she left her ad agency job, Williams knew that her income would take a serious hit, but as she later wrote, "From its inception Eve's Garden had commanded my heart."[12] Meanwhile, Joani Blank took every opportunity to express how little she cared about the mechanics of business, often declaring herself an anticapitalist. Rather than considering concepts like profit margins and earnings maximization, she instead focused on the life-transforming benefits of vibrators and the need for open discussion of sexuality.

When Susie Bright went to interview for a part-time job at Good Vibrations in 1981, working retail seemed less appealing than the other potential position on her radar, which involved moving traffic cones on the Golden Gate Bridge during rush hour. The latter was a union job that paid better. Then Blank uttered the sentence that decided Bright's future career path: "I don't care if you put a dime in the cash register all day."[13] Instead, Blank said, working at Good Vibrations was about education, talking to people, particularly women, and helping them feel more comfortable with the body, the clitoris, orgasms. At the time, "I wasn't thinking of a great career in academia or being a lawyer or a doctor," Bright told me in 2023. "I thought, *I need a job so I can have my real life, which is the revolution.*" As soon as Blank laid out her priorities, Bright immediately realized that "Joani and her little project *were* the revolution."

Bright saw that, for Blank, the store was part of the burgeoning women's health movement that had recently produced the groundbreaking reference book *Our Bodies, Ourselves*. Good Vibrations shared DNA with projects like the San Francisco Sex Information switchboard and the Institute for the Advanced Study of Sexuality, which also prioritized open discussion of sex. Blank, who was heterosexual, intuitively connected her mission with the work that grassroots gay and lesbian liberation groups were doing to liberalize queer life in the city.

"The secret strength behind Good Vibrations was bisexual and lesbian women," says Bright. Queer women were educated, enthusiastic, and curious customers who came into the store already comfortable with buying and using sex toys. They also embodied the spirit of indie creativity that lesbians were forced to develop because of establishment gatekeeping. Bright throws out examples of this can-do spirit like Mardi Gras beads tossed into a crowd. In the early 1970s, Judy Grahn and the Women's Press Collective printed lesbian erotic poetry because no one else would. (They also organized poetry readings in lesbian group households when public venues demurred.)[14] Rather than deal with New York publishers, Joani Blank started Down There Press so that books containing accurate, nonjudgmental information about sex would be available, starting with 1975's *My Playbook for Women About Sex*, which featured text hand-lettered by Blank and a cover drawn by Tee Corinne. In the 1990s, Down There published the *Herotica* series of women's erotic short story anthologies, initially edited by Blank and Bright. Other presses had rejected the concept, believing the stories to be patriarchal, politically incorrect, or lacking an audience. Regardless of whether it was driven by choice or necessity, queer women's resourcefulness fueled the sex-positivity movement.

Of course, Good Vibrations and the feminist sex-toy stores that followed its lead were themselves a DIY alternative to sleazy, profit-driven mainstream sex shops. The old-school dirty bookstores found it unfathomable that women wanted safe, high-quality items that did what people bought them for. (They were also counting on customers being so ashamed of having purchased such a thing that they would never complain when it broke.) Bright says those manufacturers would ask, "Why are you all coming to us like you want the *Good Housekeeping* seal of approval?" She told them, "Well, that *is* what we want. And you're crazy to be ignoring this!"

Stores like Eve's Garden and Good Vibrations were the first to sell toys others wouldn't. This included a line of imaginatively colored silicone dildos created by Gosnell Duncan, who was paralyzed from the waist down and initially explored the medium to produce items that would allow disabled people like him to have a sex life.[15] Bright recalls working in Good Vibrations when a man arrived from Tokyo, carrying a suitcase full of brightly colored silicone vibrators shaped like squirrels, monkeys, and lobsters. They were so playful and whimsical, Bright knew her customers would love them. The salesman was thrilled by her reaction because every other adult store he'd visited had turned him down flat. She had to explain that the mainstream sex shops only sold products made by companies they owned. Good Vibrations, on the other hand, was independent, and they were delighted to stock such innovative, inventive items. (Within a year, US companies had copied the Japanese originals, though their versions weren't nearly as good.) Bright also convinced Blank that Good Vibrations should carry a carefully curated selection of porn videos. "Clearly, women weren't going to adult theaters to sit next to raincoaters to watch these movies," she says. But after screening a lot of films in her role as a porn reviewer for *Penthouse Forum*, Bright realized there were some that would appeal to the women who shopped at Good Vibrations. Male customers would surely like them too.

In time, thanks to her columns in *On Our Backs*, a long-running podcast, and a whole shelf full of books, Bright became known as Susie Sexpert. It's striking that in the last thirty-five years, America's most accessible providers of sex education and advice have been Bright, a bisexual woman; Dan Savage, a gay man; and the owners and staffers of feminist sex-toy stores around the United States—many of whom were inspired by Betty Dodson and Dell Williams, both bisexual.[16]

For decades, queer women were completely left out of conversations about sex and sexuality. But as Searah Deysach, owner of Chicago's Early to Bed, told me, as soon as queer women started to be the people who were working at and owning sex-toy boutiques, those stores "became a safe space for a wider range of women to not only ask questions and find the toys they wanted, but maybe even explore their sexuality in a new way."[17] Perhaps it was to our advantage that straight people have little idea what we do in bed. Lesbians have sex differently, and we have a wider definition of what might be involved in "having sex." That's appealing to straight people who are trying to expand their range of options. Rachel Venning, a cofounder of the feminist sex-toy store Babeland, recalled that in the store's early years, they would often think of themselves as "translators," helping straight people to "get in touch with the fierce claiming of who we are and what we want that emerged from AIDS activism and the gay and lesbian liberation movement."[18]

Could Joani Blank really have been totally blasé about business? Anne Semans, who spent thirteen years at Good Vibrations and later worked at Babeland for more than a decade, says it was a matter of priorities.[19] Good Vibrations was a mission-driven company, and profits were always secondary to the mission. It should be noted that in the early days at least, it was possible for Good Vibrations to take this attitude because Blank had family money and was willing and able to bail out the company when needed. This generosity explains why many Good Vibrations employees jokingly called her Joani Bank.

Babeland, which opened its first store in Seattle in 1993, operated on the same principle. Founders Claire Cavanah and Rachel Venning worked toward two goals: first, said Venning, "promoting and celebrating sexual vitality and creating a space for women and queers and all kinds of people to feel safe and ask questions and flourish. And second, making money to sustain and grow the business." Cavanah adds, "There's no Babeland without a healthy bottom line. You need to be in the black and be a going concern or you can't achieve the mission we're all committed to."

Blank was a frugal person, and that attitude shaped the company culture. She believed that access to sex toys and information would make the world a healthier and happier place, and her vision was to see a sex-toy store on every corner. When Anne Semans repeated that mantra to me, I had to seek clarity. I'd seen the phrase in stories about Blank and Good Vibrations, but it surely wasn't meant literally? Semans assured me that Blank really believed vibrator stores should be as common as bodegas, but she wanted to achieve that goal without spending a lot of money. How? Her plan was to give away information and advice. "It wasn't about competition for Joani," says Semans. "She believed that if we all work on this, and we're successful, we'll change the culture."

Blank's commitment to openness and transparency was extreme. She printed the company's profit-and-loss statement in the store newsletter, the *Good Vibes Gazette*, and offered her expertise to any feminist bookstore interested in selling vibrators, even offering to provide a small starter inventory on consignment.[20] (Vibrators were "potentially very profitable," she assured the readers of *Feminist Bookstore News*.)[21] Blank went so far as to set up an internship scheme to train potential competitors. Seattle's Babeland and Boston's Grand Opening, both of which eventually became multilocation businesses, got their start from that program. (After Blank left the company, the program was abruptly killed.)

During her internship, Claire Cavanah spent a December working in the San Francisco store, learning the Good Vibrations way of doing business. But it was the company's vendor list, which most businesses would have considered valuable proprietary information and which Blank freely shared, that made the biggest difference to the soon-to-be-launched Toys in

Babeland, as the store was originally known. This was before Google, and some of the key vendors were almost impossible to track down. Back then, for example, the artist behind Dils for Does, which produced adorable silicone dildos in shapes like dolphins, cats, and corn cobs, didn't necessarily want the whole world to know about her side hustle. By providing introductions, Blank was effectively vouching for the new ventures.

Cavanah and Venning were strongly influenced by Good Vibrations, borrowing, among other things, the concept of the tryout room—leading to occasional confusion when people attempted to rent it by the hour. They were still in their twenties and active in the city's lesbian community when they opened the Seattle store. Although they stocked a wide range of vibrators, there was a dykey emphasis on dildos. The vibe was certainly not that of a lavender-scented spa.

There was an untamed energy to the place. "We played the same Breeders record for twenty-five years," Cavanah recalls. A friend applied a cool yellow-orange paint treatment to the walls, and the window displays were wild and witty. One memorable tableau featured a mannequin in a sex sling next to a sign that said, "Goodbye to gravity." Later, as the company professionalized, the windows became a little tamer, in part because one of their landlords had strict rules about what could be shown. In the early, punk-rock days, though, the mood was one of edgy playfulness. "In Seattle in 1995, we'd just put a mannequin with a strap-on in the window," Cavanah says. Venning remembers it differently: "No. More humor. More like dildos with googly eyes."

Babeland's print ads shared that same spirit of fun. In one, the slogan "Come in early and beat the crowds" appeared next to the image of a flogger. In their first mail-order catalog, Cavanah and Venning, represented by cartoon avatars created by Ellen Forney (who also drew the products that were available for sale), spoke directly to potential customers. The voice was familiar, friendly, and direct, and by 1995 there was no need to euphemize. "Getting a dildo or a vibrator may not

Welcome to Toys in Babeland. After two years of running the most beautiful sex toy store in the world (do you detect a bias?) at last we have a catalog! When we opened our store two years ago, it was for one reason: we couldn't get good lube at a good

price. While our inventory has grown, our original goal—to make it easier for women to get quality toys and reliable sex information—has stayed the same. We are acting on our belief that sexual exploration empowers people. Getting a dildo or a vibrator may not change the world, but acting in the interests of your own desire may change you!

The only downside of realizing our dream of producing a catalog is that we will no longer be able to meet each Babeland customer. Please feel free to contact us by fax, mail or e-mail with any suggestions or comments. Drop in if you find yourself in Seattle.

Babeland owners Rachel Venning and Claire Cavanah welcome readers to the company's first mail-order catalog. Their avatars were drawn by cartoonist Ellen Forney, who also created the illustrations for the catalog. Courtesy of Claire Cavanah and Rachel Venning.

change the world," the text declared, "but acting in the interests of your own desire may change you!" They signed the ad as "Claire" and "Rachel." Cavanah and Venning were entrepreneurs, but they wanted customers to think of them as the dykes next door.

Like Dell Williams of Eve's Garden thirty years earlier, Searah Deysach got into the sex-toy business after a frustrating shopping experience. When she and her girlfriend decided to buy a sex toy, their first move was to order something from the Babeland catalog. Unfortunately, it didn't work out as expected. "You're picking something from a drawing, and who knows what seven inches looks like," she told me, laughing. Undeterred, she and some friends headed to an adult store in the city, but that was also a bust. "It was so disheartening and creepy," she remembers. "There was no one there to help me. My memory is of one guy eating nachos. I didn't want to ask him about my vagina." A year later, she was in business. Early to Bed opened its Chicago storefront in 2001.

Although she has supported herself from the store since day one, Deysach admits, "There have been years where I've been in bed at night freaking out about how I'm going to pay my rent or my credit card bill." During the 2008–2009 economic downturn, she took on $70,000 of credit card debt and came close to closing on a couple of occasions, but she always received support from people passionate about the store's mission. Someone rebuilt the website, her mom extended a loan, and "people shopped even if they didn't need stuff."

The investment in the website paid off during the Covid pandemic, when the store had its best sales years ever. Of course, the internet is unpredictable. Online sales had outstripped sales from the brick-and-mortar store for more than twenty years, but that changed during the pandemic's aftermath in 2022. The shift was partly due to increased in-store sales when the shop relocated to larger premises closer to the center of the Andersonville neighborhood, a stone's throw from Women and Children First bookstore. Still, in the same period, e-commerce revenue fell by 30 percent. (While Deysach has been through too many tense years to have unqualified confidence in her store's future, Early to Bed seems to have weathered the pandemic without suffering permanent financial damage.)

When it comes to doing business online, sex-toy stores face an unfair disadvantage compared with other online sellers. Unlike competitors such as Walmart, Target, and Amazon, Early to Bed and other adult brands are prohibited from advertising on social media platforms. It's a testament to public demand that feminist sex-toy shops have been able to do so well with digital sales in spite of these restrictions. (Deysach also runs transessentials.com, selling "nonsex stuff" that supports gender expression. She set up the separate site after realizing that young people were often sitting with parents or social workers while searching early2bed.com for things like packers. Unlike the Early to Bed site, the Trans Essentials site isn't usually blocked by public servers.)

Given Joani Blank's open ambivalence about the capitalist system, it's tempting to blame Good Vibrations' failure to place a sex-toy emporium on every block on its founder's antibusiness attitude. In actuality, like Early to Bed and every other company that has tried to make a living in a field that is in any way related to sex, Good Vibrations repeatedly faced arbitrary bureaucratic obstacles. Magazines from the *Village Voice* to *Playboy* (*Playboy*!) refused to print ads for its catalog, a significant source of revenue.[22] *Ms.*, which hadn't batted an eye at the promotional copy for Eve's Garden, also refused Good Vibrations. After what seemed like years of back and forth, it transpired that *Ms.*'s objection was based on the V-word in the company name. The magazine said it was willing to print an ad that used Good Vibrations' official corporate identity, Open Enterprises.[23] It's possible, though, that since *Ms.* was already running ads for Eve's Garden, another sex-toy vendor, and a lingerie company, the magazine felt it had reached a self-imposed limit on bedroom products.

Vibrator stores still aren't eligible for the Small Business Administration loans that would help, say, a vinyl-record shop find its feet. And as Dell Williams discovered in the late 1970s, finding a place to do business is often unnecessarily complicated.

In 1994, Good Vibrations was all set to open a branch in Berkeley, on the "Girl Town" block of San Pablo Avenue that was also home to West Berkeley Women's Books and the Brick Hut Cafe, which moved there a year later. A week before the scheduled opening, the City Planning Department received a complaint from a local resident who believed the store had been improperly zoned as a retail and gift shop when it was, in fact, an adult bookstore.[24] If it were considered the latter, it would be subject to zoning laws that dictated the permitted proximity to everything from parks and libraries to residential districts. Thanks to the kind of lobbying campaign only a business staffed by political activists could mobilize on short notice, the store's permit was provisionally reinstated, but Good Vibrations had to prove that its products didn't "appeal to the prurient interest or sexual appetite of the purchaser" and that more than 51 percent of the items for sale were "educational materials and gifts." This kind of benign deception must have been torture for Blank, whose commitment to transparency and openness seemed to be limitless.

In the mid-1990s, with the opening of this new East Bay store, Good Vibrations' sales figures were growing, but so were expenses. In 1987, when the mail-order catalog generated gross sales of $118,000, the company as a whole had a net income of $62,000.[25] In 1994, despite greatly increased sales by mail and in stores, the extra costs of doing business meant that the store's net income was just $73,678.[26] Two years later, goodvibes.com, an e-commerce site, went live—a temporary life buoy, despite the unpredictability and bureaucratic hurdles of online sales.[27]

Even in the 2020s, feminist toy stores face extra hurdles and charges because of the nature of the business. At one point, Early to Bed's credit card processor abruptly refused to work with them, because the card company had changed funding banks, and the new institution had a policy against handling sex-related transactions. Deysach ran into a similar problem when she changed website platforms in 2019; finding a company that would host her business involved reams of paperwork and fees. Then, when Deysach and her partner tried to buy a building to house the store, the bank where Early to Bed had done business for twenty-one years wouldn't even discuss a mortgage. After several other rejections, they were referred to an independent, family-owned bank that was able to base its funding decision purely on financial considerations. Needless to say, Deysach is frustrated that so many powerful companies are incapable of discerning a difference between a strip club or a video-booth place and a boutique store like hers.

Blank's determination to live her values led her to turn Good Vibrations into a worker-owned cooperative in 1992, a move that transformed the dozen or so employees of the time into owners with equal shares in the business.[28] Longtime Good Vibrations employee Anne Semans remembers that period as "a freaking great social experiment. We were the boss! It was also a great business education. We learned on the job." It wasn't the most efficient structure, however. As the cooperative grew to more than one hundred member-owners, it became almost impossible to make decisions in a timely fashion (the same "too many cooks" problem that caused OWL Farm to struggle a few decades earlier). After fourteen years, the cooperative was dissolved, and Good Vibrations became a general business corporation once again.

By this point in the mid-aughts, Good Vibrations was in serious financial trouble. According to a note senior management briefly posted on the company website, competition from mainstream retailers like Amazon and a tweak to the Google algorithm had led to a precipitous decline in e-commerce revenue.[29] Sales for 2006 were around $11.9 million, a considerable shortfall from the projected $13.9 million, and the company couldn't pay its bills. This gap was much more than the Bank of Joani could have covered; besides, Blank had left Good Vibrations in 1996.[30] (Blank passed away in 2016.)[31] If Good Vibrations' stores were to survive, they needed new owners.

In 2007, a Cleveland company came to the rescue. General Video of America–Trans World News (GVA-TWN), which operated and supplied the kind of "adult" stores that Blank had wanted to provide an alternative to, bought Good Vibrations. When the sale was announced, GVA-TWN CEO Rondee Kamins told the *Bay Area Reporter* that the two companies were "a perfect fit," because "everything that Good Vibrations is GVA isn't[,] and everything GVA is Good Vibrations isn't." One year later, Kamins's uncle, Joel Kaminsky, bought Good Vibrations from his niece.[32] (So much for Good Vibrations' good feelings about selling to a woman-owned business.)

America's mainstream adult industry—the world of porn mags, peep booths, and sex superstores—is powered by multigenerational family businesses, a tradition the Kaminskys are very much part of.[33] Joel Kaminsky's brother Mel Kamins[34] (né Melvin Kaminsky) worked for Reuben Sturman,[35] the Cleveland-based business tycoon known as the "Walt Disney of Porn." These family ties helped Joel land holiday gigs in Sturman warehouses throughout high school and college. When he graduated in 1975, Mel Kamins offered his kid brother a position running ten of Sturman's stores. Although he had intended his stint in the industry to be brief, Kaminsky stuck around, managing a chain in San Diego before spending eighteen years as chief operating officer of a Sturman family firm that supplied most of the male-oriented sex-toy stores found in America's gayborhoods. When Mel Kamins announced his retirement in 2002, he named his daughter Rondee as his successor. Joel Kaminsky spent six years as her chief operating officer, the position he held when GVA-TWN bought Good Vibrations.

When he took ownership of Good Vibrations, Kaminsky felt he needed to change the company culture. "They were very educated, great people, a great staff—but bad business people," he told *StorErotica*, a trade magazine for the pleasure-product community.[36] He "dumped" most of the executive management team, decided to revamp the website, and introduced a "culture of discipline." The freedom of the co-op structure had led to what Kaminsky perceived as inefficiencies, like two or three people doing a job one person could handle.[37] He eliminated those redundancies and laid off some other employees who weren't on board with the new business-oriented approach.

Kaminsky also pushed to open more storefronts. In 2017, he bought the four Babeland stores, which continued to operate under their own name. By 2019, Kaminsky owned fifteen stores across the country. (A few closed due to the Covid pandemic.) In 2022, Joel anointed his son Casey Kaminsky as company vice president and his likely successor.[38] Before this elevation, Casey had spent ten years at Good Vibrations, working in unglamorous departments such as the warehouse, purchasing, and inventory management. Like his father, Casey is always full of praise for Good Vibrations' and Babeland's commitment to education, sex positivity, and high-quality, body-safe products.

The consensus among the current and former sex-toy-store workers I spoke with seemed to be that while it's too bad a cis-het guy now owns these historically significant women-founded sexual wellness companies, it's great that they're still in operation. (Though, as a couple pointed out, it's galling to still see publications erroneously include them on go-girl listicles promoting independent, women-owned businesses.) Crucially, fifteen years after the initial acquisition, Kaminsky appears to have maintained company values. Like other feminist toy stores, Good Vibrations refuses to stock anal desensitizers or ingestible products, and it only sells toys made from phthalate-free materials. Carol Queen, who joined Good Vibrations in 1990 and is probably America's only staff sexologist, stayed on through the ownership transitions. The Polk Street store in San Francisco houses an expanded version of the antique vibrator collection that once took up precious display space in Joani Blank's original boutique.

But why did Good Vibrations need bailing out when the sex-toy market is so robust? In 2022, the US market was valued at nearly $11 billion, and thanks to the revolution set in motion by stores like Good Vibrations and Eve's Garden, women are now responsible for nearly 60 percent of global spending on sexual wellness products.[39] What's more, feminist toy stores attract a high-spending clientele. In June 2022,

Joel Kaminsky revealed that while the average adult store sale is around $30 to $50, at Good Vibrations and Babeland, it's closer to $80, and the average web purchase is more than $100.[40]

On a basic level, it's more expensive to operate a mission-driven, education-focused business. Good Vibrations and the feminist stores that followed its example spent considerable time and money training employees to talk about sex and sex toys so they could, in turn, provide sex education to anyone who walked through the door. Unfortunately, there was no mechanism to recoup the cost of all that education. (And while Kaminsky has kept the Good Vibrations/Babeland mission in place, business now comes first.)

For all the satisfaction it provides—the transformational interactions with customers, the letters of gratitude—a sex-toy store is a demanding workplace. As everyone who has toiled in one says, it's like doing sex therapy. But therapists' working conditions are noticeably different, and they don't earn retail-store wages. As Anne Semans put it, "When Good Vibrations was smaller, and there weren't that many customers, you could just read the sex books. But once it got successful, and we were constantly trying to navigate all these interesting customer relationships in the store, that could be really exhausting." For all its undeniable successes, the women's movement did a poor job of creating high-paying jobs in feminist institutions.

At Babeland and Good Vibrations, the official job title of store workers is sex educator/sales assistant. Providing advice and education is quite different from processing sales, and while the workers saw themselves as therapists, customers sometimes treated them like clerks. In 2016, employees in Babeland's New York City stores voted to join the Retail, Wholesale and Department Store Union.[41] Their grievances included wage and training issues, as well as concerns about how discussing sex with customers could sometimes lead to harassment. Katherine Wolf told *Gothamist*, "One of the things I find most challenging is difficult customer interactions, and feeling like I have to sacrifice my own safety or boundaries in order to accommodate customers who are making sexual advances and saying inappropriate things."[42] The vote to unionize came as a "disheartening" shock to Cavanah and Venning. For Cavanah, it was "like a breakup, or as if we were being fired as being part of everything. It was really, really hard and sad. A grueling process."

The unionization drive played into the Babeland founders' decision to sell the business to Kaminsky. It made it "super not fun to go to work," says Cavanah. It wasn't the only factor, however. In addition to the original Seattle store, Babeland had opened three branches in New York and for a couple of years also operated an outpost in Los Angeles. Still, the business wasn't quite big enough to flourish. Cavanah and Venning continue to believe they were right to expand the company footprint. Spreading administrative costs over multiple stores and increasing sales volume make sense from a financial point of view, and moving into new territory furthered their sex-positive mission. Unfortunately, the competitive landscape was just too tight. Babeland had a significant online presence, where it tried to establish the kind of sensibility shoppers would also find in its stores. Still, even with blog posts, advice columns, and "voicey" product descriptions, Venning concedes, "it was still just a website." Once Amazon started selling sex toys, Babeland staffers started to notice customers "showrooming"— examining and comparing items they would later order from the cheapest online retailer.

Babeland always had very low cash reserves, and corporations' skittishness about working with completely legal, ethically run sex-toy stores also cost them money. Babeland was a bigger operation than Early to Bed, but it ran into similar issues with financial institutions. At one point, even though they were depositing thousands of dollars every day, Babeland's bank announced that it could no longer work with the company because of a directive from higher up the org chart. The Kaminsky family businesses, on the other hand, have the kind of stable, supportive relationship with bankers that highly profitable businesses traditionally command.

Undercapitalization, a word that's been whispered by bar operators, bookstore owners, and back-to-the-landers, is also relevant here. Managing cash flow is a massive headache for independent businesses, and sex-toy stores are not exempt. Sales tend to be seasonal, with the bulk occurring in the four-month period leading up to Christmas and Valentine's Day. (This explains why retailers invented Masturbation May rather than Onanist October.) As Semans explained, "You're buying all your inventory in August, and you hope you sell it, but then the bills arrive." If retailers can't pay vendors' invoices along with rent, payroll, and all their other bills, they won't have anything to sell at the most important time of the year.

Effectively, that's what happened to Good Vibrations in 2007: once their unpaid invoices reached worrisome levels, suppliers wouldn't ship more merchandise to them, so they had nothing to sell. Joel Kaminsky later described flying out to San Francisco in this period and seeing empty stores. "I thought, this is an easy fix—they just need product. Rondee had a whole warehouse full of product; [former boss] David [Sturman] had an infrastructure in the Bay Area, and I have a store management skill-set."[43] That's a textbook description of a business opportunity—and you could say, of an old boys' and old Ohioans' network. The chain of manufacturers, distributors, and stores that connect back to the Sturman empire through family or business ties is extensive, to say the least, and Kaminsky had instant access to it all.

Dell Williams also tried working with outside investors. In 1980, her sixtieth birthday just two years away, she found it "disheartening" to be struggling financially, given how hard she worked.[44] Consequently, she was receptive when Boston venture capital (VC) firm Schooner Capital, owned and operated by left-leaning businessman Vincent J. Ryan, offered to invest more than $350,000 in the business with the intention of turning Eve's Garden into a national chain.[45] The plan was for Williams to maintain her position as company president and focus on advertising and public relations, while Schooner executives would run the day-to-day operations.

Williams soon regretted her new alliance. The venture capitalists decided to close the New York stores and move the mail-order operation to Massachusetts. They also believed that if Eve's Garden were to become a mainstream hit, it needed to de-emphasize sex toys and nix the talk of liberation and orgasms in favor of sexy lingerie and fantasy masks. This new, softer focus meant that "traditional" women's magazines like *Self*, *Brides*, and *Redbook* were willing to publish the company's ads.[46] Unfortunately, customers were not so taken with the new Eve's Garden. The existing clientele wasn't interested in string bikinis, and apparently *Brides* readers didn't see anything they wanted either.

The experiment was a disaster. Instead of transforming Eve's Garden into a national brand, the VC misadventure almost killed it. As the firm prepared to cut and run, Schooner Capital advised Williams to declare bankruptcy, but she couldn't bring herself to take that step. Instead, she sold her beloved Fire Island house to pay the company's debts. Williams sold off the unwanted merchandise and eventually returned to New York, where in 1983 she reopened the discreet upper-floor retail space on 57th Street.

The experience shattered her self-confidence. In a 1982 letter to friends, she confided that she was "in a terrible panic" and "crippled with anxiety."[47] Thanks to sheer determination, Williams revived the business, owning Eve's Garden until 1998, but she lost her desire "to be a tycoon." Instead, she decided, "I just want to comfortably survive."[48] The main lesson she took away from the VC episode was "to stay small, solvent and powerful. Don't overextend yourself." Dell Williams died in 2015, at the age of ninety-two.[49]

When I started researching these businesses, I naively believed that the superior economic performance of feminist sex-toy stores would prove that the early feminist book-stores could have been commercial powerhouses if it weren't for the peculiarities of the book trade. Books were available in too many other venues, and their profit margins were too small to justify keeping thousands of them on the shelves of brick-and-mortar stores. Like Lammas and the original Amazon, Good Vibrations and Eve's Garden were mission-driven ventures, but they enjoyed several built-in advantages. Sure, the products they sold were available elsewhere, but shopping at Good Vibrations or Babeland was infinitely more pleasant than visiting a traditional adult store. Additionally, browsing a physical location, where shoppers could ask questions, get reliable advice, inspect the wares, and perhaps even take them for a spin, was preferable to purchasing online. Sex toys, unlike books, are the kind of product that people really want to hold in their hands before they buy.

Learning how disastrous outside investment was for Eve's Garden and discovering that Good Vibrations and Babeland are now owned by an adult-industry lifer provided a rude awakening. In an era of consolidation, it is almost impossible for independent businesses, especially undercapitalized women- and queer-owned independent businesses, to compete with mega-corporations, whether they're selling books or butt plugs.

Once again, though, I'm left wondering why I'm so focused on competition with the big guys. Isn't finding a balance between delighting customers and remaining excited about the mission more important? After more than twenty years, Chicago's Early to Bed is still in the hands of its founder and original owner. And it is still a single-store operation. That's very much by design. Searah Deysach told me she thinks about opening another branch "all the time," but it doesn't feel like the right move. She's seen similar-sized operations that opened second stores shutter them quickly. As her vibrator-and-dildo-stuffed office attests, she loves sex toys. "That passion is what has gotten me through the rough times. We're not as profit-driven as other stores. I can make decisions based on my feelings rather than the bottom line." There are echoes of Dell Williams and Joani Blank in that statement. "I understand capitalism," she told me. "The idea is that you're supposed to keep moving up. But what if we're at the place that we want to be? Maybe that's fine."

I'm starting to think she's right.

Enjoying the music at Sisterfire, Upper Marlboro, Maryland, 1988. Roadwork, a women's arts organization, produced the festival at the Equestrian Center, twenty miles from Washington, DC. © 1988 JEB (Joan E. Biren)

SIX

VACATION DESTINATIONS

I WAS IN MY FORTIES BEFORE IT DAWNED ON ME THAT another lesbian had lived in the neighborhood where I grew up. My childhood home was a former mining village in northern England—not as quaint as the idyllic hamlet where Miss Marple did her detecting, but like St. Mary Mead, it was a place where residents knew each other's business. The walls of the terraced houses were thin, and since most villagers got around on foot, locals were constantly under surveillance. Still, somehow, Miss D evaded my nascent gaydar.

The truth is, I'm not *positive* that Miss D—a pseudonym—was family. She dressed and did her hair like all the other (straight) ladies of her age, and as a teenager who relied on the most obvious signifiers to recognize my people, Miss D's failure to cover her clothing in buttons bearing slogans like "How Dare You Assume I'm Heterosexual" left me utterly incapable of "reading" her. But even then, I noticed something odd about the way people changed their intonation when they referred to the "friend" with whom she spent a week in Blackpool every year.

Blackpool wasn't a dyke destination at the time, but it provided a parallel world where Miss D could escape the scrutiny of nosy neighbors and the control of the domineering mother whose house she shared. The village and her mother were real life, but Blackpool was seven days—and six nights!—of respite, a place where the normal rules didn't apply.

Back then, Blackpool was the default vacation destination for people from our village. (Although I was born in the 1960s, I realize many of the customs I grew up with feel like they belong several decades earlier.) Almost everyone—Miss D was a notable exception—took their summer holidays in the same two weeks of July. This custom had its roots in the era when most residents worked in the local mills and mines; rather than cope with absences due to rolling vacations, businesses simply turned off the sewing machines and winding engines and shut down for a fortnight. Most of us spent the first week in Blackpool.

My family patronized the same bed and breakfast for many years, and that was only the first of many rituals. On Monday we'd visit the Tower Ballroom; on Tuesday we'd take a tram to Fleetwood and shop for kippers; we'd see shows featuring northern comedians at the theaters at the end of the piers; and every day we'd walk along the promenade, running into people from home, who, like us, were dressed in brand-new holiday finery. Of course, the beaches and amusement arcades were also full of people we didn't know—back then there were "no vacancies" signs on the front windows of most of the B&Bs—but they were all people like us: working-class northerners who, for one week at least, got to rule the roost. And that was the appeal of a week in Blackpool. The weather was unreliable, or reliably rainy, but the accommodations, attractions, and entertainment were priced and designed with us in mind. No judgment about accents, no sniffiness about taste, just lots of things we liked to do and could find at some point on the Blackpool tram line.

I'm grateful to have grown up in a country with a strong belief in the benefits of vacations. If Britain had a statement of values akin to the Declaration of Independence, it would probably guarantee the right to pints of beer, heated towel rails, and an annual holiday by the sea. Vacations provide a chance to recharge, spend quality time with friends or family members, and, if you happen to be queer, experience the world as you would like it to be. For my fellow villagers, Blackpool was a break from the daily grind—more leisurely, more luxurious, more self-indulgent. But in an affirming and reassuring way, it still felt like home.

I recognized that feeling when I first visited Provincetown, Massachusetts. There was no confusing this place with my "normal" life. Apart from anything else, I'd literally journeyed to the end of the American landmass to get there. (It's no accident that gay enclaves tend to sprout up in hard-to-access locations. Just as lesbian bars used to hide away on the far edge of town, queer resorts developed in places where visitors were confident they wouldn't casually run into workmates or neighbors.) Still, as soon as I stepped off the ferry, I felt as if I belonged there.

Nevertheless, it took several years of visiting Province-town before the Pilgrim Monument started to remind me of Blackpool Tower. My partner and I tended to head to this queer enclave at the tip of Cape Cod the same week every time—chosen because of where my birthday falls rather than regional practice—and our itinerary didn't vary a great deal. We'd make reservations at favorite restaurants, timed to allow for an hour or two at Tea Dance before dinner (cheers to the queer who popularized early-evening disco parties); plan excursions to the nature reserve that poet Mary Oliver, a household favorite, was known to frequent; and buy tickets to see lesbian comedians, esteemed gay authors, and anarchic drag queens performing in town. The rest of the time we'd wander up and down Commercial Street, the main thor-oughfare, running into old friends and familiar faces more often than seemed possible. It was Blackpool all over again.

There's no place in the world where LGBTQ people are a "nat-ural" majority. We're distributed at random throughout the population. While we might refer to certain zip codes as *gay-borhoods* or assign them nicknames like Dyke Slope, this gen-erally signifies that for a handful of blocks in an enormous city, recognizably queer people make up 20, 30, or maybe even 40 percent of the community. We are everywhere, but we're rarely statistically significant.

In Provincetown, though, as in a few other select spots around the world, gay is the default (at least for the summer months). This is a unique circumstance: beach or mountain resorts have served other minority communities, but those groups always had other places where they could publicly mingle. Not so for LGBTQ people, at least until the 1970s. In truth, it's hard to say if queer people constitute a majority even here, even now, but the stores, inns, entertainment venues, and outdoor gathering spaces are designed to prioritize our relationships, tastes, and culture. And that's rare enough to schlep to the tip of Cape Cod for.

Provincetown hasn't always been a queer hotspot. For the past few centuries, the land of the Nauset people has been home to Pilgrims, whalers, Portuguese sailors, artists, playwrights, poets, and these days the occasional blogger. That isn't the origin story of Fire Island, New York, home to Cherry Grove and The Pines; Rehoboth Beach, Delaware; Ogunquit, Maine; Palm Springs, California; or any other LGBTQ enclave. A few shared elements pertain: a remote location that deters casual visitors and permits a degree of anonymity; relative proximity to cities with a strong queer community; gorgeous vistas around every corner; performance spaces on every block. Still, none of these guarantee that a gay resort area is destined to spring forth. There's no set route to this status, but once a critical mass of queer visitors is reached, the network effect applies. Arty gays go to Provincetown for the same reason football fans go to sports bars and parents log on to Facebook: that's where their people are.

Each destination's story is different, but there's value in seeing how one well-known spot transformed into a queer summer haven. Fire Island is a thin strip of land just south of Long Island, some sixty-five miles from New York City. Today, its name is synonymous with gay culture—mainly due to Fire Island Pines, a vacation spot that each year attracts thousands of gay men to drink, carouse, and get to know each other. It's also home to a smaller but no less culturally rich lesbian enclave: the town of Cherry Grove.

Fire Island was operating as a getaway for weary city dwellers as long ago as 1869. Still, conditions in these early years were far from luxurious: accommodation was limited to one hotel and a smattering of modest cottages, most of which served the local fishing industry in the Great South Bay. Eventually, well-to-do visitors started to vacation on the island, but Cherry Grove lacked running water, indoor plumbing, and electricity until 1960.[1] Even then, many homeowners waited years to take advantage of those utilities. Consequently, the town's allure was rather niche, appealing only to hardy types who disliked built-up resorts or to segments of the population for whom an unpopular place would be very popular, like homosexuals. Eventually, word of Cherry Grove's burgeoning gay scene got around Manhattan's artistic and especially theatrical communities. Once there, given the challenges of cooking without electricity or refrigeration, people tended to eat their meals at the lone hotel (which had its own generator) and gather in its bar most evenings. This made it relatively easy for newcomers to break into the social scene.

In the days before Stonewall, bad news for gays as a group could have a positive impact on individuals, as when, for example, bar raids received salacious press coverage that also spread awareness of their existence. In a similar way, a number of objectively negative events helped make Cherry Grove gayer. On September 21, 1938, a hurricane devastated Fire Island, destroying at least two-thirds of Cherry Grove's cottages.[2] Although the federal government stepped up, hurricane-proofing the beaches and offering low-interest loans to property owners who wanted to rebuild, many of the straight families who had bought property there decided to leave. This allowed gay Grovers of means to buy their land— even if the cottages had drifted off into the bay. Similarly, a headline-grabbing murder case in 1949 led to weeks of newspaper stories about the strange goings-on in Cherry Grove.[3] Though it was not what the papers intended, the tales of hard-drinking debauchery held particular interest for gay and lesbian people who were following the case.

By the 1960s, gays made up a majority of the summer population on Fire Island. Its physical isolation meant that queer people could gather and flirt openly in Cherry Grove, something that was still impossible in any urban setting. One woman who was a regular Grove-goer during that period reported, "To wear slacks and to be with other people like yourself and talk to other people like yourself was for us, at that age, a simply extraordinary feeling of freedom and elation . . . because [outside the Grove] there was nothing."[4]

Even though each queer redoubt has its own idiosyncrasies— Cherry Grove is alone in having no paved roads and prohibiting private vehicles, for example—they also share many traits. Lesbians are a minority in most, though comparative gains in women's earning power and, in the case of Cherry Grove, the development right next door to The Pines, which attracts gay A-listers, have increased their presence in recent decades. (Tragically, the deaths of hundreds of thousands of gay and bisexual men during the AIDS crisis also contributed to this demographic rebalancing.) These mixed resorts may not appeal to separatists, but lesbian and bisexual women have benefitted from the scarcity of straight, cis men. One longtime Cherry Grove resident told anthropologist Esther Newton, "You could go out at night in the dark, and if there were any boys they were only disappointed you were not another boy and they never bothered you."[5] In 1993, Newton reported that in Cherry Grove the only violent crimes against lesbians had been homophobic incidents committed by men from the mainland.

These resorts also tend to be overwhelmingly white, a legacy of their origins as havens for the affluent. As the 2022 movie *Fire Island* so artfully demonstrated, places like The Pines have long been less than welcoming to nonrich, nonwhite visitors. I am reminded of something Seattle bar proprietor Erin Nestor told me in an interview.[6] Nestor, who is openly and proudly lesbian, has chosen not to run her establishments as gay bars. When I asked how she let queer customers know they were welcome, she told me that patrons need to see themselves reflected in the staff. Being helped by trans or nonbinary managers, bartenders, or waitstaff does more to make trans and nonbinary customers feel comfortable than window stickers or earnest declarations. Likewise,

Helen Caddie-Larcenia, a Black woman who co-owned Provincetown's Aspasia guesthouse for much of the 1980s, said that several Black lesbians were drawn to visit the town after hearing that she ran an inn there.[7]

Vacations stir up childhood memories the way holidays like Christmas, Passover, or New Year's remind people of the family rituals they grew up with. Walking familiar streets, dining at favorite restaurants, and ordering the customary rum punch has a nostalgic charm for me, bringing back memories of all those wet weeks in Blackpool. The allure of repetition is by no means universal, however. When I asked Tracy McDonald, a travel-loving ex, why she hadn't returned to Provincetown in decades, she told me she prefers to use her precious vacations to visit new places. There was another element that I suspected might make Ptown less appealing for Tracy: in those promenades up and down Commercial Street, it's clear there are few Black and Brown visitors. Almost all the business owners are white, and although there are some seasonal workers from Jamaica in town, they tend to be hired in behind-the-scenes roles such as cleaners and cooks rather than front-of-house positions like waiters and ice-cream scoopers.[8] Consequently, visitors of color don't get to feel the same welcoming sense of recognition that white vacationers experience. So, did Provincetown hold less appeal to Tracy as a Black woman? "It's nice being where gay is the norm. Provincetown was fun," she told me, "but the ease with which you feel at home may not be as effortless for Black and Brown lesbians."[9]

In recent years, Provincetown has made an explicit appeal to visitors of color using the same strategy that boosted women's presence in the town. Inspired by Fantasia Fair, the trans gathering first held in 1975, a group of women inn-keepers in 1984 dreamed up Women's Weekend (now Women's Week), an effort to attract more lesbian visitors and to expand the summer season into October.[10] Since that success, Ptown has enthusiastically embraced festivals targeting segments of the queer population, with events for bears, single women, leather folk, parents, and cabaret lovers and, more recently, weekends for women and men of color. (If nothing else, the transitional periods between events make for some interesting sights at the Boston ferry terminal, as in July, when a pack of bearded men disembarks and a spray of women takes their place as Bear Week fades into Girl Splash.) As siloed, and, yes, segregated as Womxn of Color Weekend and Frolic Men of Color Weekend might seem, they allow visitors of color to experience the feeling of being in the majority that white gay men and lesbians have enjoyed in Provincetown for decades. It's good to see this historical failure being addressed at last.

I lesbian for a living, so I already know with absolute certainty how strong, vital, and creative the queer women's community is. I still sometimes crave the reassurance and comfort of being among my people. When I want to experience awe, I think back to national LGBTQ marches in Washington, DC, and how life-changing it felt to see hundreds of thousands of lesbian, gay, bisexual, and trans people filling every inch of the National Mall—and packing subway trains, cafés, and supermarkets in the days before and after. Every Pride festival reminds us of the beauty, vitality, and diversity of our community. Being in Provincetown allows me to access that power on whatever random summer day I step off the ferry—and to enjoy the glory of the queer community when we're enjoying our freedoms, not just when we're fighting for them.

Reader, here I must confess something rather embarrassing: I am about three steps short of hydrophobic, which means that beaches—one of the key loci of queer conviviality—hold negative appeal for me. That's why Provincetown, whose two beaches are some distance from the town center, is my gay resort of choice. On an early trip to Ptown, I took the bus to the closest shore, Herring Cove. Once there, I listened to the Iran-Contra hearings on a transistor radio while trying to cope with sunscreen, sand, and beach towels. Even the bathing butches and floating femmes couldn't tempt me back. Provincetown's history as a center of art, theater, and poetry means that it's easy to spend many days there without thinking of the beach. Instead, there are life-drawing sessions at the art museum, openings and shows at the various galleries, and a gorgeous library right in the middle of town. Ultimately, the draw of an LGBTQ vacation destination isn't stunning beaches or attractive buildings; it's the beautiful people who dance, eat, and shop there.

Because, yes, even clothing stores can be queer. What do they sell? Fewer rainbows than you might expect—why buy a T-shirt featuring a hard-to-match splotch of color when something subtler bearing the word *Provincetown* sends the same signal? In recent years, shops specializing in gender-neutral, androgynous clothing have come to Commercial Street, alongside the more established sex-toy stores and galleries that, during Bear Week at least, specialize in portraits of portly gentlemen with lots of body hair. While LGBTQ authors are no strangers to mainstream bookstores these days, it's only in places like Ptown that readings featuring lesbian romance authors reliably draw crowds of eager shoppers. Comedy shows are as common as cornflakes, but outside Ptown, how many feature jokes about dyke haircuts, celesbians, and cunnilingus? And in Provincetown's B&Bs, no one will desperately throw out *sisters? cousins? colleagues?* before finally accepting that two women who just came out of a double room might, in fact, be a couple.

I'm always a little surprised that I crave this kind of assumed primacy. I've spent my adult life as a resident of lesbian enclaves, from Mount Pleasant in Washington, DC, through London's Stoke Newington and Seattle's Capitol Hill, to Park Slope in Brooklyn. I've always been out at work and with friends. In my self-presentation, I'm almost a parody of a middle-aged white lesbian: short hair, glasses, sensible shoes. I can't imagine why anyone would take me for straight. My life is very different from that of Miss D, or her spiritual heirs, who for reasons involving family, career, or confidence don't feel able to live an openly lesbian life at home. A few precious days by the sea aren't my only chance to creep out of the closet, but I don't want to take a step back from my comfortably queer life when I'm on vacation either. I have no desire to tense up—to straighten up, as it were—during the precious weeks when relaxing is job one.

The *most* relaxing thing about vacationing in Provincetown—or whichever queer getaway you prefer—is the guarantee that legibly gay people will be welcomed and catered to there. We breathe easier knowing that there'll be other lesbian couples in cafés and that it's OK—heck, expected even!—to ask someone of the same sex to dance at Tea. It's one of the few settings left where there's no need to make special plans to find friends and friendly strangers—just sit at a table on Commercial Street, and you'll run into someone you know or would like to know.

Felice Newman (who shared her youthful feelings about feeling isolated in lesbian bars in Chapter 1) has been coming to Provincetown with her wife, Constance, for more than twenty years and spending the entire summer there since 2011. When I asked Newman why Ptown felt special to her, she recalled a *New York Times* article published ten years earlier.[11] It was a story about the challenges of making friends after the age of thirty, when work responsibilities, busy schedules, and family life make it almost impossible for adults to get together, much less to bond. The piece mentioned three elements that sociologists have identified as being essential to making close friends: "proximity; repeated, unplanned interactions; and a setting that encourages people to let their guard down and confide in each other." Spending time in Provincetown almost guarantees the first two conditions: it's basically a two-street town; even in the height of the summer tourist season, you feel like you cross paths with every other person who's staying there at least once a day. In Newman's view, the town's geography provides the final element: "When people go to Provincetown on vacation, they're often taking stock of their lives or having a time out. Then there's something about the landscape—the openness and the ocean that encourages sharing."[12] Newman recalls numerous occasions when "I'll start talking with someone I've never met, and all of a sudden, we'll be in this deep conversation. I didn't make that happen. There's something about the town that makes it possible."

I've also had that experience. Take the usual benefits of vacation—no Zoom calls, no meetings, no dishes—and add queer kinship and the sound of the waves. Suddenly you're spilling secrets to a pipe fitter from Mahwah, New Jersey, or catching up with someone you haven't seen in twenty years. Felice Newman and I knew each other from feminist publishing circles in the 1980s and early 1990s. We staffed neighboring booths and attended business meetings together, but we never really hung out until we found ourselves in the same line at a coffee shop on Commercial Street two decades later. After that coffee-line collision, we made a point of getting together every time my partner and I visited Provincetown.

Not that we've spent a huge amount of time there. Like gay neighborhoods all over America, Provincetown has gentrified in recent decades. It's now a very expensive place to vacation, only accessible to people with lots of disposable income—especially when staying in Provincetown proper. In my twenties, when I earned peanuts in movement jobs, I could afford to spend a week there, whereas in my much more comfortable fifties, four nights was my limit. Back in the 1980s, when fewer queer people felt able to come out, a trip to this part of the Cape carried an element of danger. Nowadays, the number of people who feel comfortable associating themselves with a queer destination is much larger, while the amount of accommodation available to house them has grown only slightly.

Back in the twentieth century, it was also easier to support lesbian businesses. In the 1980s, there were as many as ten women-owned guesthouses, several of which advertised in feminist publications like *off our backs*.[13] In 2023, the Women Innkeepers of Provincetown website listed just three.[14] Most of the lesbian pioneers sold their properties to gay men in the 1990s and early 2000s, when prices were high, which at least allowed them to see some financial reward for their investment and labor.[15] Like operating a bar or bookstore, running a guesthouse is a grueling job. Innkeepers work flat-out over the course of the tourist season, which takes a toll on romantic relationships, and because they rent out as many rooms as possible, often including their own bedrooms, they spend months living in cramped spaces.[16]

Even during events like Women's Week or Girl Splash, gay men still dominate Provincetown. There are other, more lesbian-focused vacation options, though they, too, have become more expensive, and more exclusive, in recent years.

My early experience with the home-away-from-homeyness of Blackpool undoubtedly skewed my personal definition of what constitutes a vacation. In an important sense, though, any temporary break from the norm, even if it involves a short-term rejection of comfort for a chance to spend time in lesbian community, can be seen as a kind of getaway from the straight world. These escapes may not have been about having fun and relaxing, but they allowed hardy lesbians to be a part of something bigger.

Between 1981 and 2000, Britain's Greenham Common Women's Peace Camp was home to a group of women who slept in "benders," plastic sheets draped over tree branches embedded in the mud. While protesting the UK government's decision to house nuclear weapons on a nearby air force base, they faced arrest, imprisonment, and endless harassment from police and bailiffs. They also boiled kettles over open fires, dug "shit pits" in the woods, and put themselves in physical danger by blocking the gates of the base or using bolt cutters to rip holes in the perimeter fence.[17] While some women spent months or even years at the camp, others would show up for the weekend or whenever they had time off work. In 1982, the women of Greenham decided to make the camp women-only. Although it was not a lesbian-separatist project, the experience of spending time there helped many women come out. In 2021, Rebecca Johnson, who spent five years at the camp, told a reporter that because Greenham women were generally assumed to be lesbians and were treated as if they were, it was easier for her to come out to her family than it might have been if she'd never spent time at the camp.[18]

There was no charge to camp at Greenham, though women did pool their resources while there. Back in the United States, many landdyke communities welcomed short-term visitors for a nominal fee or in exchange for work, albeit in the hopes that at least some might return permanently. As we've seen, land groups were selective, only seeking new members whose ideology and temperament (and, in many cases, assigned gender at birth) were compatible with those of the existing group. Still, most had a vision of creating dynamic, ever-expanding communities, and they knew that no one would up sticks and relocate without conducting a thorough vibe check. Unfortunately, guests were often a source of stress to established residents.

Lesbians who showed up at land communities hoping for an inexpensive holiday in the countryside were often disappointed by the facilities and the degree to which they were left to their own devices. The Full Moon community in Northern California warned visitors that they must be prepared to take care of themselves, cooking their own food and providing their own camping equipment and survival tools. Full Moon women told readers of the country lesbian magazine *Maize*, "We do not have ELECTRICITY anywhere on the land. So if the intense darkness makes you uncomfortable, this would be a hard place for you to visit."[19] They also reminded potential guests that since the property was a working ranch and the chore list was long, residents rarely had time to socialize with guests.

Recognizing the tensions that could sometimes arise when visitors didn't understand what they were getting into, in 1992 *Maize* started to dedicate several pages of each issue to "Country Connections," a rudimentary listing of communities that were open for camping, lodging, or work exchange.[20] Accompanying that directory was a set of tips for how visitors should behave on lesbian land. Some of the instructions were obvious, like telling women to call or write ahead (only a small minority of landdyke communities had telephones) and to leave things the way they found them. Others were more specifically sapphic, like advising visitors of the need to ascertain the community guidelines around pets, food, scents, smoking, and chemical use in advance and reminding them that the lesbians on the land were "not likely to have more resources than [they]—no more time, energy, love, strength, money." Six years later, the directions were expanded to advise would-be visitors not to write the words *lesbian* or *dyke* on any postcards or envelopes sent through the US Postal Service and to refrain from talking to neighbors about women's land, even if they were lost.[21]

Some of the women who spent their vacations visiting lesbian land did what people often do when they're on holiday: let their hair down and relax their guard, safe in the knowledge that they would not be seen by anyone who knew them in the straight world. This was not as much fun for the permanent residents. In 1997, Sustana from Spinsterhaven in Arkansas wrote to *Maize* to remind potential visitors that "you don't come to the bible-belt with purple spiked hair. We are a community but we have to blend in with the locals enough to be accepted."[22] (Most lesbian-land groups gradually relaxed their strict rules about total isolation, but they were still cautious about drawing attention to themselves.)

It was almost impossible for lesbian-land communities to live up to the fantasies visitors projected onto them. Guests dreamed of finding utopia and instead confronted many of the same problems that plagued the rest of the world. As zana, a disabled landdyke who eschewed upper-case letters, tried to explain in a 1991 article in *Maize*, it would be wonderful if lesbian land could serve as the kind of healing retreat many women needed—"a quiet place to rest and meditate, or to go scream and discharge, a place where someone else changed the bedding and prepared delicious, healthful meals"—but that kind of caretaking is only possible in a long-term tight-knit community where women could be assured of receiving as well as giving love and support.[23] zana made no mention of money, but it seems unrealistic to imagine that the kind of restorative sanctuary visitors sought could be provided for a few dollars a day. (It strikes me that from the outside, land groups, many of which had robust spiritual practices related to goddess worship, have much in common with religious communities, albeit without the institutional underpinnings churches provided.)

While some getaways to the land may not have provided the sense of sanctuary many women hoped for, a few decades ago, women's music festivals offered a more accessible and more pleasure-focused vacation option. At their peak, women could fill their summer calendars with what scholar Bonnie J. Morris calls "lesbian mass gatherings."[24] While they were organized around music, they also provided space for workshops, religious and spiritual observances, and consciousness raising—not to mention shopping, social interaction, and sexual experimentation.

These days, thanks mostly to the controversy its "womyn-born-womyn" policy generated, the Michigan Womyn's Music Festival is the best known. While it was the biggest, it was just one stop on the circuit. Champaign-Urbana, Illinois, hosted the first, the National Women's Music Festival, in 1974.[25] By 1990 as many as twenty-five festivals took place around the country.[26] They didn't all involve sleeping under the stars, but camping was a feature of most. Now the first festival is also, if not the last, at least a lone holdout, though it, too, has radically transformed. In July 2023, the 47th National Women's Music Festival was held in a Marriott near Madison, Wisconsin.[27]

Women's music may no longer draw thousands of lesbians to rural camping grounds, but Olivia Records, the company that pioneered the genre, executed a bold and extremely successful pivot to provide a more luxurious and much more expensive kind of lesbian gathering: cruises.

As women stopped buying albums and the feminist bookstores that sold tickets for its concert tours closed, Olivia Records completely reimagined itself. Instead of Olivia artists taking their music to women around the country, the women would come to Olivia, gathering on the high seas instead of in concert halls. In 1990, singer-songwriter Cris Williamson headlined the first Olivia cruise, a four-day tour of the Bahamas. Three decades later, Olivia is probably America's most successful lesbian brand, hosting thousands of queer women from around the world every year. (The Olivia website notes that nonbinary and trans guests "are and have always been welcome.")[28]

Olivia's origins were unquestionably radical. Four of its founders had been part of the lesbian-separatist Furies collective in Washington, DC, and in its early days the company evinced little interest in making money.[29] According to a 1974 interview with *off our backs*, the founders wanted "to set up some sort of alternative economic institution which would both produce a product women want to buy and also employ women in a nonoppressive situation."[30] Artists who recorded with Olivia—without the exploitative long-term contracts other labels demanded—would have total control over what went on their records. Those albums also had a purpose: they would bring women who weren't yet involved in the women's movement "into some sort of feminist consciousness."

Olivia wasn't the only women's music label—Holly Near's Redwood Records was DC Comics to Olivia's Marvel—but whatever its provenance, the music, in all its variety, was the soundtrack of 1980s feminism. It played in women's bookstores, and the concerts provided an excuse for local communities to gather under one acoustically sound roof; it was literally a way of taking lesbian culture on the road. (In the days of dashboard cassette players, it felt surprisingly subversive to listen to lesbian love songs on the way to work—followed perhaps by lesbian breakup songs on the drive home.)

If it seems surprising that the affordable version of the one-stop lesbian cultural experience faded away while much more expensive options thrived, consider the fate of the lesbian bar. The more places queer women feel welcome, the more frills and facilities they demand. Also, as more lesbians come out, the bigger the market becomes, which allows companies to offer products at all price points, including eye-poppingly expensive. As insatiable sexpert Phoebe Sparkle told the ship's captain on the fictional Olivia voyage featured on Season 2 of *The L Word*, "For most of the women on this cruise . . . this is the only place where they're completely free to express themselves."[31] Many who board the Olivia charters had to wait years for an opportunity to dress up, openly display affection, and flirt with other women in glamorous surroundings. Now they get to watch whales while doing those things.

I attended Michigan, National, and Sisterfire, an urban festival held in the Washington, DC, area, in the 1980s, but the music was never the main attraction for me. The thrill was being with legions of lesbians. At a time when much of our queer lives played out in the shadows, it felt great to bask in the sunshine (and all too often the pouring rain). Even now, Olivia's programmers have an uncanny sense of its demographic's interests: every cruise features non-musical guests, including big-name writers, athletes, and politicians—none of whom I can imagine showing up to a muddy field in the middle of nowhere. Personally, I've never been more tempted to make a booking than when I saw that three of the Furies—a quarter of the collective!—were going to be on Olivia's fiftieth anniversary Caribbean Cruise in 2023.[32]

Lesbians have more options now. Historian Bonnie J. Morris noted, "Festivals were affected by some women's growing resistance to paying for a vacation that lacked hotel amenities, yet dared to require a workshift."[33] (Yes, some festivals, notably Michigan, required paying guests to put in at least four hours' work during their time on the land.) Just a few decades ago, lesbians were willing to sleep in tents, take cold showers in an open field, and spend a few hours of their vacation washing dishes or digging recyclables out of trash bags, all for a chance to spend five days surrounded by Amazons. Now, it seems, we want state rooms and restaurant food and to be whisked away to Amazonia.

Well, of course "we" do. Most of the women who lived the festie lifestyle in the 1980s are at least sixty now. Lesbians want to cruise rather than camp for the same reasons as straight sexagenarians: it's a luxurious, low-stress way to travel. If you can afford it, can stomach the environmental impact, and enjoy that sort of thing, it's supposedly a lot of fun.

In the glory days of women's music, according to Morris, affordable ticket prices, which could be further reduced by sliding-scale or work-exchange arrangements, allowed some women to attend three or four festivals every single summer.[34] It's hard to imagine even the mega-rich being able to take that many seaborne adventures. For many, an Olivia cruise will be a once-in-a-lifetime event.

More troublingly, something important is lost when we socialize in a walled garden—or in this case a floating fortress. With so many powerful voices amplifying homophobic and transphobic rhetoric, and without family members to model queer life stages, it's especially important for young or newly out LGBTQ people to see long-term queer coupledom, bi dating, nonbinary flirtation, trans friendship, and even dyke drama. Yes, it's expensive to stay in Provincetown, but at least for those who can get there, there's no charge to walk up and down Commercial Street, soaking in the ambient queer culture. Meanwhile, what happens on an Olivia cruise is only visible to the women who are on an Olivia cruise.

Instead of gathering at music festivals, when it's time to vacation, most of the younger queer people I know take advantage of the sharing economy and rent houses together at the beach, in the countryside, and sometimes in foreign lands. The problem is that you need queer friends before you can socialize with your queer friend group, and the loss of dedicated lesbian spaces has made it harder for some women to locate their community. (Olivia has a Solos program for unattached guests, featuring Solos dining tables and dedicated coordinators who organize mixers and other get-togethers.)[35]

Whether they are permanently queer spots like Provincetown or sites of short-term sapphism—as when fifteen thousand pool-party-seeking lesbians descend on Palm Springs, California, for the Dinah Shore Weekend; fans of the HBO show *Gentleman Jack* flock to England to celebrate Anne Lister's Birthday Week; or Autostraddle.com readers seek temporary refuge from the heteropatriarchy at A-Camp— vacation destinations are selling twin fantasies.[36] The first is that we can take a queer mulligan on rites of passage that we were shut out of the first time around: decked-out Olivians get a second chance to go to prom, women at the Dinah take another crack at spring break (albeit in the fall), A-Campers attend a summer camp where they learn to make dykey suspenders instead of lanyards, and the Anne Lister fest allows retirees to finally go on the field trips they wish they could have taken back when they were in school.

More generally, lesbian destinations let us experience, however briefly, a world without homophobia, the straight gaze, and disdain for our aesthetics and culture. It's great for as long as you can afford to be there, but it's something that must be purchased. Then, once the vacation is over, it's time to start saving for the next one. (Queer history does reveal a few off-the-grid exceptions to this rule. If the lesbian community that grew around Greenham Common Women's Peace Camp shows us anything, it's that access to a brand-new, queer world can occasionally come from taking part in a feminist protest, not just through paying gobs of money.)

Recently, I vowed to hold on to that supportive, norm-challenging vibe year-round. In the summer of 2022, my partner and I moved to Edinburgh, Scotland, a city that is both extremely walkable and constantly swarmed by tourists. For the first time, I came into regular contact with that human sidewalk blockage known as a walking tour. After spotting a group of people following a rainbow umbrella down the Royal Mile, I decided to join the crowd. I sought out an LGBTQ history tour and found Hannah Mackay Tait, a Blue Badge guide who offers specialist tours focused on Scottish women's history and Edinburgh's queer history as well as the "standard" fare.[37]

Mackay Tait's three-hour LGBTQ history walk features many of the stops you'd expect on a classic circuit, but with a queer twist: a location with a royal connection provides an opportunity to ponder whether a seventeenth-century king enjoyed intimate relationships with men, a theater facade triggers the story of a police raid, and a visit to Holyrood cues up a discussion of how, even though homosexuality remained illegal in Scotland for decades after it was decriminalized in England and Wales, by 2016 the Scottish Parliament was considered the gayest in the world.[38] Mackay Tait also points out several locales that are probably not part of the typical tour: historic cruising grounds, the locations of early Pride celebrations, and former and current queer bookstores.

It's an impressively balanced itinerary, touching on the arts, sciences, and politics and featuring lesbians, gay men, bisexuals, trans people, and a nineteenth-century military surgeon who was assigned female at birth but passed as a man for most of his life (Dr. James Barry). Nodding to the debate over Scotland's Gender Recognition Bill that was raging when we spoke, Mackay Tait says she feels it essential to include trans stories. A tour like this is an opportunity for people to explore the city, to get some exercise, and to put current events into a historical context. "They talked about themselves in different ways; they lived different lives from people nowadays, but queer and trans people have always been here, and they have always been contributing to Scottish society at all levels," Mackay Tait told me.

Of course, tours are interactive experiences. Mackay Tait says participants who were in Edinburgh in the 1970s and 1980s often contribute their own memories of people and places, while others ask for information on bars and bookshops they can visit after the group disperses. As they tramp around town visiting queer locations, a crowd that started as strangers begins to bond. In 2021, Mackay Tait offered a version of the tour as part of the Edinburgh Festival. "As we were going along, we saw a transphobic sticker on a lamppost," she recalls. "Everyone spontaneously stopped, and we peeled it off together. We'd built this little community, and we decided, *we're not going to stand for that.*"

You may not have a parliament or remnants of the monarchy where you live, but I encourage you to find traces of queer culture in your everyday surroundings. Identify the streets that once housed lesbian bars; track down the ghosts of feminist bookstores past; seek out the softball scene; support your local toy store. Most of all, remember that we are everywhere, including in your hometown.

POSTSCRIPT

LESBIAN PLACES. THE CHAPTERS OF THIS BOOK REVEAL patterns that emerge again and again, and if I want to tell the truth about queer women's spaces, those repeating patterns can't be resolved by resorting to synonyms or by simplifying the narrative. Instead, I must own our habit of hiding, or at least of adopting drab camouflage to avoid unwanted attention. I have to acknowledge that we can be terrible customers, demanding too much of the businesses we give too little support to. I'm obliged to recognize the sentimentality that tempts us to wallow in nostalgia when we'd have more fun and get more done by wholeheartedly embracing the social transformations that have made life better for almost all of us. I also can't help noticing that the straight, cis, male world will not give us a break, though it will happily swoop in and profit from our creations when we finally hang a sign on the door that reads, "Sorry, folks, I just can't do it anymore."

Mainstream society tends to venerate the tech industry's "move quickly and break things" model of innovation, but queer women get no respect for their decades of radical reinvention. Among the institutions they expertly subverted was capitalism itself. How else to explain lesbian entrepreneurs' repeated insistence that they would rather cooperate than compete?

Over and over again, so many of the people I spoke with over the course of researching this book told me that what they really wanted was a community center. When that proved impractical, they instead had to create sustainable businesses. For a lesbian business to succeed, it has to satisfy its queer customers *and* make a profit. Either task is difficult on its own, but the combination is almost impossible.

Almost impossible? Is that all? If nothing else, this book proves that queer women can make the impossible happen on a regular basis. The spaces they create may not last forever, but building long-lasting institutions was never the mission of our movement. Instead, we sought to change the lives of the women who passed through them—and in that sense, we have been remarkably successful. Besides, lesbian bars, stores, communes, and music festivals aren't the only such ventures that have closed over the last fifty years—so have most of the nonlesbian bars, stores, communes, and music festivals. Still, given lesbians' intense sense of loyalty, the keening, wailing, and gnashing of teeth that every bar or bookstore closure occasions should come as no surprise. Queer women place an unusually high premium on maintaining long-term relationships with former partners. No other set of human beings spends as much time socializing with exes as lesbian and bisexual women. People who go on vacation with an ex, the ex's current girlfriend, and that girlfriend's former partner (not to mention all their dogs) do not let business closures go unnoticed. It's easy to view every new project as a video-game-style contest, pitting the creativity of queer women against the hurdle-building skills of the patriarchy. Long-term, I wouldn't bet against the lesbians. We're a tenacious bunch.

I wanted to write this book to celebrate the lesbians who in the 1970s, 1980s, and 1990s built the spaces that helped shape my life. Researching it has introduced me to queer and trans powerhouses of today who are just as creative, just as determined, and who have already learned valuable lessons from their foremothers in the movement. They know that projects must be intersectional from the start. They have seen the disastrous consequences of holding on to outdated ideologies or failing to adapt a business model that doesn't work anymore. They are all too aware that business owners must pay attention to the mission *and* the bottom line. Oh, and they know that these places should also be fun.

The last few years have been full of bad news and appalling behavior. I understand why many queer and trans people are filled with rage and despair. But I see hope amid all the horror. I am reminded of something ALFA Omegas softball player Pici told me when we chatted in 2022. Fifty years earlier, when the Atlanta Lesbian Feminist Alliance was formed, she said,

> It was a volatile time. We were coming out of the civil rights movement, the antiwar movement, the second wave of the women's movement, the Native American movement, the

Attica prison riots, the Kent State shootings, the 1968 Democratic Convention, the murders of Martin Luther King and RFK. Everybody knew that if we didn't work together with the same goal, we were going to be destroyed.

There was something in the air—something terrifying but also galvanizing. Out of those terrible times came many of the groundbreaking spaces this book commemorates.

That sounds familiar. A new wave of queer bars, radical bookshops, and even rural trans and queer land groups have sprouted in recent years. Few will be around in fifty years, but I suspect they'll be as important to future generations as Tracks, Lammas, Babeland, and Provincetown were to me.

So, where shall we get together?

ACKNOWLEDGMENTS

This book wouldn't exist without my agent, Maggie Cooper, who does everything magnificently and makes it all look deceptively easy. She is unparalleled as an editor, a negotiator, and a provider of wise counsel. She is also a delightful correspondent and a brilliant creator of zines.

Emma Berry acquired the book for Seal Press, and her early feedback helped me find its shape and tone. Madeline Lee was the editor I needed: clear, exacting, and with an ambitious vision for what the book could be. I have been dazzled by the skills and enthusiasm of everyone involved with design, copyediting, production, marketing, publicity, rights, and sales, and I am grateful for the unerring support of publisher Lara Heimert. I'm overjoyed to have Seal Press as a publisher. It was something of a coming home, since I worked at the "original" Seal Press in the 1990s. I will forever be grateful to Barbara Sjoholm and Faith Conlon for everything they made possible.

I still can't quite believe how calm the women of Seal Press were when I told them I'd decided to move to the other side of the Atlantic in the middle of the project, but their response was extraordinarily reassuring. Thanks to all the people whose help and advice made that international relocation go smoothly, especially Hannah Bowers, Sara Burningham, Euan Fergusson, Moira Redmond, and the Old Sladians in the Red Shoes group chat.

Every "interview with the author" that appears in the endnotes represents an intrusion into someone's life. Sincere thanks to everyone who spoke with me and responded to my emails. I'm grateful for your time, insights, and honesty.

I've always loved libraries, and I now have even more reasons to be appreciative. Thanks to the workers and volunteers at the Lesbian Herstory Archives, the Quatrefoil Library, the Brooklyn Public Library, the New York Public Library, and the National Library of Scotland. I'm also grateful to all the people who dug into their personal archives, especially Joan E. Biren, whose work has been a source of sustenance and inspiration for decades. I'm delighted her photographs are a key part of this book. I am in awe of the Eugene Lesbian Oral History Project, a labor of love by Judith Raiskin and Linda Long of the University of Oregon, and of the energy archivist Morna Gerrard brings to her work at Georgia State University. Thanks also to the endlessly patient Julie R. Enszer, editor and publisher of *Sinister Wisdom*, and to Merril Mushroom, who kindly allowed me to use a stanza from her poem "Work Ethic: 1975."

Slate has been my professional home for more than twenty-five years, and I love all its pixels and people. Special thanks to Lakshmi Gopalkrishnan and Jack Shafer, who pulled me from the slush pile and showed me what to do. Julia Turner and John Swansburg brought their immense editorial skills to my 2011 series "The Gay Bar: Its Riotous Past and Uncertain Future," which in many ways sowed the seeds that grew into this book. Thanks to the Slatesters who shared their insights into the art and science of book writing, including Henry Grabar, Josh Levin, Laura Miller, Dana Stevens, Seth Stevenson, and Jacob Weisberg. I've been making podcasts since 2005, and every episode has been a blast, thanks to all the supersmart cohosts and talented producers I've worked with. Much love to Isaac Butler, Cameron Drews, Rumaan Alam, Kevin Bendis, Karen Han, and the entire Working crew, past, present, and future. A grateful shoutout to Emily Charash and Daisy Rosario, whose help at a crucial point in the writing of this book allowed me to meet a key deadline. Queer cheers to the entire Outward family, especially Christina Cauterucci, Jules Gill-Peterson, and Bryan Lowder, a cherished longtime collaborator.

Writing a book is hard on friendships, so I'm grateful to pals Alison Bechdel, Andy Bowen, Dominic Bowers, Kim Walden Bowers, Claire Buck, Susan Davis, Sian Gibby, Ian Hodder, Paula Krebs (my first journalism teacher, tough but fair!), Karen McManus, and Colm Redmond for putting up with me these last few years.

Thanks to all my dentists, near and far, especially Dr. Susan Isaacson and Dr. Gwen Engelhard.

Ta to my parents, Edith Thomas and the late Alan Thomas. They sent me off on an educational path that took me many miles from home, and they did so at great sacrifice and without complaint.

My favorite place in the world is wherever Rosemary Warden is. This book wouldn't have been possible without her genius, love, and patience.

NOTES

Introduction

1. Calculating the size of the LGBTQ population is notoriously difficult, in part because different researchers focus variously on behavior, attraction, and identification. In 1948, with the publication of his book *Sexual Behavior in the Human Male* (Philadelphia, W. B. Saunders Company), Alfred Kinsey declared, "At least 37% of the male population has some homosexual experience between the beginning of adolescence and old age." Five years later, in *Sexual Behavior in the Human Female* (Philadelphia, W. B. Saunders Company, 1953), he concluded that 20 percent of women had some kind of same-sex experience. In 1977, the first director of the National Gay Task Force examined Kinsey's somewhat complex findings and concluded, more succinctly, that 10 percent of the US population was gay or lesbian. While studies suggest men are more likely to be exclusively gay, whereas women are more likely to be bisexual, it still seems reasonable to posit that approximately half of the queer 10 percent are women. Kinsey's methodology now seems archaic, but contemporary data scientists have found the 10 percent estimate "reasonable," at least when it comes to sexual behavior. By some estimates, the numbers are rising. A 2022 Gallup Poll found that almost 21 percent of Gen Z Americans identified as LGBTQ. For more on this topic, see Spiegelhalter, David, "Is 10% of the Population Really Gay?," *Guardian*, April 5, 2015, https://www.theguardian.com/society /2015/apr/05/10-per-cent-population-gay-alfred-kinsey-statistics; Jones, Jeffrey, "LGBTQ Identification in U.S. Ticks Up to 7.1%," Gallup, February 17, 2022, https://news.gallup.com/poll/389792 /lgbt-identification-ticks-up.aspx; and Gates, Gary J., "How Many People Are Lesbian, Gay, Bisexual, and Transgender?," Williams Institute,

April 2011, https://williamsinstitute.law.ucla.edu/publications/how-many-people-lgbt.

2. The first three issues of the monthly magazine of the Daughters of Bilitis, *The Ladder*, used a PO box as their return address. Martinac, Paula, *The Queerest Places: A Guide to Gay and Lesbian Historic Sites* (New York, Henry Holt and Company, 1997), p. 269.

3. Loftin, Craig M., *Letters to ONE: Gay and Lesbian Voices from the 1950s and 1960s* (Albany, SUNY Press, 2012), p. 8.

4. Packer, Vin, *Spring Fire* (1952; repr., San Francisco, Cleis Press, 2004), p. vi.

5. Marijane Meaker, interview with the author, conducted by phone, January 16, 2016.

6. Packer, *Spring Fire*, p. viii.

7. Rauch, Jonathan, "The Unknown Supreme Court Decision That Changed Everything for Gays," *Washington Post*, February 5, 2014, https://www.washingtonpost.com/news/volokh-conspiracy/wp/2014/02/05/the-unknown-supreme-court-decision-that-changed-everything-for-gays.

8. Shaffi, Sarah, "Librarians Sue Arkansas State over Law Banning Them from Giving 'Obscene' Books to Children," *Guardian*, May 31, 2023, https://www.theguardian.com/books/2023/may/31/librarians-sue-arkansas-state-over-law-banning-them-from-giving-obscene-books-to-children.

9. The April 21, 1966, action, now known as the "Julius Sip-In," was an attempt to gain clarity regarding the New York State Liquor Authority's rules. See Johnson, Thomas A., "3 Deviates Invite Exclusion by Bars," *New York Times*, April 22, 1966, p. 43. For more on New York's "masquerade" laws, see Ryan, Hugh, *The Women's House of Detention: A Queer History of a Forgotten Prison* (New York, Bold Type Books, 2022), e.g., p. 157.

10. Information about women's exclusion from credit markets before the passage of the Equal Credit Opportunity Act is taken from Krippner, Greta R., "Democracy of Credit: Ownership and the Politics of Credit Access in Late Twentieth-Century America," *American Journal of Sociology*, Vol. 123, No. 1, July 2017, https://doi.org/10.1086/692274.

11. Spain, Daphne, *Constructive Feminism: Women's Spaces and Women's Rights in the American City* (Ithaca, Cornell University Press, 2016), Location 2298, Kindle Edition.

12. Ibid., Location 2211, Kindle Edition.

13. Esrig, Barbara, "Women Unlimited: Gainesville, Florida," *Hot Spots: Creating Lesbian Space in the South, Sinister Wisdom* 109, Winter 2018, p. 33.

14. Culver, Corky, "Transforming Lesbian Cultural Politics in Gainesville, Florida," *Hot Spots: Creating Lesbian Space in the South, Sinister Wisdom* 109, Winter 2018, p. 36.

15. Oral history interview with Barb Ryan, Eugene Lesbian Oral History Project, July 9, 2018, https://oregondigital.org/concern/documents/df73c318d.

16. Linda Long, email exchange with the author, March 28, 2023.

17. Annise Parker, interview with the author, conducted via Zoom, December 7, 2022. (For more on Phyllis Frye, see Sontag, Deborah, "Once a Pariah, Now a Judge: The Early Transgender Journey of Phyllis Frye," *New York Times*, August 29, 2015, https://www.nytimes.com/2015/08/30/us/transgender-judge-phyllis-fryes-early-transformative-journey.html.)

18. In *Let the Record Show*, her magnificent history of ACT UP New York, Sarah Schulman shares several stories of people who became AIDS activists because they happened to be at the center when ACT UP was holding a meeting. See Schulman, Sarah, *Let the Record Show: A Political History of ACT UP New York, 1987–1993* (New York, Farrar, Straus and Giroux, 2021), p. 213. For other examples, see also pp. 38, 46, and 63.

19. Bechdel, Alison, *Fun Home* (Boston, Houghton Mifflin Company, 2006), p. 118.

Chapter 1: Lesbian Bars

1. Gates, Gary J., "How Many People Are Lesbian, Gay, Bisexual, and Transgender?," Williams Institute, April 2011, https://williamsinstitute.law.ucla.edu/publications/how-many-people-lgbt.

2. *Gayellow Pages USA*, Gayellow Pages, http://www.gayellowpages.com/wholebook.pdf.

3. Petronius, *New York Unexpurgated* (New York, Matrix House, 1966), p. 177.

4. Maggie Collier, interview with the author, conducted by phone, April 27, 2011.

5. Chauncey, George, *Gay New York: Gender, Urban Culture, and the Making of the Gay Male World, 1890–1940* (New York, Basic Books, 1994), p. 229.

6. Bannon, Ann, *Beebo Brinker* (1962), reprinted in *The Beebo Brinker Omnibus: Ann Bannon's Pulp Classics* (San Francisco, Cleis Press, 2015), Location 14559, Kindle Edition.

7. Aldrich, Ann (pseudonym of Marijane Meaker), "Introduction to the 2006 Edition," in *We, Too, Must Love* (1958; repr. New York, Feminist Press at the City University of New York, 2006), Location 93, Kindle Edition.

8. Carter, David, *Stonewall: The Riots That Sparked the Gay Revolution* (New York, St. Martin's, 2004), p. 74.

9. These examples are taken from de la Croix, St. Sukie, *Chicago Whispers: A History of LGBT Chicago Before Stonewall* (Madison, University of Wisconsin Press, 2012).

10. David K. Johnson estimates that "as many as five thousand suspected gay or lesbian employees may have lost their jobs with the federal government during the early days of the Cold War." Johnson, David, K., *The Lavender Scare: The Cold War Persecution of Gays and Lesbians in the Federal Government* (Chicago, University of Chicago Press, 2004), p. 166.

11. Ibid., p. 11.

12. Ibid., p. 152.

13. Cartier, Marie, *Baby, You Are My Religion: Women, Gay Bars, and Theology Before Stonewall* (Durham, Acumen Publishing, 2013), p. 11.

14. Johnson, *The Lavender Scare*, p. 212.

15. Kinsey, Alfred C., *Sexual Behavior in the Human Female* (Philadelphia, W. B. Saunders Company, 1953), p. 460.

16. Loftin, Craig M., *Letters to ONE: Gay and Lesbian Voices from the 1950s and 1960s* (Albany, SUNY Press, 2012), p. 5.

17. Gallo, Marcia M., *Different Daughters: A History of the Daughters of Bilitis and the Rise of the Lesbian Rights Movement* (New York, Carroll & Graf, 2006), p. 5.

18. Meeker, Martin, *Contacts Desired: Gay and Lesbian Communications and Community, 1940s–1970s* (Chicago, University of Chicago Press, 2006), p. 90.

19. Unless otherwise indicated, Elaine Romagnoli quotes and biographical details originate in an in-person interview with the author, conducted April 6, 2011.

20. Hearings Before the General Subcommittee on Labor of the Committee on Education and Labor, House of Representatives, First Session on H.R. 8259, Part 1, June 29, 1965, p. 1061.

21. Stegall, Gwendolyn, "A Spatial History of Lesbian Bars in New York City," master's thesis, Graduate School of Architecture, Planning, and Preservation, Columbia University, May 2019, p. 83. Available at the Academic Commons of the Columbia University Libraries, https://doi .org/10.7916/d8-k46h-fa23.

22. Ibid., p. 67.

23. Jay, Karla, "The First Lesbian Dance: A Political Memoir," *Womanews*, Vol. 2, No. 6, June 1981, p. 1.

24. Duberman, Martin, *Stonewall* (New York, Plume, 1994), p. 248.

25. *Gayellow Pages (NYC/NJ Edition)*, Issue 6, November 1977 (New York, Renaissance House, 1977), p. 48.

26. Bahlman, Lynn, "A Sapphic Bar Guide to Gotham," *Christopher Street*, September 1977, p. 47.

27. *Purple Rage*, November–December 1972, p. 13.

28. *Gayellow Pages (NYC/NJ Edition)*, p. 48.

29. Found in "Bars, October 11, 1980–July 1, 1989" in the Lesbian Herstory Archives Subject Files, Park Slope, Brooklyn, New York.

30. Elaine Romagnoli was a great bar operator and a terrible copy editor. In public-facing materials like holiday cards or even magazine display ads, she would sometimes write "Bonnie & Clyde's" instead of "Bonnie & Clyde" or "Cubbyhole" instead of "Cubby Hole."

31. Greenfield, Fran, "Duchess Faces Grim Future After Police Raid," *Womanews*, Vol. 3, No. 9, October 1982, p. 1. According to a May 27, 2022, email exchange with the Public Information Department of the New York State Liquor Authority, that screen-law provision was in force until 1998.

32. The Duchess stayed open as a "juice bar," serving nonalcoholic drinks, for several months. Other lesbian bars later took over that space, including, in 1989, Duchess II.

33. Burton, Krista, *Moby Dyke: An Obsessive Quest to Track Down the Last Remaining Lesbian Bars in America* (New York, Simon & Schuster, 2023), p. 207.

34. Note dated January 8, 1981, accessed via Lesbian Herstory Archives Subject Files, "Bars."

35. Byron, Peg, "B&C's Bites the Dust," *Womanews*, Vol. 2, Issue 2, February 1981, p. 6.

36. Stegall, "A Spatial History of Lesbian Bars in New York City," p. 110.

37. Tourguide, Jane, "A Quick Sex Trip to New York," *Rites for Lesbian and Gay Liberation*, Vol. 3, Issue 7, December 1986–January 1987, p. 7.

38. See, e.g., Musto, Michael, "Immaculate Connection," *OutWeek*, March 26, 1991, p. 36.

39. Reyes, Nina, "Landmark Lesbian Bar Shuts Its Doors for Good," *OutWeek*, December 26, 1990, p. 18.

40. Event listing, *OutWeek*, November 21, 1990, p. 66.

41. Reyes, "Landmark Lesbian Bar Shuts Its Doors for Good," p. 30.

42. Writing in *Womanews* in October 1982, Fran Greenfield tried to discern why the Duchess had suddenly been targeted, given that it had been operating as a lesbian bar since 1972. Unfortunately, there was no obvious, clear-cut explanation. Greenfield observed, "There does not appear at this time to be any state wide backlash against gays and both gubernatorial candidates are going out of their way to court the gay vote." She did note a rising tide of conservatism in the country at large, but her tentative conclusion was that the New York State Liquor Authority had chosen to crack down on vulnerable lesbian and leather bars to distract attention from a recently released report indicating that an estimated five thousand unlicensed premises were selling liquor in the state. (Greenfield, "Duchess Faces Grim Future After Police Raid," p. 1.)

43. Stegall, "A Spatial History of Lesbian Bars in New York City," p. 123.

44. The ad ran in several publications, including *Sappho's Isle*, Vol. 8, No. 2, February 1995, p. 22.

45. For coverage of the controversy, see, e.g., "Homosexuality: Born or Bred?," *Newsweek*, February 23, 1992, https://www.newsweek.com/homosexuality-born-or-bred-200636. Thanks to Al Miller for directing my attention to this common error.

46. The ad ran in many publications, including *Sappho's Isle*, Vol. 4, Issue 7, August 1991.

47. Ad, *Sappho's Isle*, Vol. 6, Issue 12, December 1993, p. 36.

48. Al Miller, email exchange with the author, July 12, 2023.

49. Romagnoli, Elaine, "Letters," *OutWeek*, May 22, 1991, p. 5.

50. "A Letter to Our Customers from Shescape," dated February 1987, "COOL (Committee of Outraged Lesbians)" folder, Lesbian Herstory Archives.

51. Jacqueline Woodson, interview with the author, conducted via WhatsApp, January 9, 2023.

52. COOL flyer, undated, found in "COOL (Committee of Outraged Lesbians)" folder at the Lesbian Herstory Archives.

53. De Luca, Nancy, "Lesbians Picket Shescape," *Gay Community News*, Vol. 14, No. 33, March 8–14, 1987.

54. Settlement agreement dated December 17, 1987. Also marked as "Exhibit A" and "Joint Statement," in "COOL (Committee of Outraged Lesbians)" folder at the Lesbian Herstory Archives.

55. De Luca, "Lesbians Picket Shescape."

56. Stegall, "A Spatial History of Lesbian Bars in New York City," p. 111.

57. For more on Luke and Leroy's, see, e.g., Sicha, Choire, "The Guide," *New York Times*, October 17, 2004, https://www.nytimes.com/2004/10/17/arts/the-guide.html; for more on Le Royale, see, e.g., Ryzik, Melena, "Hipsters Leap to Club-Party Hopscotch," *New York Times*, December 31, 2007, https://www.nytimes.com/2007/12/31/arts/music/31club.html.

58. Pleading received via a Freedom of Information Law request to the State of New York Division of Alcoholic Beverage Control.

59. Carmel, Julia, "Elaine Romagnoli, Longtime Fixture of Lesbian Nightlife, Dies at 79," *New York Times*, November 8, 2021, https://www.nytimes.com/2021/11/08/nyregion/elaine-romagnoli-dead.html.

60. Waters, Chocolate, "The Problem with Women's Bars in This Town," *Big Mama Rag*, Vol. 7, Issue 11, December 1979, p. 13.

61. McCann, Mac, "The Trouble with Bars…Anywhere," *Big Mama Rag*, Vol. 8, No. 1, January 1980, pp. 2, 18.

62. Mandel, Marjorie, "No Man's Land: Battle over Women's Bar," *St. Louis Post-Dispatch*, September 9, 1979, pp. 1, 14.

63. Mandel, Marjorie, and Abby Cohn, "Blast, Fire Destroy Women's Bar on Grand," *St. Louis Post-Dispatch*, September 11, 1979, p. 1.

64. See the Lesbian Bar Project, https://www.lesbianbarproject.com. These figures are accurate as of October 15, 2023.

65. Loftin, *Letters to ONE*, p. 203.

66. The United States' high minimum legal drinking age—most European countries allow people to purchase and consume alcohol in bars at least three years earlier than the US threshold of twenty-one—excludes thousands of young people from an important homosocial setting.

67. Cartier, *Baby, You Are My Religion*, preface.

68. Córdova, Jeanne, "The Lesbian Bar," *Lesbian Tide*, November 1973, p. 12.

69. Cohen, Leslie, *The Audacity of a Kiss: Love, Art, and Liberation* (New Brunswick, Rutgers University Press, 2021), p. 118.

70. Stegall, "A Spatial History of Lesbian Bars in New York City," p. 112.

71. Newman, Felice, "Why I'm Not Dancing," in *Lavender Culture*, ed. Jay, Karla, and Allen Young (New York, New York University Press, 1978), p. 142.

72. Felice Newman, interview with the author, conducted by phone, January 31, 2022.

73. Lea DeLaria, interview with the author, conducted by phone, June 8, 2021.

74. For information on the history of the Woman's Christian Temperance Union, see Okrent, Daniel, *Last Call: The Rise and Fall of Prohibition* (New York, Scribner, 2010), Location 401, Kindle Edition; Spain, Daphne, *Constructive Feminism: Women's Spaces and Women's Rights in the American City* (Ithaca, Cornell University Press, 2016), Location 243, Kindle Edition.

75. Okrent, *Last Call*, Location 298.

76. House, Penny, "The New York Women's Coffeehouse," *Dyke: A Quarterly*, Vol. 1, Issue 1, 1975, p. 10.

77. Ibid., p. 12.

78. Ibid., p. 11.

79. Chauncey, *Gay New York*, p. 165.

80. Ibid., asterisked footnote.

81. Faderman, Lillian, and Stuart Timmons, *Gay L.A.: A History of Sexual Outlaws, Power Politics, and Lipstick Lesbians* (New York, Basic Books, 2006), Location 49, Kindle Edition.

82. Stryker, Susan, and Jim Van Buskirk, *Gay by the Bay: A History of Queer Culture in the San Francisco Bay Area* (San Francisco, Chronicle Books, 1996), p. 49.

83. Meaker, Marijane, *Highsmith: A Romance of the 1950s* (San Francisco, Cleis Press, 2003), p. 12.

84. Buchsbaum Genter, Alix, "Risking Everything for That Touch: Butch-Femme Lesbian Culture in New York City from World War II to Women's Liberation," PhD diss., Rutgers, State University of New Jersey, 2014, p. 58.

85. Blume, M., "The Food's Bad but the Ideology Is Strong," *International Herald Tribune*, 1974.

86. "Dolores Alexander, Interviewed by Kelly Anderson, March 20, 2004, and October 22, 2005, Southold, NY," Voices of Feminism Oral History Project, Sophia Smith Collection, Smith College, https://compass.fivecolleges.edu/object/smith:1342617.

87. Jerome, Jim, "Feminists Hail a Restaurant Where the Piece de Resistance Is an Attitude, Not a Dish," *People Weekly*, June 2, 1975, p. 10.

88. "Dolores Alexander, Interviewed by Kelly Anderson."

89. Ibid.

90. Testi, Arnaldo, "My Failed Encounter with the First Feminist Restaurant in America, with a Short History of Mother Courage Restaurant (1972–1977)," *Short Cuts America*, January 9, 2020, https://shortcutsamerica.com/2020/01/09/my-failed-encounter-with-the-first-feminist-restaurant-in-america-with-a-short-history-of-mother-courage-restaurant-1972-1977.

91. Joan Antonuccio and Sharon Davenport, interview with the author, conducted via Zoom, September 28, 2021.

92. Davenport, Sharon, "LGBT Pride: Remembering the Brick Hut," KQED, June 23, 2011, https://www.kqed.org/bayareabites/29308/lgbt-pride-remembering-the-brick-hut-cafe-part-1.

93. "Mary Watkins on Olivia Records," Queer Music Heritage, https://queermusicheritage.com/olivia-mw.html.

94. "The Bar Tapes," *Pearl Diver*, July 1977, pp. 1–19.

95. River, Julie, "The Lesbian Bar Project Seeks to Save the Dying Lesbian Bar," *Outfront*, May 10, 2023, https://www.outfrontmagazine.com/the-lesbian-bar-project-seeks-to-save-the-dying-lesbian-bar.

96. "30 Years Is a Whole Lotta History," Henrietta Hudson, https://henriettahudson.com/history.

Chapter 2: Feminist Bookstores

1. The information on 1990s feminist bookstores is taken from Corrigan, Theresa, "Feminist Bookstores: Part of an Ecosystem," *Sojourner*, November 1993, p. 6B. For more on contemporary bookstores, see, e.g., "List of Feminist Bookstores," Charis Books & More, https://www.charisbooksandmore.com/list-feminist-bookstores.

2. "Coming Out Story" (1993), originally published in *Gay Comics #19*, reprinted in *The Indelible Alison Bechdel* (Ithaca, Firebrand Books, 1998), pp. 35–37.

3. Alison Bechdel, interview with the author, conducted by phone, December 29, 2020.

4. Enke, Finn, *Finding the Movement: Sexuality, Contested Space, and Feminist Activism* (Durham, Duke University Press, 2007), p. 66.

5. Ibid.

6. Ibid., p. 67.

7. Lehmann, Nancy, "Shaping the New Woman at Meechee Dojo," *Black Belt*, December 1976, p. 77.

8. "Julie Morse Quist," LegiStorm, https://www.legistorm.com /person/bio/60496/Julie_Morse_Quist.html.

9. Quoted in Seajay, Carol, "Happy Anniversary!," *Feminist Bookstore News*, Vol. 17, No. 6, March/April 1995, p. 19.

10. Enke, *Finding the Movement*, p. 68.

11. The ad, from 1971, was reproduced on p. 24 of the November/ December 1995 issue of *Feminist Bookstore News*.

12. Enke, *Finding the Movement*, p. 68.

13. Ibid., p. 226.

14. Quarter-page ad in *Gold Flower*, September 1973, p. 14.

15. Enke, *Finding the Movement*, p. 69.

16. Quarter-page ad in *Gold Flower*, September 1973, p. 14.

17. Koivisto, Mickey, "Honoring Women Who Honor Women: Amazon Turns 25," *Lavender Lifestyles*, September 29, 1995, p. 27.

18. Ellen Hart, interview with the author, conducted by phone, January 17, 2021.

19. Matthesen, Elise, "Amazon Celebrates Silver Anniversary: Nation's Oldest Feminist Bookstore," *Lavender Lifestyles*, September 29, 1995, p. 24.

20. Koivisto, "Honoring Women Who Honor Women," p. 27.

21. Ibid.

22. Enke, *Finding the Movement*, p. 252n29.

23. "Amazon Bookstore," *Feminist Bookstore News*, Vol. 9, No. 3/4, January/February 1987, p. 12.

24. "ABA, Third World Women's Bookfair, and News," *Feminist Bookstore News*, Vol. 8, No. 6, July/August 1986, p. 10.

25. "Amazon Bookstore," p. 11.

26. Moskowitz Grumdahl, Dara, "The Pride Behind Pride," *Mpls.St. Paul Magazine*, June 21, 2020, https://mspmag.com/arts-and-culture /the-pride-behind-pride.

27. Seajay, Carol, "News from the Bookstores," *Feminist Bookstore News*, Vol. 13, No. 6, March/April 1991, p. 15.

28. "News from the Bookstores," *Feminist Bookstore News*, Vol. 15, No. 6, March/April 1993, p. 26.

29. Reprinted in *Feminist Bookstore News*, Vol. 17, No. 5, January/February 1995, p. 54.

30. Seajay, "Happy Anniversary!," p. 19.

31. Wieser, Barb, "Taking Care of Business: Thriving Amazon," *Feminist Bookstore News*, Vol. 18, No. 3, September/October 1995, p. 29.

32. Quoted in Seajay, "Happy Anniversary!," p. 19.

33. Wieser, Barb, "Taking Care of Business: Thriving Amazon," p. 29.

34. Ibid.

35. "News from the Bookstores," *Feminist Bookstore News*, Vol. 19, No. 5, January/February 1997, p. 15.

36. "News from the Bookstores," *Feminist Bookstore News*, Vol. 20, No. 4, November/December 1997, p. 15.

37. Seajay, Carol, "News from the Bookstores," *Feminist Bookstore News*, Vol. 19, No. 4, November/December 1996, p. 19.

38. Wieser, Barb, "An Open Letter to the Friends of Amazon Bookstore," originally published in *Minnesota Women's Press*, reprinted in *Feminist Bookstore News*, Vol. 22, No. 1, May/June 1999, p. 24.

39. Kirch, Claire, "The Struggle Continues," *Publishers Weekly*, October 13, 2003, https://www.publishersweekly.com/pw/print/20031013/23146-the-struggle-continues.html.

40. Quoted in Thomas, June, "When Amazon Went to War with Lesbians," *Slate*, October 21, 2013, https://slate.com/human-interest/2013/10/amazon-com-versus-amazon-bookstore-the-1999-legal-tussle-was-rancorous.html.

41. Chait, Jonathan, and Stephen Glass, "Amazon.Con: Earth's Biggest Bookstore? Pshaw. Cheaper, Faster, and More Convenient? Pshaw Again," *Slate*, January 5, 1997, https://slate.com/news-and-politics/1997/01/amazon-con.html.

42. Mutter, John, "Amazon.com to Battle Amazon in Court," *Publishers Weekly*, April 19, 1999, https://www.publishersweekly.com/pw/print/19990419/35526-amazon-com-to-battle-amazon-in-court.html.

43. Mieszkowski, Katharine, "Battle of the Amazons," *Salon*, October 28, 1999, https://www.salon.com/1999/10/28/amazon_3.

44. Ibid.

45. Soto Ouchi, Monica, "Amazon at 10: Will It Keep Clicking?," *Seattle Times*, July 10, 2005, https://web.archive.org/web/2017050 2101450/http://old.seattletimes.com/html/businesstechnology/2002 371700_amazon10.html

46. Matthesen, "Amazon Celebrates Silver Anniversary," p. 24.

47. Kirch, "The Struggle Continues."

48. Seajay, Carol, "News from the Bookstores," *Feminist Bookstore News*, Vol. 18, No. 2, July/August 1995, p. 43.

49. Seajay, Carol, "Amazon.com Settles with Amazon After Dyke-Baiting Fails," *Feminist Bookstore News*, Vol. 22, No. 6, Spring 2000, p. 16.

50. Seajay, Carol, "Amazon Is Moving to a New Building," *Feminist Bookstore News*, Vol. 22, No. 6, Spring 2000, p. 31.

51. Ellen Hart, interview with the author, conducted by phone, January 17, 2021.

52. Kirch, "The Struggle Continues."

53. Ibid.

54. Goetzman, Amy, "The Stuff of Herstory: Original Amazon Bookstore to Close," *MinnPost*, June 5, 2008, https://www.minnpost.com/arts-culture/2008/06/stuff-herstory-original-amazon-bookstore-close.

55. Goetzman, Amy, "How a Feminist Bookstore Got a Zero-Hour Reprieve," *MinnPost*, June 20, 2008, https://www.minnpost.com/arts-culture/2008/06/how-feminist-bookstore-got-zero-hour-reprieve.

56. Webster, Maryjo, "The Long Climb Back: A Decision That Forever Changed Bookstore Owner's Life," *Pioneer Press*, September 19, 2012, https://www.twincities.com/2012/09/19/the-long-climb-back-a-decision-that-forever-changed-bookstore-owners-life; Hertzel, Laurie, "Saying Goodbye to True Colors," *Star Tribune*, February 24, 2012, https://www.startribune.com/saying-goodbye-to-true-colors/140316273.

57. Seajay, "Amazon.com Settles with Amazon After Dyke-Baiting Fails," p. 25.

58. For more on women and credit in the 1970s, see Krippner, Greta R., "Democracy of Credit: Ownership and the Politics of Credit Access in Late Twentieth-Century America," *American Journal of Sociology*, Vol. 123, No. 1, July 2017, https://doi.org/10.1086/692274.

59. Grimstad, Kirsten, and Susan Rennie, *The New Woman's Survival Catalog* (New York, Coward, McCann & Geohegan, 1973), p. 21.

60. Bryant, Linda, "A Personal History of Charis by Linda Bryant," Charis Books & More, https://www.charisbooksandmore.com /personal-history-charis-linda-bryant-0.

61. Borrelli, Christopher, "More Than a Bookstore," *Chicago Tribune*, November 10, 2009.

62. Dorothy Allison, interviewed by Kelly Anderson, November 2007, Voices of Feminism Oral History Project, Smith College, https:// compass.fivecolleges.edu/object/smith:1342618, p. 12.

63. Norman, Rose, "'You Had to Be Passionate and Crazy': Feminist Booksellers in the South," *Sinister Wisdom* 116, Spring 2020, p. 28.

64. Grimstad and Rennie, *The New Woman's Survival Catalog*, p. 180.

65. *Just Us: A Directory of the Washington Gay Community* (Washington, DC, Washington Area Gay Community Council, 1975), p. 26.

66. Grimstad and Rennie, *The New Woman's Survival Catalog*, p. 180.

67. Mary Farmer, interview with the author, conducted via Zoom, October 3, 2021.

68. Grimstad and Rennie, *The New Woman's Survival Catalog*, p. 25.

69. Deb Morris, interview with the author, conducted via Zoom, October 4, 2021.

70. Gelb, Joyce, *Feminism and Politics: A Comparative Perspective* (Berkeley, University of California Press, 1989), p. 36.

71. Sara Look and E. R. Anderson, interview with the author, conducted via Zoom, October 5, 2021.

72. Sturgis, Susanna, "Editor's Notes," *Lammas Little Review*, Vol. 4, No. 1, Summer 1983, p. 2.

73. Hoover, Eric, "Fading Places," *Washington City Paper*, October 13, 2000, https://washingtoncitypaper.com/article/266060/fading -places.

74. See, e.g., "From the Boys on Publishers Row," *Feminist Bookstore News*, Vol. 7, No. 1, September 1983, p. 43.

75. Seajay, Carol, "*Patience and Sarah* Back in Print," *Feminist Bookstore News*, Vol. 7, No. 1, September 1983, p. 13.

76. Seajay, Carol, "Womanbooks Closes," *Feminist Bookstore News*, Vol. 10, No. 3, October 1987, p. 26.

77. *Judith's Room Newsletter*, Vol. 4, No. 1, Fall 1993.

78. Publisher's Opinion, "Judith's Room Closes Its Doors," *Sappho's Isle*, January 1995, p. 3.

79. Corrigan, Theresa, "Feminist Bookstores," *Womyn's Press*, January/February 1994, p. 10.

80. Seajay, Carol, "Notes from the Computer Table," *Feminist Bookstore News*, Vol. 8, No. 1, June 1985, p. 1.

81. Ibid.

82. I'm not aware of any published source for the total number of feminist and/or gay bookstores that have existed in the United States and Canada. My estimate is based on a close reading of *Feminist Bookstore News* and other feminist and LGBTQ publications.

83. Linda Semple, interview with the author, conducted via Zoom, January 20, 2023.

84. Rodwell, Craig, "The Tarnished Golden Rule," *Queen's Quarterly: The Magazine for Gay Guys Who Have No Hangups*, Vol. 3, Issue 1, February 1971, p. 5.

85. Tobin, Kay, and Randy Wicker, *The Gay Crusaders* (New York, Paperback Library, 1972), p. 70.

86. Ibid., p. 71.

87. Ibid., p. 70.

88. Price, Naomi, "Welcome to Our Reading Room," *Christian Science Journal*, June 1979, https://journal.christianscience.com/shared/view/26xsgc7hgi0.

89. Email correspondence with Committee on Publication of the First Church of Christ, Scientist, October 26, 2021.

90. Tobin and Wicker, *The Gay Crusaders*, p. 71.

91. Duberman, Martin, *Stonewall* (New York, Plume, 1993), p. 166.

92. Quoted in Marotta, Toby, *The Politics of Homosexuality* (Boston, Houghton Mifflin Company, 1981), p. 168.

93. Shilts, Randy, *The Mayor of Castro Street: The Life and Times of Harvey Milk* (New York, St. Martin's Press, 1982), p. 65.

94. Ibid., p. 256.

95. Bajko, Matthew S., "Political Notes: HRC Set to Move Out of Historic Castro Storefront amid Talks to Make Property a National Park Site," *Bay Area Reporter*, March 5, 2021, https://www.ebar.com/story.php?ch=news&sc=latest_news&sc2=&id=302659.

96. Don Kiser, interview with the author, conducted via Zoom, October 6, 2021.

97. "Mission & History," Women & Children First, https://www.womenandchildrenfirst.com/wcf-history-and-purpose.

98. Adams, Barry, "Room of One's Own Headed to Historic Building on Atwood Avenue," *Wisconsin State Journal*, February 16, 2021.

99. Smith, Kelundra, "The Country's Oldest Feminist Bookstore, Charis, Finds a New Home at Agnes Scott," *Atlanta*, April 18, 2019, https://www.atlantamagazine.com/news-culture-articles/the-countrys-oldest-feminist-bookstore-charis-finds-a-new-home-at-agnes-scott.

100. Cafe Con Libros, https://www.cafeconlibrosbk.com.

101. Christina Pascucci-Ciampa, interview with the author, conducted via Zoom, January 18, 2023.

102. Casey, Kathleen B., "The Renaissance of Feminist Bookstores," *Ms.*, January 21, 2023, https://msmagazine.com/2023/01/21/feminist-bookstores.

103. Edinburgh is home to both Lighthouse ("About," Lighthouse, https://lighthousebookshop.com/about) and Rare Birds Books ("About Us," Rare Birds Books, https://rarebirdsbooks.com/pages/about-us).

104. "Series of Tubes," Wikipedia, https://en.wikipedia.org/wiki/Series_of_tubes.

105. Sara Look and E. R. Anderson, interview with the author, conducted via Zoom, October 5, 2021.

106. Schnall, Marianne, "Timeless Wisdom from Gloria Steinem," Feminist.com, https://www.feminist.com/resources/artspeech/interviews/timeless-wisdom-from-gloria-steinem.html.

Chapter 3: The Softball Diamond

1. "Willie Tyson—Full Count," Discogs, https://www.discogs.com/release/2301040-Willie-Tyson-Full-Count/image/SW1hZ2U6Odc0OTE2ODA=.

2. "Court Nominee Comes to the Plate," *Wall Street Journal*, May 11, 2010, p. 1.

3. Quoted in Weiner, Juli, "The Wall Street Journal Runs Front-Page Picture of Elena Kagan Playing Softball, of All Things," *Vanity Fair*, May 11, 2010, https://www.vanityfair.com/news/2010/05/the-wall-street-journal-runs-front-page-picture-of-elena-kagan-playing-softball-of-all-things.

4. Mimi, "Another Lesbian Custody Case Lost," *off our backs*, May–June 1975, p. 12.

5. "ACLU Challenges Anti-lesbian Bias," *Bay Area Reporter*, Vol. 21, No. 6, February 7, 1991, p. 20.

6. "Women Musicians in Oregon Victorious in Bias Settlement," *Wisconsin Light*, June 13–26, 1991.

7. Chesnut, Saralynn, and Amanda C. Gable, "'Women Ran It': Charis Books and More and Atlanta's Lesbian-Feminist Community, 1971–1981," in *Carryin' On in the Lesbian and Gay South*, ed. Howard, John (New York, New York University Press, 1997), p. 253.

8. "Lorraine Fontana Oral History Interview, 2019-06-26," Special Collections and Archives, Georgia State University Library, https://digitalcollections.library.gsu.edu/digital/collection/GSB/id/10266.

9. K[nowlton], Elizabeth, "How to Start a Lesbian-Feminist Organization (or Any Kind of Non-hierarchical Group)," Lesbian Herstory Archives, Organization Files, ALFA, 1984, p. 1.

10. "Frances Pici Oral History Interview, 2014-06-07," Special Collections and Archives, Georgia State University Library, https://digitalcollections.library.gsu.edu/digital/collection/lgbtq/id/4769. (Note: "Frances Anne Pici" is her legal name, but she prefers to go by Pici.)

11. Unless otherwise stated, timeline events are taken from "ALFA/Lesbian Time-Line," created to commemorate ALFA's tenth anniversary in 1982, in the Atlanta Lesbian Feminist Alliance Archives, ca. 1972–1994, Duke University Library, Box 1, Folder 32, accessed via Gale Archives of Sexuality and Gender database.

12. Kaye, Diana, "Lesbians on the Move," *Great Speckled Bird*, August 21, 1972, p. 15.

13. Wells, Susan, and Vicki Gabriner, "How to Start a Lesbian Organisation," written for *The Lesbian Resource Book*, published by the National Gay Task Force. Reprinted in *Atalanta*, Vol. 5, No. 8, August 1977, p. 3.

14. *ALFA Newsletter*, No. 7, March 1974, p. 3.

15. *ALFA Newsletter*, No. 8, April 1974, p. 3.

16. *ALFA Newsletter*, No. 11, July–August 1974, p. 2.

17. *ALFA Newsletter*, No. 12, September 1974, p. 7.

18. Gabriner, Vicki, "How a Skinny Jewish Kid from Brooklyn Found Happiness on the ALFA Omega Softball Team," *Great Speckled Bird*, March 6, 1975, p. 15.

19. Gabriner, Vicki, "Come Out Slugging!," *Quest*, Vol. 2, No. 3, Winter 1976, pp. 52–57.

20. *ALFA Newsletter*, No. 12, September 1974, p. 7.

21. Gelfand, Rachel, "'Come Out Slugging!': The Atlanta Lesbian Feminist Alliance, 1972–1975," *Southern Cultures*, Vol. 26, No. 3, Fall 2020, https://www.southerncultures.org/article/come-out-slugging.

22. Elizabeth [Knowlton], "From the Stands," *ALFA Newsletter*, July 1976, p. 1.

23. Pici, interview with the author, conducted via Zoom, August 10, 2022.

24. Wells and Gabriner, "How to Start a Lesbian Organisation," p. 4.

25. Elizabeth, "From the Stands," p. 1.

26. "Frances Pici Oral History Interview, 2014-06-07."

27. "Lesbian Softball Revisited," *Atalanta*, Vol. 5, No. 6, June 1977, p. 4.

28. Gabriner, Vicki, "A Hystory of the Atlanta Lesbian/Feminist Alliance 1972–1978, as Told by One Womin," printed by Gabriner as part of her work as a typesetter; also published in the December 1980 issue of *Atalanta*.

29. Cage, Carolyn, *The Amazon All-Stars: A Musical Comedy in Two Acts*, Act 1, Scene 4, in *The Amazon All-Stars: Thirteen Lesbian Plays with Essays and Commentary*, ed. Curb, Rosemary Keefe (New York, Applause Books, 1996), p. 135.

30. For more on the Mary Vazquez Women's Softball League, see Castledine, Jacqueline L., and Julia Sandy-Bailey, "'Stop That Rambo Shit…This Is Feminist Softball': Reconsidering Women's Organizing in the Reagan Era and Beyond," in *Breaking the Wave: Women, Their Organizations, and Feminism, 1945–1985*, ed. Laughlin, Kathleen A., and Jacqueline L. Castledine (New York, Routledge, 2011). Also see *In League with Us: The Story of the Mary Vazquez Women's Softball League*, a documentary directed by Lacey Johnston, available through the Internet Archive at https://archive.org/details/40211InLeague WithUs.

31. Castledine and Sandy-Bailey, "'Stop That Rambo Shit,'" p. 202.

32. "Rules, Regulations, Responsibilities, and Courtesies," Mary Vazquez Women's Softball League, http://www.maryvsoftball.org /rules.

33. "We Have to Be Our Own Spark: An Interview with Gente Third-World Lesbian Softball Team," *Lesbian Tide*, July 1974, p. 6. Players weren't quoted by name. According to the piece, "They work and think as a team. This is their collective statement."

34. Zipter, Yvonne, *Diamonds Are a Dyke's Best Friend* (Ithaca, Firebrand Books, 1988), p. 158.

35. "We Have to Be Our Own Spark," p. 25.

36. Ibid., p. 7.

37. For more on the Motown Soul Sisters, see Enke, Finn, "Pioneers, Players, and Politicos: Women's Softball in Minnesota," *Minnesota History*, Vol. 58, No. 4, Winter 2002–2003, pp. 210–223, https://www.jstor.org/stable/20188348.

38. Zipter, *Diamonds Are a Dyke's Best Friend*, p. 188.

39. Enszer, Julie R., ed., *Sister Love: The Letters of Audre Lorde and Pat Parker, 1974–1989* (Dover, A Midsummer Night's Press/Sinister Wisdom, 2018), p. 138.

40. "We Have to Be Our Own Spark," p. 25.

41. Johnson, Susan E., *When Women Played Hardball* (Seattle, Seal Press, 1994), p. xii.

42. Hunter, Dianna, *Wild Mares: My Lesbian Back-to-the-Land Life* (Minneapolis, University of Minnesota Press, 2018), p. 13.

43. Ibid., p. 15.

44. "About BASL," Big Apple Softball League, https://www.bigapplesoftball.com/about.

45. Annise Parker, interview with the author, conducted via Zoom, December 7, 2022.

46. Conversations with players at three BASL games on June 11, 2022.

47. Alina Butareva, interview with the author, conducted via Zoom, June 10, 2022.

48. E. R. Anderson, interview with the author, conducted via Zoom, June 15, 2022.

Chapter 4: Lesbian Land

1. Sue, Nelly, Dian, Carol, and Billie, *Country Lesbians: The Story of the WomanShare Collective* (Grants Pass, WomanShare Books, 1976), p. 62.

2. Ibid., pp. 64, 66.

3. Ibid., p. 64.

4. Statement by Carol Newhouse, "On Wimmin's Land Panel, Oct. 12, 2022, University of Oregon," video posted to YouTube, https://www.youtube.com/watch?v=kKBDOyqGb6I.

5. Anahita, Jensine (Sine), "Landdyke Landscapes: The Politics, Participants, and Praxis of the Lesbian Land Movement," PhD diss., Iowa State University, 2003, https://lib.dr.iastate.edu/rtd/562.

6. *Landykes of the South: Women's Land Groups and Lesbian Communities in the South, Sinister Wisdom* 98, p. 6, attributes this quotation to Shewolf, originally made on an online discussion forum.

7. Raphael, Rina, "Why Doesn't Anyone Want to Live in This Perfect Place?," *New York Times*, August 24, 2019, https://www.nytimes.com/2019/08/24/style/womyns-land-movement-lesbian-communities.html. In her 2003 PhD dissertation "Landdyke Landscapes," Sine Anahita offered a higher estimate of 200 to 220 "rural settlements whose members collectively identify as members of the landdyke movement in the U.S."

8. *Maize: A Lesbian Country Magazine 2022 Lesbian Land Connections Directory*, Issue 130, Spring 2022.

9. Burmeister, Heather Jo, "Rural Revolution: Documenting the Lesbian Land Communities of Southern Oregon," Dissertations and Theses, Paper 1080, 2013, p. 26, https://doi.org/10.15760/etd.1080; Luis, Keridan N., *Herlands: Exploring the Women's Land Movement in the United States* (Minneapolis, University of Minnesota Press, 2018), p. 46.

10. Burmeister, "Rural Revolution," p. 61; "Percentage of the U.S. Population Who Have Completed Four Years of College or More from 1940 to 2022, by Gender," Statista, https://www.statista.com/statistics/184272/educational-attainment-of-college-diploma-or-higher-by-gender.

11. Burmeister, "Rural Revolution," p. 10.

12. Kopp, James J., *Eden Within Eden: Oregon's Utopian Heritage* (Corvallis, Oregon State University Press, 2009), p. 155.

13. Radicalesbians, "The Woman Identified Woman" (Pittsburgh, Know, Inc., 1970), p. 1.

14. Ibid., p. 4.

15. Frye, Marilyn, "Some Thoughts on Separatism and Power," *Sinister Wisdom* 6, Summer 1978, p. 32. (The *Sinister Wisdom* essay was distilled from a conference paper given at the December 1977 meeting of the Society of Women in Philosophy.)

16. Bunch, Charlotte, "Perseverance Furthers: Separatism and Our Future," *The Furies*, Vol. 1, Issue 7, Fall 1972, p. 4.

17. Grahn, Judy, *A Simple Revolution: The Making of an Activist Poet* (San Francisco, Aunt Lute Books, 2012), p. 197.

18. Thomas, June, "The National Register of Historic Places Adds Its First Lesbian Landmark," *Slate*, May 6, 2016, https://slate.com

/human-interest/2016/05/furies-collective-joins-national-register-of
-historic-places.html; "The Furies Collective," National Park Service,
https://www.nps.gov/places/furies-collective.htm.

19. Berson, Ginny Z., *Olivia on the Record: A Radical Experiment in
Women's Music* (San Francisco, Aunt Lute Books, 2020), Location 2628,
Kindle Edition.

20. Ginny Z. Berson, interview with the author, conducted via Zoom,
September 4, 2021.

21. Sankey, Marea, and Martha Benewicz, "A Country Lesbian Manifesto," *So's Your Old Lady*, Issue 2, April 1973, pp. 20–21.

22. Traveler, Helen, "A Traveler's Tale," *WomanSpirit*, Spring 1977,
pp. 28–30.

23. Burmeister, "Rural Revolution," p. 61.

24. "Atkins, Gail, and Demeter, Gwen—interviewed by Rose Norman," Southern Lesbian-Feminist Activist Herstory Project, Duke
University Libraries, October 12, 2013, https://repository.duke.edu/dc
/slfaherstoryproject/19b23808-a7eb-4f96-8a3f-e3f3bd4b336a.

25. "Ellison, Kate—interviewed by Rose Norman," Southern
Lesbian-Feminist Activist Herstory Project, Duke University Libraries,
November 10, 2012, https://idn.duke.edu/ark:/87924/r41c1zw0s.

26. Silverowl, Dark Artemis, "Missouri," *WomanSpirit* 32, Summer
Solstice 1982, p. 11.

27. Reid, Coletta, "Taking Care of Business," *Quest*, Vol. 1, Issue 2,
Fall 1974, pp. 6–23.

28. Sue, Nelly, Dian, Carol, and Billie, *Country Lesbians*, p. vi.

29. Ibid., pp. 108–110.

30. Ibid., p. 145.

31. Shosana, "Kvindelandet," in *Lesbian Land* (Minneapolis, Word
Weavers, 1985), p. 63.

32. *The Blatant Image*, Issue 1, 1981, p. 7.

33. Mushroom, Merril, "Work Ethic: 1975," in *Landykes of the South:
Women's Land Groups and Lesbian Communities in the South, Sinister
Wisdom* 98, p. 33.

34. Shewolf, "Woman's World," *Maize*, Issue 24, Spring 9990, p. 11.
(During the period when *Maize* was published by Word Weavers, dates
like 1990 were presented as 9990, because, as Word Weavers' Nett Hart
told me via email in early 2023, "women invented agriculture approximately 10,000 years ago.")

35. "Boudreaux, Shewolf (Jean)—interviewed by Barbara Esrig and Kate Ellison," Southern Lesbian-Feminist Activist Herstory Project, Duke University Libraries, January 2013 to February 2013, https://repository.duke.edu/dc/slfaherstoryproject/a011eb7c -d271-4631-9555-5021403c7746.

36. Sallie and Sashie, "Greenhope," in *Lesbian Land* (Minneapolis, Word Weavers, 1985), p. 56.

37. Shosana, "Kvindelandet," in ibid., p. 65.

38. Weed, Susun, "Laughing Rock Farm," in ibid., p. 76.

39. Cheney, Joyce, "The Story of the Stories," in ibid., p. 9.

40. "Ellison, Kate—interviewed by Rose Norman."

41. Sue, Nelly, Dian, Carol, and Billie, *Country Lesbians*, p. 10.

42. Lee, Anna, "A Black Separatist," in *For Lesbians Only*, ed. Hoagland, Sara Lucia, and Julia Penelope (London, Onlywomen Press, 1988). Reproduced by Feminist Reprise at https://feminist-reprise.org/library /resistance-strategy-and-struggle/a-black-separatist.

43. "Sassafras: A Land in Struggle," *Big Apple Dyke News*, August–September 1983, pp. 4–6.

44. "MAAT DOMPIM/The Womyn of Color Land Project," *Maize: A Lesbian Country Magazine 2022 Lesbian Land Connections Directory*, Issue 130, Spring 2022, p. 26.

45. Newhouse, "On Wimmin's Land Panel."

46. "About NativeWomanshare," NativeWomanshare, https://www .nativewomanshare.com/about.

47. Paz, Juana Maria, "Where Do Dreams Go When They Die?," in *Lesbian Land* (Minneapolis, Word Weavers, 1985), p. 73.

48. Lee, Pelican, "Nozama Tribe," in ibid., p. 161.

49. Cheney, Joyce, "Redbird," in ibid., p. 117.

50. Ibid., p. 120.

51. Haggard, Jae, "Lesbian Land, Serafina, New Mexico," *Maize* 27, Winter 9991, p. 11.

52. Newhouse, "On Wimmin's Land Panel."

53. "Topless Bather Arrested in Cape Code Protest," *New York Times*, August 26, 1984, p. 23, https://www.nytimes.com/1984/08/26/us /topless-bather-arrested-in-cape-cod-protest.html.

54. Shosana, "Kvindelandet," p. 64.

55. Thomas, Sherry, and Jeanne Tetrault, *Country Women: A Handbook for the New Farmer* (Garden City, Anchor Books, 1976), p. 23.

56. "August 4–9, 2015, the 40th and Final Michigan Womyn's Music Festival," Michfest, available through the Internet Archive, https://web .archive.org/web/20170112002104/http://michfest.com.

57. Macdonald, Jocelyn, "Setting the Record Straight About Michfest," *After Ellen*, October 24, 2018, https://web.archive.org /web/20181219081617/https://afterellen.com/general-news/565301 -setting-the-record-straight-about-michfest.

58. See, e.g., "Lesbian Natural Resources," *Maize* 37, Summer 9993, pp. 28–29, for information on the grants LNR made that year.

59. Archibald, Sasha, "On Wimmin's Land," *Places*, February 2021, https://placesjournal.org/article/on-wimmins-land-the-heartland -of-lesbian-separatism.

60. For more information on land trusts and other legal and ethical issues affecting lesbian-land projects, see "On Our Own Terms: Access, Ownership, Conservation, and Transfer of Lesbian Land," a 2017 publication available from Lesbian Natural Resources (http://www .lesbiannaturalresources.org/publications).

61. Guthrie and Roz, "Notes on a Land Trust," *WomanSpirit*, Spring 1977, p. 34.

62. Sierra, "Herstory of the Oregon Women's Land Trust," *WomanSpirit*, Spring 1977, pp. 10–11.

63. Bowoman, Diann, "Moving On Is Hard," *Maize* 54, Summer 97, p. 18.

64. Guthrie and Roz, "Notes on a Land Trust," p. 34.

65. Although the story of the pregnant woman was mentioned in two landdyke publications, *WomanSpirit* and *Lesbian Land*, I could find no further information about her fate.

66. Sierra, "A Herstory of the Oregon Women's Land Trust," p. 11.

67. Raven, "Twenty Years: A Reminiscence," *Maize* 37, Summer 9993, p. 5.

68. Lee, Pelican, "Journey to Lesbian Lands," *Maize* 33, Summer 9992, p. 7.

69. Fran, "Oregon Gathering," *Maize* 53, Spring 97, p. 9.

70. Gwynn, Bethroot, "Landdykes, Part 2," Zoom panel organized by Old Lesbians Organizing for Change, video posted to YouTube, February 5, 2022, https://www.youtube.com/watch?v=-yNspi7XVFM, at 54:16.

71. "VICTORY! Jordan Cove LNG Terminal & Pacific Connector Pipeline," Western Environmental Law Center, https://westernlaw.org /jordan-cove-lng-terminal-pacific-connector-pipeline.

72. Gwynn, "Landdykes, Part 2," 54:16.

73. Gwynn, Bethroot, "Oregon Gathering," *Maize* 53, Spring 97, p. 7. Gwynn was paraphrasing Jean Mountaingrove.

74. I also want to discourage readers from assuming that all lesbian-feminists active in the 1970s were trans-exclusionary. In 1977, Olivia responded to protesters who were criticizing the collective for working with transwoman Sandy Stone by saying, "Our daily political and personal interactions with her have confirmed for each of us that she is a woman we can relate to with comfort and with trust." (Enszer, Julie R., "'How to Stop Choking to Death': Rethinking Lesbian Separatism as a Vibrant Political Theory and Feminist Practice," *Journal of Lesbian Studies*, Vol. 20, No. 2, 2016, p. 187; for more see the full article at https://julierenszer.files.wordpress.com/2012/01/how-to-stop-choking-to-death-rethinking-lesbian-separatism-as-a-vibrant-political-theory-and-feminist-practice.pdf).

75. Lorde, Audre, "Man Child: A Black Lesbian-Feminist's Response" (1979), originally published in *Conditions Four*, reprinted in *Zami, Sister Outsider, Undersong* (New York, Quality Paperback Book Club, 1993), p. 78.

76. Whittier, Nancy, "Political Generations, Micro-cohorts, and the Transformation of Social Movements," *Sociological Review*, Vol. 62, October 1997, pp. 760–778, https://www.jstor.org/stable/2657359.

77. "Oregon," *Maize: A Lesbian Country Magazine 2022 Lesbian Land Connections Directory*, Issue 130, Spring 2022, pp. 23–25.

Chapter 5: Feminist Sex-Toy Stores

1. For more on the NOW gathering, see Johnston, Laurie, "Women's Sexuality Conference Ends in School Here," *New York Times*, June 11, 1973, p. 10, https://www.nytimes.com/1973/06/11/archives/womens-sexuality-conference-ends-in-school-here-older-women-attend.html. For more on Betty Dodson's contributions to the conference, see Dodson, Betty, *Sex by Design: The Betty Dodson Story* (New Providence, Betty A. Dodson Foundation, 2015).

2. Bright, Susie, *Big Sex, Little Death: A Memoir* (New York, Seal Press, 2011), p. 229.

3. Gevins, Adi, "She's Bringing You Good Vibrations," *Berkeley Barb*, July 17–25, 1977, p. 5.

4. Legacy Business Registry Application, San Francisco Office of Small Business, p. 12.

5. Laura Miller, interview with the author, conducted via Zoom, March 1, 2023.

6. Williams, Dell, and Lynn Vannucci, *Revolution in the Garden: Memoirs of the Gardenkeeper* (Silverback Books, 2005), p. 179.

7. Ibid., p. 141.

8. Ibid., p. 146.

9. Ibid., p. 183.

10. Ibid., p. 203.

11. Strictly speaking, Eve's Garden wasn't the first calm and clean boutique-style store to offer sex toys in Manhattan. In 1971, gay men Duane Colglazier and Bill Rifkin opened The Pleasure Chest in the West Village. When a *New York Times* reporter came to investigate this new kind of erotic emporia, Rifkin told her, "We treat our customers just as though they were walking into Gimbels to buy a table and chairs" (Klemesrud, Judy, "Sex Boutique: 'Middle Ground Between Drugstore Approach and Smut Shop,'" *New York Times*, January 13, 1972, p. 36, https://www.nytimes.com/1972/01/13/archives/sex-boutique-middle-ground-between-drugstore-approach-and-smut-shop.html). For more on the fascinating history of The Pleasure Chest, see Lieberman, Hallie, *Buzz: A Stimulating History of the Sex Toy* (New York, Pegasus Books, 2017).

12. Williams and Vannucci, *Revolution in the Garden*, p. 182.

13. Susie Bright, interview with the author, conducted via Zoom, March 9, 2023.

14. Grahn, Judy, *A Simple Revolution: The Making of an Activist Poet* (San Francisco, Aunt Lute Books, 2012), p. 173.

15. Lieberman, *Buzz*, p. 93.

16. Independently owned feminist sex-toy stores in the United States include Early to Bed in Chicago; Feelmore in Oakland; Self Serve in Albuquerque; Smitten Kitten in Minneapolis; She Bop in Portland, Oregon; and Sugar in Baltimore.

17. Searah Deysach, interview with the author, conducted via Zoom, February 27, 2023.

18. Claire Cavanah and Rachel Venning, interview with the author, conducted via Zoom, March 5, 2023.

19. Anne Semans, interview with the author, conducted via Zoom, March 6, 2023.

20. Comella, Lynn, *Vibrator Nation: How Feminist Sex-Toy Stores Changed the Business of Pleasure* (Durham, Duke University Press, 2017), p. 57.

21. Seajay, Carol, "Vibrators for Sale," *Feminist Bookstore News*, September 1984, p. 15.

22. *Good Vibes Gazette*, Fall 1989.

23. Lieberman, *Buzz*, p. 227.

24. Ibid., p. 265.

25. Blank, Joani, "The Year-End Financial Report, 1987," *Good Vibes Gazette*, No. 4, February 1988.

26. Lieberman, *Buzz*, p. 259.

27. Legacy Business Registry Application, San Francisco Office of Small Business, p. 6.

28. Ibid., p. 13.

29. Cassell, Heather, "Good Vibrations Announces Merger," *Bay Area Reporter*, October 3, 2007, https://www.ebar.com/story.php?238350.

30. Lieberman, *Buzz*, p. 266.

31. Rainey, Libby, "Joani Blank, Feminist Activist Who Founded Good Vibrations, Dies," *SF Gate*, August 18, 2016, https://www.sfgate.com/bayarea/article/Joani-Blank-feminist-activist-who-founded-Good-9171689.php.

32. Warren, Peter, "Joel Kaminsky Leaves GVA-TWN to Focus on Good Vibrations," *AVN*, October 28, 2009.

33. Rodriguez, Ariana, and Nicolas Yanes, "Family Ties: A Look at How Kinship Drives the Pleasure Industry Forward," *XBIZ*, December 15, 2022.

34. Kaplan, Larry, "Store Chain Spotlight: The Good Shepherd," *StorErotica*, June 2022, https://storerotica.com/the-good-shepherd-good-vibrations-2.

35. Eric Schlosser provides an excellent summary of the twists and turns of Reuben Sturman's career in the adult industry in *Reefer Madness: Sex, Drugs, and Cheap Labor in the American Black Market* (Boston, Mariner Books, 2004).

36. Kaplan, "Store Chain Spotlight."

37. Comella, *Vibrator Nation*, p. 219.

38. Murphy, Casey, "Casey Kaminsky Shares Vision for Barnaby Ltd.'s Retail Brands," *XBIZ*, December 8, 2022, https://www.xbiz.com/features/270004/casey-kaminsky-shares-vision-for-barnaby-ltd-s-retail-brands.

39. "Market Analysis Report, Sex Toys Market Size, Share & Trends Report," Grand View Research, 2022, www.grandviewresearch.com/industry-analysis/sex-toys-market.

40. Kaplan, "Store Chain Spotlight."

41. For more on the Babeland organizing effort, see Comella, *Vibrator Nation*, pp. 215–217.

42. Whitford, Emma, "Babeland Becomes First Sex Shop to Join Retail Workers Union," *Gothamist*, May 24, 2016, https://gothamist.com/news/babeland-becomes-first-sex-shop-to-join-retail-workers-union.

43. Kaplan, "Store Chain Spotlight."

44. Williams and Vannucci, *Revolution in the Garden*, p. 218.

45. "DW Letter Explaining Financial Crisis with Venture Capital," summer 1982, Dell Williams Papers, Collection 7676, Division of Rare and Manuscript Collections, Cornell University Library.

46. "Carten, Marilyn, Business-Related Correspondence, 1981–82," Dell Williams Papers, Collection 7676, Division of Rare and Manuscript Collections, Cornell University Library.

47. "DW Letter Explaining Financial Crisis with Venture Capital."

48. Flanigan, Judy, "Eve's Garden Grows Again," *New Directions for Women*, January/February 1984, p. 7.

49. Fox, Margalit, "Dell Williams, Founder of Sex Boutique, Dies at 92," *New York Times*, March 13, 2015, Section D, p. 8, https://www.nytimes.com/2015/03/14/nyregion/dell-williams-founder-of-sex-boutique-dies-at-92.html.

Chapter 6: Vacation Destinations

1. Newton, Esther, *Cherry Grove, Fire Island: Sixty Years of America's First Gay and Lesbian Town* (Durham, Duke University Press, 2014), p. 73.

2. Ibid., p. 55.

3. Ibid., p. 94.

4. Ibid., p. 106.

5. Ibid., p. 293.

6. Erin Nestor, interview with the author, conducted by phone, March 1, 2022.

7. Krahulik, Karen Christel, *Provincetown: From Pilgrim Landing to Gay Resort* (New York, New York University Press, 2005), p. 176.

8. Myers, K. C., "Jamaican Business Owners Come to the Front of the House," *Provincetown Independent*, August 11, 2021, https://provincetownindependent.org/news/2021/08/11/jamaican-business-owners-come-to-the-front-of-the-house.

9. Tracy McDonald, email exchange with the author, March 17, 2023.

10. For more on the history of Fantasia Fair and Women's Week, see Krahulik, *Provincetown*, pp. 178–179.

11. Williams, Alex, "Why Is It Hard to Make Friends over 30?," *New York Times*, July 13, 2012, https://www.nytimes.com/2012/07/15/fashion/the-challenge-of-making-friends-as-an-adult.html.

12. Felice Newman, interview with the author, conducted by phone, January 31, 2022.

13. Krahulik, *Provincetown*, p. 174.

14. "Where to Stay," Women of Provincetown Innkeepers, http://womeninnkeepers.com/where-to-stay.

15. Krahulik, *Provincetown*, p. 184.

16. Information about innkeepers' experience taken from Lapidus, Jackie, "Making Lesbian Space: Women Guesthouse Owners Interviewed," *Womantide*, Summer–Fall 1985, pp. 10–13, 28.

17. "Helen Moore," Greenham Women Everywhere, https://greenhamwomeneverywhere.co.uk/wp-content/uploads/2020/08/Helen-Moore.pdf.

18. Savage, Rachel, "A Time of Coming Out: Greenham Lesbians Reflect on U.K. Peace Camp," Thomson Reuters Foundation, October 18, 2021, https://www.reuters.com/article/britain-lgbt-documentary-idUSL8N2RE25D.

19. "Full Moon Enterprises, Hopland, California," *Maize* 32, Spring 9992, p. 6.

20. "Country Connections," *Maize* 34, Fall 9992, p. 41.

21. "Tips for Visitors to Lesbian Land," *Maize* 57, Spring 1998, p. 23.

22. "Letters," *Maize* 55, Fall 97, p. 36.

23. zana, "The Shock That It Is Not Utopia," *Maize* 29, Summer 9991, pp. 15–18.

24. Morris, Bonnie J., *The Disappearing L: Erasure of Lesbian Spaces and Culture* (Albany, SUNY Press, 2016), p. 65.

25. "Women in the Arts, Inc.," National Women's Music Festival, https://www.nwmf.info/wia.

26. Morris, *The Disappearing L*, p. 76.

27. National Women's Music Festival, https://www.nwmf.info.

28. See under "The Travel Experience" at "FAQ & Contact," Olivia, https://www.olivia.com/faq-and-contact.

29. Ginny Z. Berson, email exchange with the author, March 20, 2023.

30. "The Muses of Olivia: Our Own Economy, Our Own Song," *off our backs*, Vol. 4, No. 9, September–October 1974, pp. 2–3.

31. "Land Ahoy," Episode 2 of *The L Word*, Season 2, first aired on Showtime on April 24, 2005.

32. "Week at a Glance, 50th Anniversary Caribbean Cruise II, February 26–March 5, 2023," Olivia, https://info.olivia.com /hubfs/Marketing/PDFs/OBM/WeekAtAGlance/WAAG_2023 -50thCarib2.pdf.

33. Morris, *The Disappearing L*, p. 193.

34. Ibid., p. 76.

35. "Travel Solo with Olivia," Olivia, https://www.olivia.com /solos-program.

36. For more on these events, see "Club Skirts Dinah Shore Weekend," Wikipedia, https://en.wikipedia.org/wiki/Club_Skirt s_Dinah_Shore_Weekend; Anne Lister Birthday Week, https://www .annelisterbirthdayweek.com; "About A-Camp," A-Camp, http://a-camp .org/about-autostraddle-camp-2-1.

37. Hannah Mackay Tait, conversation with the author, conducted via Zoom, March 17, 2023.

38. Bennhold, Katrin, "Scotland Embraces Gay Politicians in a Profound Cultural Shift," *New York Times*, October 23, 2016, https:// www.nytimes.com/2016/10/23/world/europe/scotland-gay-politicians .html.

INDEX

Index

Index

Index

Index

Index

Index

primitive conditions on, 157–158
sexual conflicts/nonmonogamy on,
   170–171
skills needed for living on, 158–161
troubled individuals drawn to, 177–178
visitors (vacationers) on, 232–235
Lesbian Land (anthology), 164, 170–171
lesbian-land movement, 146. *See also*
   lesbian land
lesbian mass gatherings, 235
Lesbian Natural Resources, 175
Lesbian Resource Center
   (Minneapolis), 71
Lesbians Empowered for Action and
   Politics, 10
lesbian separatism, 6, 148–155
   exclusionary politics of, 149–150,
     166–168, 174–175, 182–185
   and group houses, 122–123, 151–155
   See also lesbian land
lesbian spaces
   author's personal discoveries in, 17–18
   author's personal search for, 1–3
   creation of, quest for community
     and, 3–5
   emerging questions about, 14
   focus on key locations, 5–6
   inclusive description of women involved
     in, 14
   lessons from, 15
   outsized significance of, 4
   overall cultural forces affecting, 14–15
   patterns of, 245
   physical, importance of, 13, 113
   pioneers, credit due to, 245–246
   refuge from male (heterosexual) gaze in,
     6, 142, 172, 241
   reinvention/future of, 63–64, 247–248
   success, despite closures, 109, 246–248
   virtual, 12–13, 112
   See also specific spaces
Lesbian Tide (periodical), 48,
   133–134, 135
Lesbos, 1
Letterman, David, 32–33
LeVay, Simon, 35

Librería Mujeres, 68
London
   gay and lesbian bookstores in, 103–105
   lesbian enclaves in, 154, 228
Long, Linda, 11–12
Look, Sara, 91
Lorde, Audre, 75, 183
Los Angeles
   as hotbed of activism, 10
   post office seizure in, 7–8
   See also specific spaces
Louisiana, lesbian land in, 163

Maat Dompim, 167–168, 175
Madison, Wisconsin, feminist bookstore
   in, 109
Madonna, 32–33, 35
Madrid, Spain, feminist bookstore in, 68
Mafia, 8, 28, 48, 56
magazine section, of feminist bookstores,
   99–100
mail, restrictions on, 6–8
Maize (periodical), 163, 171, 175, 233–235
male (heterosexual) gaze, refuge from, 6,
   142, 172, 241
male spectators, lesbian bars at, 18,
   29–30, 142
Mama Bears, 59
Mama's Home Fried Truck Stop, 11
Manchester, England, radical bookstore
   in, 67
Mary Vazquez Women's Softball League,
   131–132
Massachusetts
   feminist bookseller in, 110–112
   feminist sex-toy store in, 198
   softball in, 131–132
Mattachine Society, 105–107
Maxine's, 20
McCann, Mac, 44–45, 47
McDonald, Tracy, 225
Meaker, Marijane, 7, 20, 56
Michigan Womyn's Music Festival, 155,
   173–175, 236
Milk, Harvey, 107–109
Miller, Al, 37

Index

Index

Index

Index

Index

Credit: Rachel Hein

June Thomas is a journalist and cohost of *Slate*'s *Working* podcast. Thomas was formerly senior managing producer of *Slate* podcasts and was the founding editor of Outward, *Slate*'s LGBTQ section. Her work has appeared in outlets including *Bloomberg Businessweek*, *Marie Claire*, the *New York Times*' *T* magazine, and the *Advocate*. After forty years in America, Thomas now lives in Edinburgh, Scotland.